Wild Unrest

Wild Unrest

Charlotte Perkins Gilman
and the Making of
"The Yellow Wall-Paper"

Helen Lefkowitz Horowitz

OXFORD
UNIVERSITY PRESS

2010

OXFORD
UNIVERSITY PRESS

Oxford University Press, Inc., publishes works that further
Oxford University's objective of excellence
in research, scholarship, and education.

Oxford   New York
Auckland   Cape Town   Dar es Salaam   Hong Kong   Karachi
Kuala Lumpur   Madrid   Melbourne   Mexico City   Nairobi
New Delhi   Shanghai   Taipei   Toronto

With offices in
Argentina   Austria   Brazil   Chile   Czech Republic   France   Greece
Guatemala   Hungary   Italy   Japan   Poland   Portugal   Singapore
South Korea   Switzerland   Thailand   Turkey   Ukraine   Vietnam

Published by Oxford University Press, Inc.
198 Madison Avenue, New York, New York 10016

www.oup.com

Oxford is a registered trademark of Oxford University Press

Library of Congress Cataloging-in-Publication Data
Horowitz, Helen Lefkowitz.
   Wild unrest : Charlotte Perkins Gilman and the making of "The yellow wall-paper" /
Helen Lefkowitz Horowitz.
      p.   cm.
   Includes bibliographical references and index.
   ISBN 978-0-19-973980-6 (hardcover : alk. paper)   1. Gilman, Charlotte Perkins,
1860–1935.   2. Gilman, Charlotte Perkins, 1860–1935. Yellow wallpaper.   3. Authors,
American—19th century—Biography.   4. Feminists—United States—Biography.   I. Title.
   PS1744.G57Z69 2010
   813'.4—dc22   2010009109

1 3 5 7 9 8 6 4 2

Printed in the United States of America
on acid-free paper

TO DAN, as we begin
our next half century . . . .

ACKNOWLEDGMENTS ·

It is a great pleasure to acknowledge the individuals and institutions who aided me in the development of this book. My deepest debt is to Smith College. Its generous sabbatical and leave policy allowed me the necessary time for research and writing. The Katharine Asher Engel Lecture gave me the opportunity to present my work to lively and informed colleagues. At two moments during the lecture I realized how deeply the college was intertwined with my work. At one point I looked out to see in the audience Ronald Perera, who premiered at Smith his magnificent opera *The Yellow Wallpaper*, and Jane Bryden, who sang the part of the narrator. At another moment, I saw Rick Millington, with whom I had taught Gilman's story for many years in our collaborative American studies course. I am grateful to those at the talk, particularly Michael Gorra and Annie Jones, who sent me good suggestions for reading. Smith provided some of the early readers of the manuscript: the college's former president Mary Maples Dunn, as well as my colleagues Daniel Horowitz, Richard Millington, and Kevin Rozario. Through Smith came travel funds and research assistants who provided substantial help: Judith Shumway, Sarah Miller, Anne-Marie Hawkes, and Laura Putnam. At Smith I have had the opportunity to work with American studies majors in a symposium that has provided an ongoing forum for ideas about the relation of mind and body in illness and health. Librarians at Neilson and the staff of the Sophia Smith Collection have always been generous with time. I have indeed been fortunate to have been part of this great college dedicated to the higher education of women.

I would like to acknowledge the other institutions that have materially aided my project. The National Endowment for the Humanities provided a fellowship at just the right moment. The Arthur and Elizabeth Schlesinger Library holds the many collections of Charlotte Perkins Gilman and her world, and its friendly and helpful staff made work there a pleasure. I am particularly grateful to Ellen M. Shea, Diana Carey, Sarah Hutcheon, and Lynda Leahy. I am also thankful for the collections and the assistance of librarians at the Countway Medical Library, the Houghton Library, and the Baker Library of Harvard University. Farther afield, I wish to thank the Bancroft Library, the Huntington Library, the College of Physicians of Philadelphia, the Duke University Medical Center Library, Drexel University Libraries, and the National Library of Medicine (NLM). I was fortunate to be able to develop the higher education module for the NLM's banner exhibit, "The Literature of Prescription," and wish to acknowledge Manon Parry and Jiwon Kim for their interest and kindness. Stephen Greenberg's initiative and persistence enabled me to both do important research a the NLM and present my ideas to an engaged audience. It was a particular joy to spend a lovely day in Los Alamos with Gilman's grandson, Walter Chamberlin, and his wife, Sally, and to see their marvelous collection of family paintings.

I am grateful to the Schlesinger Library for permission to quote from the papers of Charlotte Perkins Gilman, Grace Ellery Channing, and Charles Walter Stetson. I also wish to thank, for permission to publish excerpts of materials they hold, the Rhode Island Historical Society, the Wisconsin Historical Society, the Baker Library Historical Collections and D&B, and the Bancroft Library, University of California, Berkeley. I wish to acknowledge the courtesy of the providers of illustrations: the Schlesinger Library, the Bancroft Library, and the collection of Christopher and Melinda Ratcliffe.

Countless scholars helped shape my thinking about nervous illness and Charlotte Perkins Gilman, and many are acknowledged in my notes. I owe a particular debt of gratitude to the labors of Gary Scharnhorst, whose bibliography helped guide me at many points, and Denise D. Knight, whose manifold scholarly contributions were always illuminating. At Harvard, I have profited by the good counsel of Anne Harrington, Allan Brandt, and Charles Rosenberg, and the hospitality of the History of Science Department. Julie Reuben of the Graduate School of Education was especially helpful at a critical moment. The Radcliffe Institute brought me a generous reading by and wise advice of Susan Faludi. Writing is a solitary experience, but a writing group is a wonderfully collective one. At a critical moment my writing group pitched in and helped me out. Presenting my ideas at the American Historical Association gave me the collaboration of panelists Patricia Cline Cohen and Gail Bederman, the generous hosting of Lynn Dumenil, and the helpful comments of Jesse Battan and the audience.

I am fortunate in having Sandy Dijkstra as my agent and cheerleader. I wish to thank Susan Ferber, my editor at Oxford University Press, for her insightful reading, thoughtful guidance through revision, and close attention to issues large and small. I also wish to thank Martha Ramsay for her careful copyediting and Jessica Ryan and Marc Schneider for shepherding the manuscript to its final destination.

CONTENTS ···

Wild Unrest

Introduction

> Can I, who suffer from the wild unrest
> Of two strong natures claiming each its due,
> And can not tell the greater of the two;
> Who have two spirits ruling in my breast
> Alternately, and know not which is guest
> And which the owner true.

When Charlotte Perkins Gilman was twenty-three, she was in the middle of the central crisis of her life. In an untitled poem dated April 1, 1883, she wrote that she suffered from "wild unrest."[1] Her deep distress, she believed, sprang from the inner war between her "two strong natures." One, her female side, desired a man's love and its full expression in marriage and children. The other, the self that in her mind had no sex, felt the need to be independent to act in the world—to write, convince others of her ideas, and become famous.[2] Which of her spirits was the true "owner" of Charlotte? Which was the "guest"?[3]

She later posed that struggle in a different form in "The Yellow Wall-Paper." Writing in 1890, as she neared thirty, she distilled much of her conflicted life into this harrowing short story. Since its rediscovery over a generation ago, it has been read and reread by millions in classrooms and libraries and in the privacy of dormitories and homes. More than an assignment or pleasure reading, "The Yellow Wall-Paper" continues to shock and move readers.

Today we believe that a woman can both marry and be an autonomous adult, but in Charlotte's time and place she thought she had to make a choice. When she wrote of her wild unrest, it was 1883 and she lived in Providence, Rhode Island. She was in love and planning to wed. She was lively, beautiful, athletic, intelligent, bold, and unconventional. Her husband-to-be enjoyed all these attributes, but he wanted a traditional wife. He was buttressed by a culture of male striving and female domesticity and a legal system that recognized few rights for a woman in marriage. All around her she could see the common lot of many married women and the unusual achievements of a few who remained single. In her case, battling her aspirations and will for the single life was her loneliness and desire. She wanted to love and be loved and to find sexual fulfillment in marriage. She imagined that love and marriage would bring happiness, and that remaining alone might entail deep self-denial.

Charlotte experienced this deep conflict between love and work within the context of severe depressive episodes. Mysterious in their origin and frightening in their impact, they had come on for some years, alternating with longer periods of well-being. Living through the numbness and the dark that enveloped her during a despondent time was one thing when she was younger and alone in her mother's house. It took on new dimensions as she matured and became intimate with a man who loved and wanted to marry her.

Two months after writing of her wild unrest, Charlotte chose to marry. A year's wait followed; she wed in May 1884 and gave birth to a daughter almost eleven months later. In this period of marriage and early motherhood, she found not happiness but recurring and ever deepening periods of depression. When she broke down in April 1887, she sought the rest cure of the famed neurologist S. Weir Mitchell. After his therapy did not restore her health, she fought to find her own way out of despair. She separated from her husband, wrote and lectured, and by fits and starts began to improve physically and mentally.

Much of the power behind "The Yellow Wall-Paper" derives from its author's intimate knowledge of mental affliction. In this chronicle, a troubled woman—kept isolated by her physician-husband in an upstairs room in a country house, prevented from writing, and deprived of the stimulation of company—descends from nervous illness into madness. The story's central character and narrator takes the reader on every step of her downward course.

Those who teach the story often use it to convey the deeply painful effects of nineteenth-century limitations on women's freedom. This work of fiction stands as a cry of pain against the combined forces of constricting marriage, prejudiced medical practice, restrictive social roles, and narrowed expectations that could and did drive women mad.

The oft-told tale of its origin has heightened the story's impact. Later in her life, Charlotte Perkins Gilman testified that she had lived what she wrote in "The Yellow Wall-Paper." Details were changed, but, she insisted, the essential story was true. "For many years," she wrote in 1913, "I suffered from a severe and continuous nervous breakdown tending to melancholia—and beyond." She went to Dr. Mitchell, took his rest cure for a month, and received, she claimed, his "solemn advice to 'live as domestic a life as far as possible,' to 'have but two hours' intellectual life a day,' and 'never to touch pen, brush, or pencil again' as long as I lived." She followed his instructions, she declared, and "came so near the borderline of utter mental ruin that I could see over." She emphasized that she wrote her short story with a single purpose—to save others from her fate and to get Dr. Mitchell to change his methods. Although Mitchell never acknowledged receiving the copy she sent, Gilman alleged that he "admitted to friends" that after reading the story, "he had altered his treatment of neurasthenia." At the close of her life, she repeated the essentials of this narrative in her autobiography, *The Living of Charlotte Perkins Gilman.*[4]

According to this telling, the creation of the story is itself a testament to Gilman's will to resist the doctor's life sentence. Defying his instructions, she eluded madness, got out of confinement, and wrote. Moreover, her subsequent extraordinary life provided its own testimony. Denied, like the sister of Shakespeare whom Virginia Woolf imagined, a room of her own, she struggled to earn one. As she lectured and wrote, she advocated for all women what was forbidden her story's protagonist—escape from the trap of traditional domesticity, opportunity to work in the public sphere, and social equality.

This book examines Gilman's life and story from the other end of the telescope. It moves forward from her coming of age, not back from her recollections late in her life. It attempts to read "The Yellow Wall-Paper" in light of its author's experiences of love, ambition, and depression in her twenties. Gilman's autobiographical statements have influenced many efforts to understand her breakdown, her treatment, and this short story, but they can be misleading. This book puts aside the myths Gilman created about "The Yellow Wall-Paper" to present her at the time as she understood herself and as she was portrayed by others close to her.

The materials available for this study are a historian's dream. Gilman wrote and published throughout her adult life. The rich treasure trove of her papers includes her daily journal, in which she noted what she did each day and what she read. Her typically terse accounts generally present a running view of her activities, only on occasion allowing access to her feelings. By contrast, her drafts of poems and essays and letters to intimate friends in the same years convey passionate feelings of love and despair, hope and betrayal, opening a window into her interior struggles.

Other sources present the points of view of her husband and her neurologist. Charles Walter Stetson, the man she married in 1884, kept a voluminous diary throughout the 1880s. He set down his thoughts and emotions, sought to report conversations verbatim, and copied letters from Charlotte that would otherwise have been lost. Much of his diary has made its way into print, but important passages remain only in manuscript. Although there is no specific mention of her in the abundant papers of Dr. S. Weir Mitchell, much can be learned in them about her rest cure, the accepted treatment for women suffering from what were then called neurasthenic or hysterical symptoms. Mitchell popularized his therapies for a national audience in a number of books and described them in professional terms to fellow physicians.

Finally, a rich record of the several years of Gilman's life following Mitchell's rest cure resides in her journals, her letters to friends, her friends' letters to others, and public records. All of these sources provide new ways to ground and understand "The Yellow Wall-Paper" anew, building on a wealth of important scholarship on Gilman since the 1970s.[5]

This treasure trove of material must be examined with care and a historian's eye, for language can be deceptive. Words in the past may seem transparent, their meanings fixed by a dictionary, but they carry connotations that can be specific to time, place, and social position. Although the nouns and verbs Charlotte used are current today, they were penned in a different cultural world and can relate to ideas and phenomena no longer known today. Exploring what she read makes it possible to discover the meaning of key words to her at the time she uttered them.

Charlotte was unusual as a young woman not only in her intelligence, talent, handsome presence, striking personality, and energy but also in her isolation. Circumstances of her early upbringing and erratic schooling removed her from both peers and the constant influence of adults other than her mother. As she matured, this one relationship became fraught with tension. In the vacuum she read voraciously, fiction, poetry, and popular science. What is important was not just the amount of her reading but its impact on her.

She learned from articles and books, gaining insight from writers known today, such as Herbert Spencer and George Eliot, and from those less known, such as William Carpenter and contributors to the *Alpha,* a monthly magazine treating sexual matters and women's rights. What she read did more than just inform her; it shaped her consciousness. Understanding her reading sheds much light on how she imagined herself as she lived in her body and experienced the shifting tides of ambition, love, sexual feeling, depression, and creative expression. This book makes a fresh contribution by exploring Charlotte's reading to interpret her language and thought.

Charlotte was both of her time and ahead of it. She shared many of the assumptions of her era about love and marriage, even as she fought to free herself from them. Bound by legal constraints governing marriage, limitations on women's political rights and obligations, and structures of inequity in employment and public life, she joined the fight for women's emancipation. In 1898, she gained immediate and lasting fame both in the United States and abroad with *Women and Economics,* a wide-ranging work that examined and theorized the causes of women's subordination to men. From its publication, she was a major public figure as a lecturer, author, poet, reformer, and suffragist.

She married a second time in 1900, taking the name Charlotte Perkins Gilman. Throughout the remainder of her long life, she continued to write important books and advocate for broader freedom for women. She gave particular attention to the practical and ideological traps of domestic confinement, envisioning housing that freed women from kitchen, laundry, and child care to work in the public sphere. As women read her words and listened to her lectures, many would decide to earn a living and seek the vote.

This book focuses not on the public Gilman but on the private Charlotte. As a young woman, she wrote, "There will be times when this frenzy for freedom boils up with force, which, ungratified, would bring misery to myself and those around me; and there will be times when the woman's heart will wake and cry with heartrending loneliness."[6] This book captures that time and tells that story.

Charlotte Comes of Age

"Gentle reader, wouldst [thou] know me?" So began Charlotte Anna Perkins on January 1879, as she put her pen to her first journal. "Verily, here I am. 18 years old. 5 feet 6 ½ in. high," weighing 120 pounds. Charlotte described her looks as "not bad. At times handsome. At others decidedly homely." Where she excelled was in her health, which she pronounced "perfect," and her strength, "amazing." About her character, Charlotte was a bit more restrained, for she felt she was working to overcome her laziness and to develop self-command. She described herself as definitely "<u>not</u> sentimental. Rather sober and bleak as a general thing." She must have written this in one of her darker moments, which alternated with other times when she was enthusiastic, or to use a nineteenth-century term, whole-hearted.[1]

She was born in 1860 into the distinguished Beecher family of New England, but to a branch that fell on hard times.[2] Her father, Frederick Beecher Perkins, a grandson of the great revival preacher Lyman Beecher, was also related by his sister's marriage to the illustrious Hale family of Boston. During her childhood, Charlotte claimed as relatives the famous (and scandalous) preacher Henry Ward Beecher, the antislavery novelist Harriet Beecher Stowe, and the revered author and minister Edward Everett Hale. Her mother, Mary Westcott Perkins, was the daughter of a Rhode Island merchant. After their marriage, Frederick and Mary Perkins settled in Providence. What may have seemed like a promising beginning deteriorated when Frederick, a writer and librarian, left the household when his surviving children, Thomas and Charlotte, were young. Thereafter he supported them and his wife only intermittently. Mary sought and gained a divorce in the early 1870s. Impoverished, the female-headed family often depended on others to take them in.

Charlotte never blamed her father for his desertion and neglect, but she did fault her mother for her unhappy childhood—and much else besides. Years later, in private letters and in her autobiography, Charlotte complained that her mother withheld from her expressions of love in the effort to make her self-reliant. She told how Mary refused even to kiss her good-night, leading her to pretend to fall asleep in order to get the kiss her mother denied her when she was awake. In addition to her other privations, Charlotte had only irregular schooling as a child.

She was, however, highly imaginative. In 1887 she wrote that when she was young, she enjoyed "visions of unattainable delights" on going to sleep. She penned fictions in childhood of brave princesses and their derring-do, fantasies of power and rescue. She also read novels, delighting in Scott and Dickens from an early age. Narrative poems and novels of the period gave mixed messages—of heroism and villainy, of love found and love lost, of brave action and valiant sacrifice. In these books there were clever girls and women, heroines and anti-heroines who offered many alternatives to domestic ideology, at least before submission at the novel's end. Intense, passionate feeling underlay much of the literature she imbibed, but she also was exposed to satire, farce, and light humor.

At age twelve, Mary Perkins told Charlotte to end her inner life of fantasy, and, according to a letter Charlotte wrote in her twenties, she complied. For a time, perhaps influenced by the tirades against fiction by ministers and writers on health who feared stimulating licentious impulses, Mary also insisted that Charlotte give up novels. This lasted only a short while before mother and daughter returned to fiction, often reading aloud to each other.

Charlotte had remarkable curiosity about the world and growing ambition. She suffered, however, from inconsistent formal education. Her mother was her earliest teacher, giving her a good start, but over the course of her childhood and its many changes of address, she went to seven schools, on and off for a total of only four years. At age fourteen she was able to attend a good private school for roughly a year, but her secondary education ended when she was fifteen. Her absent father was an important influence. A published author of short stories, Frederick Perkins became a librarian in Boston and later in San Francisco. As the compiler of the reference book *The Best Reading,* he helped shape the literary choices of the nation and his daughter.[3] As Charlotte matured, she found a way to reach her father by asking him to suggest books for her reading. In the late 1870s, he sent her regular bundles of *Popular Science Monthly.*[4] After she demonstrated talent in art, he paid for her training during the academic year 1878–79 at the newly opened Rhode Island School of Design.

As early as age fifteen, Charlotte began to experience times when she was very low in spirits. As she wrote to her father, these frequent intervals of "depression" made her feel "hopelessly despairing, at my total inability to <u>work</u>."[5] During her year of art training, her brother Thomas came down with diphtheria, and she missed many days of academic work in nursing him. She tried to resign herself to familial duties without success, and in February 1879 she recorded in her journal a depressive episode. She found herself thinking of death and the peace of dying. After her mother took sick, Charlotte wrote in her journal, "Mother is very cross and fretty. As for me, I weep."[6] Two years later, in February 1881, as she again nursed her mother through illness, she noted to herself that she worked "in a season of moroseness and depression" and in "all pervading gloom."[7]

As she matured, Charlotte increasingly went her own inner way, leading to conflicts with her mother. These intensified as Charlotte reached maturity. Mary Perkins believed that she had the right and responsibility to monitor Charlotte's behavior and control her personal life. Although Charlotte was successful in evading much of Mary's oversight once she stepped out of the house to run errands and visit friends, her mother continued to open her letters, advise her on how to answer them, and tell her which invitations she could accept and which she must refuse. As a result, Charlotte occasionally felt denied some of the ordinary pleasures of heterosexual social life enjoyed by her female Providence friends, such as going to the theater with a man. Like many a girl growing into womanhood, Charlotte resented her mother's intrusions and fought for independence. This she found increasingly as she moved into a world of friends in Providence and on visits with the high-spirited Hale family in Boston, where she tasted a freer social life and enjoyed the company of her male cousins and their Harvard classmates.

In the summer of 1881, all was relatively stable in the Perkins household. Frederick was able to contribute to the rent of a generous part of a house in Providence in which Charlotte lived with her mother and an aunt. It was pleasantly situated in a residential area of large wooden dwellings on the city's east side, not far from Brown University.[8] Thomas was far away in Nevada, working as a railroad supervisor. His father had paid for him to go to the Massachusetts Institute of Technology, but he had flunked out. Money was scarce, for Frederick offered only partial support and Mary earned only a small income from teaching private pupils. Charlotte was developing her skill as a painter of flowers, and she put them on greeting cards, stationery, and objects for sale among friends and acquaintances. Assisted by an older cousin who worked for the Providence soap manufacturer Soapine, she

Charlotte as young woman, c. 1884. Schlesinger Library, Radcliffe Institute, Harvard University.

designed decorative trade cards for the firm.[9] She paid her mother for board and her room on the third floor. She had many friends, including a very special one, Martha Luther. She read constantly and wrote poetry and prose. In excellent health, she was an avid walker and runner.

On July 3, 1881, Charlotte celebrated her twenty-first birthday.[10] It was, she believed, a turning point. For some time she had chafed under her mother's intrusiveness into her private life. Now, with her coming of age, she demanded that her mother treat her like an adult and respect her right to personal privacy. She insisted that she be able to receive and send letters without her mother's monitoring eye or censorship. This allowed Charlotte to write down her feelings and reflections freely.

Thus she luxuriated in letters to and from Martha, her beloved friend, during the summer of 1881. At last free to write just what she pleased, Charlotte could give her letters an intimate turn. She wrote long, detailed letters almost daily to Martha, who was vacationing in New Hampshire. They are exuberant testaments to what it is to be young—questing, self-fashioning, seeking to find companions and like-minded intimates, longing to be admired, reaching out for love.

The two young women had known each other for a number of years, brought together in the casual world of young women who met in school or on outings and at parlor visits for tea. As an intimate friendship gradually blossomed, they came to spend many hours together. In the spring of 1881, they bought identical bracelets to wear as symbols of their affection. In the 1880s, it was still customary for girls to have romantic relationships with female friends. Those close to them, such as mothers and teachers, often encouraged such romantic attachments among daughters and pupils, seeing them as safer than intimacy with males.[11]

Charlotte had many things on her mind that summer. She was trying to organize a gymnastics class for the year. Like a growing number of women of her time, she was enthusiastic about physical exercise and had an intense commitment to building up her bodily strength. She also hoped to start an essay club among her female friends. Such informal groups offered mutual support to women as they aspired to understand the world of ideas and express themselves orally and on the page. Summer offered the chance to be outdoors and the easy pleasures of outings. Whole days were spent in social visiting.

Young men came to call or walked her home, and a particular young man, Jim Simmons, was very much on her mind. An attractive Brown graduate, he presented himself as a gentleman caller. She was drawn to him, but she did not like the way he browbeat her as they conversed about ideas and religion. At some point in late July, she made a decision that she would distance herself from him, and by mid-August he had ceased to call. In reflecting on this, she wrote to Martha that she did not want male friends "until my head sitteth more firmly on my heart, not until brain exercise has enlarged and strengthened that organ."[12]

Sam Simmons, Jim's brother, was neither a suitor nor one who challenged her beliefs, and Charlotte turned to him as a confidant. She wrote to Martha that she had talked to Sam about "the frightful incompatibility between mother & myself, my rebellion and utter inefficiency in this unsound sort of life, my gradually strengthening and now unconquerable desire for mental culture and exercise; my determination to drop my half-developed <u>functional</u> womanhood, and take the broad road of individuality apart from sex, and all the bother and uncertainty resulting from Mother's inability to live without me, and my surviving relics of overdrawn hereditary conscience." In this densely packed sentence Charlotte conveyed a great deal about herself. She was uneasy about constantly judging herself, a heritage she believed came from her ancestors. She felt deeply at odds with her mother and disliked her domestic and scattered life. She worried that her mother would be dependent on her, hampering her freedom. Charlotte wanted to grow mentally and physically. Most of all, she feared what lay in store for her if she followed a conventional woman's path to courtship and marriage, and she imagined herself as developing her individual gifts alone, away from men. She related that Sam took her words very seriously and said to her, "Go ahead!"

Charlotte dreamed of living apart from her mother as an unmarried, independent woman, able to focus her energies and control her destiny. In such moments she began to think of herself, as she put it, as "a <u>strong-minded</u> woman."[13] Her ambition remained undefined, but she continued to dream of doing big things in the world.

To this young woman's eye, strong-minded women could not have courting men in their lives, as they threatened them with subordination and maternity. But she imagined that such women could have each other without fear. While Martha was away, Charlotte spent time with Cassie, a slightly older female friend, a teacher in a neighboring town. After Charlotte described dressing up for her in a letter to Martha—in satin and lace, long white gloves, silver bells, a fan, and her hair high—she added, "Cassie was smashed," the familiar schoolgirl term for same-sex attraction. Then she followed with an enticement to Martha, "And I have vowed a vow to wear good clothes in the future whenever I can. <u>Won't it be nice, 'little girl.'</u>" Trying at this moment to woo Martha away from a male suitor, Charlotte wrote to her that if she were a betting person, she would wager that Martha would make up to her "for husband and children and all that I shall miss." Thus at the time she turned twenty-one, Charlotte had a clear image of female twosomes who resisted the dominant heterosexual pairing of marriage.[14]

Charlotte wrote to Martha that she was "really getting glad not to marry," for she reasoned that "the mother side" of herself was so strong that, if she married, she would experience "an interminable war between plain duties & irrepressible instincts." Even now, she felt "rage" at domestic confinement. Were she married, she would dissipate her energy and get nowhere.[15] Charlotte's judgment was that if she stayed single, if she "let that business alone," she could expand her "individual strength and development of personal power of character, <u>myself as a self</u>." She contrasted this to growth "merely as a woman, or that useful animal a wife and a mother." Although she would give up a "happiness that part of me would so enjoy," she believed she would gain in the balance "usefulness and effect."[16]

With this she conveyed her dream that the two of them might live together. As she did so, she used terms that denied much of what she was feeling for Martha. She stated that in not marrying a man she would repress the feminine and maternal side of herself with its associated "irrepressible instincts."[17] Following this logic, a woman could satisfy her instincts only if she married and had children.

As she experienced love for Martha, Charlotte did not understand or chose not to see her strong homoerotic feeling. Expression of such yearning abounded—pet names, baby talk, expression of the desire to live with Martha. Under the heading "Private!" she wrote to Martha, "I would like to put my hand under your chin, and look way down into your big eyes, ask questions, deposit kisses."[18] Then, imagining that someone lacking the proper taste or culture to understand might see what she had written, Charlotte wrote, "Even if the Philistines ever should see it, what care I! If I am not ashamed of having sentiments I am not ashamed of admitting them, and why shouldn't I love my little comfort when I haven't anything else to love?"[19]

Martha must have challenged Charlotte's use of the word *love*. After recounting at some length her conversation with Sam about her ambitions and dreams for the future, Charlotte attempted to respond to Martha's likely concern. "Why in the name of heaven," Charlotte wrote, "have we so confounded love with passion that it sounds to our century-tutored ears either wicked or absurd to name it between women. It is no longer friendship between us, it is love." Charlotte tried to turn love into a distinction between friendship, which was for the multitudes, and a feeling for one person only. She reserved the word *passion* for the love of someone of the opposite sex.[20] The ardent language she used when she wrote to Martha, however, belied that limitation.

Many years later, when Charlotte reconnected with Martha, she wrote, "No one has ever taken your place, heart's dearest. No one has ever given me the happiness that you did, the peace, the rest, the everpresent joy."[21] Recalling the summer of 1881, Charlotte wrote, "I doubt if most people have as much happiness in all their lives as I had then."[22] The emphasis must be on the "I." Although only Charlotte's letters remain, Martha was clearly resisting many of Charlotte's effusions, either by ignoring them or distancing herself through pleading that she and Charlotte were different. At one point, Charlotte wrote her, "Here I show you my heart and you don't take the slightest notice."[23]

Martha was involved in her own drama at the time. She was being courted by a young lawyer from Hingham, Massachusetts, Charles Lane, whom she admired, and was deciding whether or not to marry him. Charlotte put up a brave front. "You are to be your own sweet lovely self, marry all you please, and be loved and cared for to your heart[']s content. But be your home as charming as it may, I am to have a night-key, as it were, and shall enjoy in you and yours all that I don't have myself. Halicarnassus [Charles Lane] will like me I know, and as for the children—look out for your laurels."[24] Toward the end of the summer, Charlotte had the insensitivity to write Martha of her fantasy that she, Charlotte, would move into a big house with Martha and Charles, he would die, and then, "lo, I will be all in all!"[25] Charlotte's failure to read situations and others appropriately or to see her own behavior as others might would remain constant.

Alongside her declarations of love, another important aspect of her letters to Martha was Charlotte's eagerness to be and do. The letters are filled with life—social fun and gossip. She also wrote Martha about her vaunting ambitions and her desire for intellectual growth. She set out her reading program and discussed a decision to learn Latin. Her precise goals for the future were at this point indeterminate. Once she had written to her father of her desire to become a doctor or go on the stage. Now she only wrote only in generalities that included doing good and becoming famous.

In the fall of 1881, despite the paucity of Charlotte's formal education, she took on the daughter of a prominent Providence family as a private pupil and gradually began to have other young students, teaching them a range of subjects, including art.[26] She read a great deal of ancient history, most likely in conjunction with a correspondence course she took. She continued to decorate stationery and cards for paying customers. An enthusiastic athlete, she rowed, walked, and ran. The gymnastics class started, and she reveled in her exercise there several days a week. Encouraged by a minister, she conducted a regular boys' club meeting on Saturday afternoons and a Sunday school class. She went to lectures and theatricals.

Charlotte's journal that autumn conveys little of her inner life but much of her constant motion and her striving to make the most of every moment. She lived in a social world in Providence of daily visiting, frequent gift-giving, and nightly bouts of whist or chess. She had ups and downs. Punctuating bursts of activity were times of feeling "blue." Underlying this was the realization that she was losing Martha to Charles Lane, confirmed by Martha's engagement at the beginning of November. A few years later, she wrote that this was "a desperate grief to me."[27]

In mid-November, she poured out her deep sadness in a letter to Sam Simmons. At the end of a typical day of teaching, running around, and studying, she had an evening of quiet to write to him as her mother and aunt were out attending a lecture. During the afternoon she had not stopped off at Martha's for tea—"I hardly cared to go half a mile out of my way tonight just to hear about Hingham"— and she now felt bereft. Charlotte described herself without Martha as an amputee. After surviving the surgery, "I complain no longer of the <u>pain</u>, but feel the <u>loss of the limb</u> as sensibly as ever." The hurt, however, had come back recently, evoked by kindness. When an older friend, Caroline Hazard, reached out, Charlotte poured out a bit of her grief-stricken heart. Caroline stroked her hand, saying, "my poor stormy child!" With these words, Charlotte once again felt the intense pain of her loss.[28]

Sam had apparently tried to comfort her by saying that he would only feel closer to a male friend who became engaged. For female friends, Charlotte responded, it was different. As she saw it, once a woman married, she became a wife and belonged to a man, who took her both physically and emotionally away from her friends. But that was not enough to describe the difference. In her letter Charlotte groped for words to explain to Sam what she was feeling, realizing that it was difficult for him to "compass such an abnormal state of affairs." She had found the one person who filled her every need, but Martha now had someone who offered her more. Charlotte asked Sam to imagine "that there was some one who could give your friend <u>everything</u> which you had so gladly rendered, and a world beside."[29] The words of this letter challenge the clear distinction Charlotte had attempted to draw between love and passion.

A private poem addressed to Martha, labeled merely "Unsent," reveals the extent of Charlotte's grief.[30] Preceded by nine pet names for Martha, the poem begins with the statement that each name carries memories, and now "Each little name and all the thoughts behind / Hath arrows poison tipped." Invoking a pet name, she calls up the associated emotion and the caresses. She alternates the sweet endearment she had once used in addressing Martha with rebukes.

> "My little girl!" My little girl! No more,
> Never again in all this weary world
> Can I with clinging arms & kisses soft
> Call you "my little girl!"

Invoking one of the names, Charlotte addresses Martha directly, telling Martha what she meant to her:

> "Sweetheart!" You were my sweetheart. I am none,
> To any man, and I had none but you.
> O sweet! You filled my life; you gave me all
> Of tenderness, consideration, trust,

Confiding love, respect, regard, reproof,
And all the thousand thousand little things
With which love glorifies the hardest life.

Charlotte recalls the time a year ago "When you and I asked nothing of the world / But room, and one another" and gave each other their hearts. Charlotte asks Martha to remember the moments "when we could hardly dare / Be seen abroad together lest our eyes / Should speak too loud." Not only do such words evoke passionate feeling, they and the throwaway line to Sam about the "abnormal state of affairs" suggest a suppressed awareness on her part of a forbidden love that needed to be hidden from the world.

The poem then turns to Charlotte's sense of betrayal. Martha took Charlotte's heart and held it in her hands, but only kept "it warm until another came." Martha gave the heart back, and now Charlotte's heart, like a newborn baby, cries. As Charlotte closes and says farewell, she suggests that what is left for her—with unrequited love and no male sweetheart—is only "hard work."

The poem, dated December 13, was unsent, but not unread. Charlotte reported in her journal that when Martha visited a week later, she read the poem aloud to her, and Martha wept. Writing and reading it to Martha seems to have exorcised the demon of grief for a time. As January 1, 1882 approached, Charlotte picked herself up and set out her resolutions for the new year.

I have in my mind this year three cares. (So far.)

1. Others first.
2. <u>Correct</u> & <u>necessary</u> speech only.
3. Don't waste a minute!

If I can form the ground work of these habits in a year it will be well.

Furthermore I wish to form a habit of <u>willing</u> as much as I can.[31]

A page from Charlotte's journal, 1882. Schlesinger Library, Radcliffe Institute, Harvard University.

"Groundwork of habits," "habits of willing"—such phrases may remind some readers today of the distance between Charlotte's mental universe and their own. She was a highly intelligent and energetic young woman, irregularly educated, of modest means, living with her mother and working at home, with a talent for drawing and poetry and an intense desire to achieve. Where did she learn about life, where did she find the words and images that allowed her to interpret her experience and imagine her future?

Charlotte was a reader. She read history and science to broaden her education, and she read novels and narrative poems for pleasure. Her journals and diaries chronicle vast reading that she accomplished in her late teen years. She read alone, and she read aloud to her mother, aunt, and friends. As Charlotte reached out to the larger world, the printed page opened her to wide influences. It fed her ideals and gave her concepts and a language with which to understand and articulate what she was feeling.

As Charlotte emerged from her girlhood, she was an avid follower of the new science of bodily functioning, what was called in her day "reform physiology."[32] Influenced in school by a talk by Mary J. Studley, Charlotte began her quest for health. A physician trained at the Woman's Medical College of New York, Studley taught natural sciences at State Normal School in Framingham, Massachusetts. In addition to advocating moderation and self-control, she admonished her youthful audience to get plenty of fresh air and exercise, eat healthful foods, and wear clothes that were nonbinding and comfortable.[33] Charlotte took this advice on diet, exercise, and dress reform to heart.

In Charlotte's case such advice was especially well received, for the ground had been prepared by her great-aunt Catharine Beecher, whom she never knew. Beecher was a towering figure in the early and mid-nineteenth century who, in addition to her famous work on household economy and her leadership in women's education, wrote many books on health, developed calisthenics for girls in her schools, and promoted her ideas about the importance of physical culture. In writing to Martha about her various schemes over the summer, Charlotte jokingly said, "Truly the manageress and reformer worketh within me! Shades of Aunt Catherine!"[34]

Charlotte developed a specific interest in gymnastics at a girls' school in Providence she attended in 1875, where Dr. John P. Brooks taught classes.[35] In the years that followed, she took brisk walks around Providence, especially during her year at the Rhode Island School of Design. In 1879, she bought William Blaikie's newly published *How to Get Strong and How to Stay So* and embraced it as a personal guide. This work by the New York lawyer and fitness enthusiast championed the ideas and system of Dudley Allen Sargent, the director of Harvard's new Hemenway Gymnasium. Blaikie took a general concern for the physical and mental health of the American populace, male and female, as the starting point for his book and promised improvement through a structured program of physical exercise. As he presented Sargent's exercises and apparatus, Blaikie challenged girls and women to build up their bodily strength as a preventative against the "chronic debility" that could lead a woman to be a "source of anxiety and a burden to her friends, when instead of this she might have been a valued helper." He was critical of the girls he saw. "Instead of high chests, plump arms, comely figures and a graceful and handsome mien, you constantly see flat chests, angular shoulders...narrow backs and a weak walk....few have vigor and force." He recommended strenuous exercise to repair and strengthen the brain through increased respiration and circulation.[36] In urging his case, he wrote, "Are not the majority of our women to-day, especially in town and city, physically weak? The writers on nervous disorders speak of the astounding increase of such diseases among us, of late years, in both sexes, but especially among the women. General debility is heard of nowadays almost as often as General Grant."[37] Charlotte began regular exercise at home, measuring her body, and following Blaikie's directions each night "with the greatest assiduity."[38]

In the summer of 1881, Charlotte went to Dr. Brooks to ask him to set up a women's exercise room in conjunction with his

Providence Gymnasium, frequented by men. Aided by the wealthy Mrs. Roland Hazard II, the mother of her friend Caroline, Charlotte rounded up a class of young women and girls.[39] Brooks's Providence Ladies Sanitary Gymnasium opened on the fifth floor of a building in downtown Providence, "a large light airy hall...stocked with apparatus selected by Dr. Sargent of Harvard University."[40] Charlotte was an enthusiastic participant. For several years she went to the gym several times a week, including a regular Saturday demonstration in front of an audience. She helped recruit others to the gym and regarded herself as its leading participant. At one point, when the woman who directed the group failed to inspire, Charlotte proudly wrote, "I take hold, lead the marches, & give lots of vim to it."[41]

Charlotte's journal implicitly demonstrated the way reform physiology shaped her thinking about herself. The assumption that one could make a healthy body and maintain it through diet, sleep, comfortable clothing, and exercise underlies her entries in the years before her marriage. Each day she watched herself carefully and noted the times she rose and went to bed, what she ate, the work she accomplished, and the exercise she took. She gloried in walking and, once she had a pedometer, put in her diary the distances, as many as five and a half or ten miles at a stint. She identified an energetic body with larger health that included mind and spirit. For example, as the year 1884 began, she wrote in her journal, "Begin a course of diet, by means of which, and other changes, I trust to regain my old force & vigor."[42] That evening she went to the gymnasium and tested her strength on the rope and the rings.

Charlotte also tried to build up her brain by systematic reading and in the fall of 1881 began to take a course from the Society to Encourage Studies at Home, based in Boston.[43] The society was created in 1873 by Anna Eliot Ticknor as a correspondence program for women who, for a range of reasons, could not pursue higher education in established institutions. Ticknor got well-educated but generally unemployed women to volunteer their time to set up courses of study in the liberal arts and sciences and guide students through reading. Through flyers and word of mouth, Ticknor gathered interested girls and women. Initially the numbers were small, but by the early 1880s, when Charlotte began her work, a thousand students were enrolled.

Ticknor asked prospective students a few questions and then assigned them teachers who would correspond with them once a month, assigning books, asking them questions, and reading their essays. Included in the faculty were some well-known names: Ellen Swallow Richards, the creator of home economics; Vida Scudder, professor of English at Wellesley College; and Alice James, the sister of William and Henry, Jr.[44] Working under the direction of A. Fanny Alden of Hingham, for two years Charlotte read ancient history, including the history of the Hebrews and early Christians, wrote essays, and received reports. Over time, the relationship between teacher and student became personal, and Charlotte visited with Fanny Alden at the home of mutual friends and received letters from her.[45]

In her later lecturing and writing, Charlotte's wide reading in ancient history served her in good stead, helping to buttress some of her important arguments about the sources of female subordination. However, in the 1880s, her studies did not answer the kinds of questions she had about herself. Here her most important educator was not a teacher or a sequence of books but a magazine, *Popular Science Monthly*. In its pages, she learned about her animal nature, evolutionary theory, the new field of psychology. Here she learned to think of her "brain" as an organ to be enlarged and strengthened, and she read the newest scientific thought about what it meant to be a woman.

Although Charlotte read Charles Darwin's *Descent of Man* as early as 1880, her primary understanding of evolution came from *Popular Science Monthly*'s presentation of the works of Herbert Spencer, the British philosopher. His ideas remained with Charlotte for the rest of her life. The language of evolution and human will was, of course, in the very air Charlotte breathed, but in her struggle to train her mind as well as her body, she made regular visits to Providence libraries, noting them in her journal. In addition to works of ancient history, she found there pleasure books and the leading periodicals of the day, such as the *Century, Scribner's, Harper's,* and the humor magazine *Punch.* But most of all, she imbibed the latest current issues of *Popular Science Monthly.* She wrote to Martha in the summer of 1881 that she had read a particular copy of *Popular Science Monthly* with "starved eagerness."[46] Through its articles, editorials, notes, and book reviews, she was exposed to a broad range of issues and thinkers. Except for her year at the Rhode Island School of Design and her correspondence course in ancient history, she had no formal higher education. *Popular Science Monthly* became her university.[47]

Founded in 1872 by Edward Livingston Youmans to bring the work of Herbert Spencer to a broad American public, *Popular Science Monthly* was immediately successful, quickly entering the homes of eleven thousand subscribers. This attractive and accessible monthly compendium of useful and theoretical science presented Spencer's newest work along with an eclectic mix of reports on scientific and advances and new inventions, offerings of the new social sciences, and discussions of philosophical issues alongside controversies with religious opponents. The primary thrust of the magazine was, as its name suggested, popular science. Articles about comets and new varieties of seed sprinkled its pages, but these can be seen as lighter fare surrounding the more serious. Youmans wanted his journal to work for the common good through the diffusion of scientific knowledge. He defined science broadly as "the most accurate knowledge that can be obtained of the order of the universe by which man is surrounded, and of which he is a part." Insight began with the physical world and widened to include human nature and society. What made a work science was not what it studied but how. Science was "a method of the mind."[48] The monthly's appeal was best captured by Oliver Wendell Holmes, Sr., in an 1874 letter to Youmans in which he wrote that *Popular Science Monthly* "comes to me like the air they send down to the people in a diving bell. I seem to get a fresh breath with every new number."[49]

Through presenting the work of Spencer in ninety-one articles (by the time of Youmans's death in 1887), *Popular Science Monthly* offered an evolutionary perspective on human beings that emphasized the aspects of human nature that derived from instinct and unconscious forces. This approach drew clear distinctions between women and men, determining that women were less evolved and thus less differentiated, less capable of sustained thought and judgment, and more controlled by their bodies and instincts.

Spencer drew on major scientific principles of his time—evolution, the persistence of force, equilibrium—to put together a comprehensive understanding of the world, its structure and functioning, in which all discrete phenomena seemed to fit together and make sense. Trained as a civil engineer, Spencer derived great meaning from the principle of the conservation of energy, what he called the "persistence of force," which ordained that all matter and motion existed from the beginning, changing over time in form only. Although Spencer was an evolutionist before Darwin published his *On the Origin of the Species* and the first to write the phrase "survival of the fittest," he took strength from Darwin's principle of struggle.[50]

Through *Popular Science Monthly*, Charlotte learned that natural and human history formed a single continuum. Over eons, the cosmos moved from simple to complex, from homogeneity to heterogeneity, from uniformity to differentiation. So did biology, as the chain of evolution progressed from single-celled animals to its apex, humankind. Charlotte shared with a long generation of readers in Britain and America the excitement of Spencer's formulation, which conveyed to them a "sense of a whole world operating at different yet related levels" and offered dynamic, unexpected analogies from different realms of being.[51]

When Spencer wrote about humanity, he used the word *man*. While it was customary for nineteenth-century writers to employ this word as a generic term covering woman, in Spencer's case, he meant it specifically. He argued that in order to develop the most complex, heterogeneous, and differentiated society, western European man had to be joined to a differently constituted being, woman. In Spencer's understanding, the sexes had evolved differently.

Human females, Spencer argued, had become adapted to survive and reproduce in ways that made their bodies and characters quite distinct. He adhered to the Lamarckian theory of the inheritance of acquired characteristics, but he also believed that natural selection favored "the predominant transmission of traits to descendants of the same sex."[52] In the case of humans, men succeeded by battle and conquest, but women conserved their nutrition, to better bear and feed their young. As a result they were smaller, weaker, and softer and were forced to rely on men to protect them and their infants. They matured earlier in ways that arrested their mental development, leaving their brains smaller and therefore capable of less thought. When their brains stopped growing in their teen years, what remained undeveloped were "those two faculties, intellectual and emotional, which are the latest products of human evolution—the power of abstract reasoning and that most abstract of the emotions, the sentiment of justice."[53] Only western European men, whose physical and mental maturation continued until their twenties, had fully developed brains and mental capacities.

Spencer saw women as acquiring distinct gifts as they successfully adapted to the dominant men, who both protected and abused them. Women had "the ability to please, and the concomitant love of approbation." They had the arts of persuasion and remarkable "powers of disguising their feelings." And they had the power of intuition, essentially "an aptitude for guessing the state of mind through the external signs" that enabled them to "distinguish quickly the passing feelings of those around." These feminine capacities had enabled some women, dependents in a world dominated by powerful, barbarous men, to become mothers and pass on their traits to their female children. Their abilities were sex-linked, further differentiated by their need to attach themselves to strong and potent men, who in turn passed their male characteristics to their sons.[54]

Charlotte would work with these ideas throughout her life, gradually modifying them as she absorbed the more progressive possibilities that Edward Bellamy, Lester Frank Ward, and women's rights advocates posed. At this point, as she came of age, however, she felt the rank injustice of Spencer's positioning of women. She sought to strengthen her body and brain and refashion herself as an independent being capable of acting in the world. Her inchoate sense of mission and her strenuous activity can be understood as implicit attempts to counter Spencer's limitations on female capacity.[55]

Aiding those efforts was a way of seeing herself that she shared with some other women of her time. Opposing Spencerian notions, Charlotte imagined herself as composed of two sides. As she expressed it to Martha, she saw one, "the mother side," as that part of herself that existed "merely as a woman" and disparaged it as "that useful animal a wife and a mother." She thought, however, that satisfying its claims might give her "happiness" to "enjoy." Against this side was her individual self, the "personal power of character," what she called "myself as a self." This aspect of her was unbounded by sex distinction and therefore had the capacity to be equal to that of a man. A goodly number of other vibrant women in this era, such as the educator M. Carey Thomas, saw their mothers' generation as tied down by marriage and maternity.[56] Hoping for the autonomy to reach and grow that they saw in males, they pitted an individual self that they believed had no sex against a part of themselves that they thought was bound by their female bodies. As Charlotte gained her maturity she, too, saw female "animal" versus autonomous "self" as the central dichotomy in her life.

She gave this division profound expression in a poem, "In Duty Bound," first written in 1881, perhaps in the time of her depression during her mother's illness. In its initial iteration, the poem consisted of three stanzas. Charlotte presents the other side of her sense of mission to achieve in the world—the feeling of aspiration unrealized because it exists in the frame of a woman's body. Charlotte imagined a lone woman with a life "hemmed in," pressed by the circumstances of womanhood and poverty to bend to a lesser life. She uses as the central image a woman in "A house with roof so darkly low" that she "cannot stand erect without a blow."

Charlotte expressed starkly in this poem the conflict between the claims of womanhood and dreams of a higher life:

An obligation preimposed, unsought;
Yet binding with the force of natural law.
The pressure of antagonistic thought

Aching within, each hour
A sense of wasting power.

Rejecting the one "chance of breaking out"—"sin"—the woman of the poem can only hope for death, "a grave more wide" than the constricting house of womanhood.[57]

"In Duty Bound" gave a desolate picture of female existence. Seeking a way out, Charlotte hoped she could escape from the trap of being a female "animal" by building up her autonomous "self," which she imagined as free of sex, and by avoiding the counting company of men. Just as she exercised and fortified her body, she would, she wrote to Martha, engage in "brain exercise" to enlarge and strengthen "that organ."

At this time in her life, two resources that might have helped Charlotte were absent. The women's rights movement was over three decades old, and two older members of the Beecher family were directly involved in it. Henry Ward Beecher was the nominal head of the relatively conservative American Woman's Suffrage Association, and Isabella Beecher Hooker was active in the more radical National Woman's Suffrage Association. Both Catharine Beecher and Harriet Beecher Stowe represented women's advancement but had advocated retaining the domestic path to women's influence. Although Charlotte caught glimpses of the drive for female emancipation in her reading, inexplicably, she stood aloof from it until around 1883. Had her exposure to the movement been wider, she might had been able to link her ambition more fully to others and to see that, in some cases, women's achievement was compatible with marriage.

Charlotte also had limited knowledge of sexuality. More than many adolescent girls, she had been sheltered and educated at home, missing the peer world of boarding school and college that shaped some of her contemporaries. She was aware of smashes and pairs of women who lived together, but the potential sexual component of women's relationships likely remained obscure. The broader culture had long sanctioned and valued female intimacy, and in the decades that preceded Charlotte's majority, it was normal for middle-class women to share expressions of affection such as hand-holding, kissing, embracing, sleeping in the same bed, and caressing—what the era called "spooning" or "petting." Within this world, women generally enjoyed the privacy of romantic feeling.

By Charlotte's era, elements of intimate female expression were beginning to come under question as unhealthy, particularly as boarding school and college practices became more known to the public. As this happened, what had earlier been regarded as appropriate for all women was increasingly relegated to schoolgirls. Avowed sexual relationships among women were not openly acknowledged or a part of public discussion in 1881. Thus, despite kisses and caresses and the experience of powerful feelings of love for Martha, Charlotte held on to the abstractions of public discourse that limited the object of a woman's instinct and passion to a man. Simply put, this created a cognitive gap between what she felt and what she knew.

Charlotte's explicit need, as she sought to act in the world, was to reconcile evolutionary doctrine with human freedom. Spencer himself laid out a groundwork for a science of right behavior that influenced her at a later point, but earlier on, *Popular Science Monthly* offered her new thinking in psychology that applied evolutionary biology to the brain and mind and found room for the will and thus for individual liberty. Charlotte was exposed to the British writer William B. Carpenter, the most respected psychological thinker, both directly and indirectly in *Popular Science Monthly*. His writings appeared in the magazine from its first year, and as it continued to publish work by him, it also contained articles by others who drew on and cited his work. The influence of Carpenter and of those who agreed with him pervaded the magazine.[58] Charlotte's personal program of self-development offered a living example of his instructions.

It was a hard balancing act to accept the central dictates of evolutionary biology on the importance of instinct and habit and to restore simultaneously a place for human will, but Carpenter attempted it in ways that influenced a generation. In response to Thomas Huxley's famous materialist dictum that humans were "automata," that mental activity was merely a secretion of the brain, Carpenter countered that "in virtue of the Will…we are *not* mere thinking Automata."[59]

What specifically influenced Charlotte's thinking was Carpenter's argument that "the control which the Will can exert over the *direction* of the thoughts" and the propelling force behind feelings enabled the human psyche to be free.[60] He developed a theme that became important to Charlotte: that human beings could alter their behaviors and ideas by initiating actions through acts of will; if repeated, these willing acts could become established habits. For a person such as Charlotte who sought to have an impact on the world, Carpenter encouraged the subordination of emotion to reason and will.

As Charlotte sought in various ways to strengthen herself, she responded to distinctive and significant elements of Carpenter's work. He wrote, for example, of the importance of learning how to fix one's attention—in today's parlance, to focus. This enabled the Will to direct the "power over the current of Thought and

Feeling, which characterizes the fully developed Man." Attention was important both for intellectual activity and for the "due regulation of our Emotional nature." It was necessary to fix attention on states of feeling that one wanted to intensify, and conversely "by withdrawing it from those we desire to repress," it was possible to "keep in check what we know to be wrong or undesirable."[61] The Will had no direct power over emotions. "We can no more avoid feeling *mental* 'hurt' than we can avoid feeling *bodily* 'hurt.' But we have exactly the same power of *withdrawing the attention* from the mental 'hurt,' that we have of withdrawing it from bodily pain, by *determinately fixing it upon some other object.*"[62]

Charlotte set herself on a course of shaping her behavior and controlling her thoughts through repeated acts of will. Thus we can understand her gloss on the resolutions she made, as the new year approached, to think first of others, to limit her speech, and to not waste time: "If I can form the ground work of these habits in a year it will be well. Furthermore I wish to form a habit of *willing* as much as I can."[63]

Here Charlotte was directly trying to apply to her own life Carpenter's edicts, which she understood in the context of Spencer's larger framework. More generally, her wide early reading continued to inform her and shape her reactions, judgments, and reasoning and gave her a language to talk about her feelings. Spencer and Carpenter formed an intellectual base on which she continued to build as she read, wrote, listened, and talked. These sources would serve her well—and ill—in the years ahead.

Walter Enters

On January 12, 1882, Charlotte met Charles Walter Stetson, a twenty-three-year-old fellow artist. Theirs was an arranged meeting. A mutual friend had taken her the previous day to a lecture by Walter on etching and followed up on January 12 by escorting her to Walter's studio. Charlotte wrote in her journal, "I like him and his pictures." A Providence painter at the beginning of his career, Walter was handsome and charming. Ten days later, after their first time alone, Charlotte reported in her journal that they had "a nice talk. I introduce myself as fully as possible, and he does the same. We shake hands on it, and are in a fair way to be good friends."[1]

Charlotte was immediately drawn to Walter but warned him at the very beginning of their friendship, "I am not of the combining sort. I <u>don't</u> combine, and I don't want to." What she meant was that she had decided not to marry. Repeating to him what she wrote to Martha, Charlotte conveyed her dream of an independent life. As she wrote, "My life is one of private aspiration and development, and of public service which only awaits to be asked."[2]

Her choice of the word "combine" for marriage is unusual, but it sprang from a tradition with long roots. As a fledging poet, she would have known Anne Bradstreet's line from the seventeenth century: "If ever two were one, then surely we." Two becoming one in marriage was more than a poetic figure of speech. It was also the law of the land.

As a citizen, Charlotte was subject to the common law doctrine governing marriage. The eighteenth-century British jurist William Blackstone had set out the essential understanding of the marriage contract in common law in his great compendium *Commentaries on the Laws of England,* a work that guided nineteenth-century legal practice in the United States. Blackstone placed discussion of wedlock with "master and servant" and "parent and child" among "private economical relations":

> By marriage, the husband and wife are one person under law: that is, the very being or legal existence of the woman is suspended during the marriage, or at least is incorporated or consolidated into that of the husband under whose wing, protection, and cover, she performs every thing…and her condition during her marriage is called *coverture.*

In exchange for her husband's protection, the wife owed obedience. Although a civil contract, marriage was distinct, for it was lifelong, and its terms were not subject to negotiation.[3]

In practical terms, what this meant was that in addition to the civil disabilities that females had by virtue of their sex—lack of suffrage, ineligibility to hold public office or serve on juries—women suffered even more losses on marriage. A husband possessed whatever wages a wife earned, and she had no ability to sue her husband or testify in court against him. She did not have the right to custody of her children.

All of this was being challenged by 1882. A number of states had altered laws governing property, especially that held by a woman at the time of marriage, and had liberalized divorce.[4] Charlotte knew firsthand that a marriage could dissolve and that a wife could win a divorce if, as in Mary Perkins's case, her husband deserted the family. Charlotte knew that a mother could retain custody of children, at least if her husband did not contest it. Although at this point in her life Charlotte was removed from the full force of the woman's movement, she knew something from her reading of *Popular Science Monthly* of ongoing nineteenth-century efforts to give women equal power within marriage.[5]

Charlotte was hardly alone in her aspiration to keep her autonomy by not marrying. She did not attend a four-year liberal arts college, but her broad reading and her aspirations fostered in her goals paralleling those of many female college graduates. In the late nineteenth century, a time when roughly 10 percent of American women did not marry, almost half of all women with a B.A. degree remained single.[6] Some unmarried women lived together in romantic twosomes, a possibility Charlotte envisioned with Martha.

Statistics are cool on the page. The inner struggle of individual women, by contrast, was hot in its intensity. In Charlotte's case, what complicated her desire for independence and work in the world was a passionate nature and a sudden, unanticipated eagerness for a man's love and its physical expression.

Charlotte did not simply state to Walter that she was not to marry. She told him of her struggle to subdue her sexual feelings. After telling him that she was not "of the combining sort," she exploded on the page:

> Having calmly accepted the fact that the happiness of most women was no happiness for me; having lost forever the one joy that made hardships trifles; having bowed quietly to a fate that forbade the indulgence of each and every individual instinct; having settled my shoulders firmly to the yoke which grows harder to bear as the years pass; holding in control such of my wild horses as are already mastered, and taming new ones every day; plodding steadily on with no light save the self-made radiance of my future home—I turn

a sudden corner, and find—! I cover my eyes as yet. Cover my eyes and plod on, but with a new light in the dreary landscape, a wild sweet music beating through the harsh noises around me, a glowing background for my thoughts to rest upon—when I dare to let them go.

In this extraordinary outpouring, she told Walter that as she held in her womanly instincts, controlling her "wild horses," she found in him "a wild sweet music." Walter rightly understood from this that she found him desirable. In closing the letter, she intimated that she also found him dangerous. Forgetting her intense suffering at Martha's forsaking of her to marry, Charlotte wrote, "I half wish you were a woman. I have a haunting dread that in this joy there may lurk some danger."[7]

According to Charlotte's journal, on Sunday, January 29, three days after she wrote this letter and seventeen days after they first met, Walter proposed to her. She recorded, "I have this day been asked the one question in a woman[']s life, and have refused."[8] That it was truly a proposal we have only her word, but it is clear that on that day she pushed Walter to make some sort of declaration of his feelings and then to suggest prematurely his hopes. From her perspective, any expression of a desire for heterosexual love and its sexual expression was intrinsically linked to matrimony. This allowed her to interpret what Walter said to her as an offer of marriage.

Two days later, in an extended note to herself, she wrote her "Reasons for living single." She did this, she said, because she was now "cool and clear," and she feared that at a later point "the force of passion" would come to "cloud my reason, and pervert or benumb my will." She wrote a long list, but essentially there were two reasons why she should live alone. One was that she liked her newfound freedom to come and go and to make all her own choices as to what to eat, wear, think, and say. The second was that to be bound up with others—obviously, but without stating it, she was thinking of being a wife and mother—would limit her

Walter as a young man, 1880. Schlesinger Library, Radcliffe Institute, Harvard University.

usefulness, her power to do good in the world. Again, Charlotte was vague about the specific good she might do, in this case making it seem like she was to be a ministering angel to the multitude. For this, she wrote, "I decide to <u>Live</u>—Alone."[9]

Decide whatever she might, Charlotte openly sought Walter's companionship, responding with enthusiasm to his company. He visited her in her home every Sunday evening, and they had shorter visits during the week. They wrote long letters to each other almost every day. Of this vast correspondence, only a tiny fraction remains in her papers, but Walter copied some of her letters in his diary. In them, Charlotte announced in explicit terms that she wanted only friendship. Undertones reveal, however, that she wanted more than that. Charlotte wanted to be loved and petted.

One can see all this in a poem for Walter, dated February 10–12, written as an answer to a letter from him. It seems that in pleading his case for their love, he had called her desire for independence a shirking of "A woman's highest, holiest work: / For pleasure I much preferred." He had reduced her ambitions, choosing among her "reasons...the mean and small," suggesting that she believed that by refusing to consider marriage, she gave up nothing. In the poem she fought back. What she had renounced were, in fact, "the passionate dreams of youth," "the Eden wide / That lies at the feet of a happy bride." She returned to the hurt of losing Martha, dwelling on it for two stanzas. Then she shifted to meeting him, "a brother soul," a person she saw as "a new friend." Yet instead of the unencumbered love she sought, he demanded that she give up her life of purpose to become his wife, the mother of his children. After what seems like an accusation against Walter, the poem turns to her longing for him, for the "love that is more than life!...a heart to be all my own." And at the end, she questions her mission:

And I think of the hours of hopeless grief
Which I know I shall have to see—

Till I long to turn from my journey wild
And throw myself like a tired child
Into arms that are waiting for me.[10]

In several letters to Walter written in late February, her inner conflict between love and autonomy was stark.[11] She wrote that she dreamed of a single life in which she would be self-supporting and work for good in the world. She stated that she also had emotional and physical needs that could be satisfied only in marriage, what she identified as the normal life of womankind. "I knew of course that the time would come when I must choose between two lives, but never did I dream that it would come so soon, and that the struggle would be so terrible."[12]

Independent life for a woman allowed friendship only, not love. She projected her dilemma onto Walter and blamed him for it.

It seemed as if I was at last to find what I had hardly known enough to long for—companionship.
And now—
Why did you? O why did you!
If only you <u>didn't</u>; if only you could help it—if only we might have given me what I wanted and not this—![13]

This letter declared that the problem was not in herself but came from Walter, his declaration of love. As she wrote him soon after, "How can I offer even the warmest friendliness to one who asks for love?" She continued, "I feel helpless and dumb. The feeling of delighted companionship with which I met you so gladly at first fades to insignificance before the look in your eyes that asks for more than I dare give."[14]

Her difficulty was intensified by her uncertainty about the future. She had ambitions, hopes, and dreams, but she was a fledgling, untried and unproven. What if she could not make it? A part of her deeply wanted a chance to try and thus postpone any true courtship for a few years to find out if success on her own in the world was possible. She weighed the option of risking "loss of a few years['] possible happiness" against that of "endurance of a lifetime's possible <u>pain</u>" if she never attempted independence. Although he initially disguised his feelings, Walter wanted her to live a traditional woman's life, to subordinate her strivings to his work and the care of his household and future children. This life he defined as a woman's true destiny, her duty. He labeled her desire for work and self-sufficiency as selfishness. One side of her was partially convinced by him, a side impelled by her "childhood's ultra conscientiousness, and by the new humility which you have taught me."[15]

Strengthening Walter's case was her own sexual desire. "Here is a force—the strongest known to human nature, which says 'Yield!'" And buttressing it was the power of tradition and culture. As she put it, "The voice of all the ages sounds in my ears, saying that this is noble, natural, and right; that no woman yet has ever attempted to stand alone as I intend but that she had to submit or else repented in dust and ashes—too late!"

Readers today understand Charlotte's words—the "force" calling her to "yield"—as signifying a recognition of her own strong sexual desire. But it is important to realize how she distanced herself from this drive. She must have imagined at the moment of writing that this "force—the strongest known to human nature" was separate from her real self, for she continued with these key words: "I stand quietly against it." Thus for her, at this time, her real self, the real "I," was the resisting self. She followed with a comparison of herself to women like Martha and her own mother: "I am different from if not better than all these, and…my life is mine in spite of a myriad lost sisters before me."[16]

Yet at the very moment of writing, she had doubt. "The resisting force is sapped by the underlying possibility of presumption and mistake.[17] It is no easy thing to refuse one great work on the ground—self asserted and unproven—that I can do a greater." What if she failed at her unspecified great work?[18]

Moreover, there were moments when the force of nature was not so distant, so separate from what she regarded as her real self.

As she put it in another letter, explaining why she found it difficult to write to him: "I am crushing my heart under foot."[19] From the outset Charlotte was genuinely torn. She had ambitions *and* she desired Walter; and she saw no way to reconcile the two.

She reached for guidance. Not from a mother she did not trust or from friends who could hardly understand but in her own characteristic way. In the days immediately after writing this letter, Charlotte went to the public library and over the next two weeks absorbed John Stuart Mill's work *The Subjection of Women*.[20] Mill stood against Spencer and the biological arguments of his time and opposed women's subordination. Arguing on grounds of justice and utility, Mill addressed his words to both attitudes and institutions. He directed his reform proposals to women's lives in the public domain and advocated educational equality, the right to vote, and women's economic rights.

During these weeks, Walter persisted. On March 2, Charlotte wrote, "Mr. Stetson called at a little past 8:30[.] Some talk. He understands."[21] Perhaps she used Mill to try and convince him that they needed to be equals. She left no direct commentary on her reading, but it is likely that Mill's work gave her hope that a woman's marriage to a man did not have to mean subordination. Walter seems to have picked up the cue, and Charlotte, perhaps believing that he accepted this possibility, began to take her foot off her heart. On March 6, the day she finished Mill's tract, she wrote to Walter, "I am beginning to wonder how I ever lived through this winter, before you—; beginning to see how tired I was, how depressed and pessimistic. You want to give me something! You are giving me back myself!"[22] At this point, she made a shift. She identified her real self not as the resisting "I" standing apart from womankind but as the one who yearned for emotional and sexual intimacy with Walter.

Charlotte and Walter then began what appeared to be a promising courtship. With the onset of warm weather, they took walks as long as ten miles, giving themselves a realm of privacy away from the observing eyes and ears of Charlotte's mother and aunt.

In May she wrote in their mutual language of calling each other King and Queen, "O my grand lover! My heart's King! Truly I was ready to have you turn my face to yours with gentle force; ready to give my heart to you when our lips met."[23] Always interested in clothing, she gave special attention to her appearance and reported that on June 29 she met him in "tissue skirt, bunting, over thing, lace, pearls, silver stars, bracelets & rose." As she put it, "A party for one. Charles Walt. appears, & enjoys it."[24] By early summer 1882, although there is no direct mention of marriage in Charlotte's writings, they offer a conventional depiction of the courtship of a devoted couple headed to the altar.

In contrast to Charlotte's accounts, Walter left his own chronicle of the progress of their love story in his diary.[25] While Charlotte's journal entries are terse, his are expansive and offer an intriguing counterpoint to her perspective. While focused on his needs and desires, his diary allows us to see Charlotte from the outside and gain a better understanding of her and of their relationship.

Walter was an aspiring painter, and much of his journal chronicled his successes and failures as he attempted to find buyers and patrons and worked on his art. As he sold little of his work, Walter lived with his parents and was responsible for their partial support. His father was an impecunious minister without a pulpit who traded in patent medicines. His mother was often ill. His prospects were modest, for he was untrained and had not taken the trip to Europe deemed necessary to see and copy its artistic glories.

Some established and wealthy persons believed in Walter's gift, but that did not keep him from deep debt and financial misery. During the 1880s, he found a patron in George Vaux Cresson, the president of the Narragansett Pier Casino, a dining and entertainment spot on the Rhode Island shoreline designed for the elite by the prestigious architectural firm of McKim, Mead, and White. George Cresson, a wealthy manufacturer, and his wife, Mary, were a childless couple who lived in grand style outside Philadelphia. Cresson did more than buy paintings and commission a portrait; he sought to find other buyers for Walter's paintings, including the department store owner John Wanamaker. Although these efforts proved unsuccessful, the Cressons invited Walter to visit and gave thoughtful and generous gifts. Walter also had Providence supporters, especially the physician E. B. Knight, and he was commissioned to paint the official portrait of the city's mayor.

After meeting Charlotte, much of Walter's diary revolved around his romantic feelings toward her, but even more of it was centered on his ambition to make his way as a painter, his hopes for commissions, his relationships with potential and real clients, and his worries about money. By the standards of his time, he was in no position to marry and establish his own household.

Nonetheless, his diary reveals him to be a man searching for true love. Walter was a romantic who dreamed of consummation with a pure woman. He accepted fully his sexual urges as part of the virile manhood he would bring to a marriage. As an artist he believed that the love of a pure woman would elevate not only his lust but also his art.[26]

At the outset Walter, found Charlotte to be beautiful, athletic, and unusually bold in her manner. On first meeting, she immediately invited him to walk with her on Sunday afternoons. He reported in his diary, "She said frankly, 'Mr. Stetson, I must know you better!'" As he wrote in his diary, Charlotte was "strong, vivacious, with plenty of bounding blood."[27] He was intrigued by her unconventional manners and her intimate talk. His reference to her flow of vital blood meant that he imagined her capable of strong passion. He made it clear that he was drawn to her sexually.

Charlotte responded to him frankly and passionately but complexly. Early on, in response to a little remark, she "covered her face and said: 'It seems too good to be true!' And then in a deep rapturous way, 'I like you—for what you are.'" They began regular visits on Sunday afternoon, when she knew they had a chance to be alone. In these first visits Walter saw in her "a warm, soft, sensuous nature held in check and overcome by a strong will, a sound intellect & a good moral nature."[28]

In his telling, the January 29, 1882, conversation with Charlotte was nothing like the simple proposal of marriage she logged in her journal. According to his diary entry that evening, it was Sunday afternoon, and they were alone. Charlotte had taken him into her study to look at her books and pictures. As they went back into the parlor, she said, "Do you want to please me a little.... want to give me a few sugar plums so to speak?"[29]

Walter responded that he would be happy to oblige if he knew what she wanted. She then requested that he tell what he admired in her, saying, "I never was admired before and—I like it. I want to know just what you admire." He then spoke of admiring her purpose in life and her honesty and willingness to think for herself. She then asked for "some artistic reasons" why he admired her. Walter asked,

> "Do you want me to tell you what I admire that is physical?"
> "Yes," she said.
> So I made a soberly detailed account of her physical qualities that pleased me.
> "I do heartily enjoy having you admire me!"

As Walter began to put his coat on to leave, Charlotte told him that the way he at times looked at her troubled her. He answered,

> "How do I look at you?"
> "As if you—might grow fond of me."
> "Well, suppose that I should?"
> "I can but fear that something will go wrong and mar our happiness."

She stated that she feared that they might come to love each other. She continued, "Let us talk plainly—for I cannot marry, although I am fitted to enjoy all that marriage can give to the utmost. Were I to marry, my thoughts, my acts, my whole life would be centered in husband and children. To do the work that I have planned I must be free." With this stated, the two discussed whether or not it would be better to part at once before falling into love. Charlotte conveyed her sense of inner struggle. She told of why their parting should happen soon, then interjected, "But I need you—you can be so much to me. And if I could only feel that all would go well I could be glad and give you everything but my life."

Walter asked why she knew his love for her might hinder her. She responded, "Oh, on the simplest of physiological grounds I know that a love begun should be consummated: and consummation would mean relinquishment of all my plans—and it would feed the side of my nature which I am holding in check. I am pretty evenly balanced, animal & spiritual. Were I to give up—I fear I should give all up and become of no more use than other women."

Charlotte made her goal of an autonomous life clear, but at the same time she complicated it by drawing attention to her bodily attractions and telling him of the strong physical nature that she held in check. It was in the midst of these confusing signals that Walter declared his love. He put it this way: Yes, they would be friends, but friendship combined with love was "a thousand times better." As he put it, "You have both; I give you both. Your life will be different from now, I am sure." When Charlotte drew back, declaring her need of independence, Walter stated that although marriage need not rob her of her expressive powers, they were talking prematurely of marriage. Charlotte told him that it was best to consider the outcome at the beginning. Walter then said, "Can you not see that you have already hastened my love by showing me that it is possible that I may be loved in return?" In his telling, her final answer to the question of continuing to see each other was hardly ambiguous. She said with strong emotion, "I will risk all." As she followed him out of the door, she bent over the railing to take his hand, an act that at the time signaled more than friendship.[30]

Two very different portrayals of the same event raise the question of who to believe. Did Walter propose? From her perspective, yes. Charlotte pushed him to declare his love. She moved logically from love to marriage, and he did not disavow his desire to wed her ultimately but suggested only that any discussion of this future was happening too early in their relationship. From Walter's point of view, he was pushed prematurely. He came with the intention only of a courting visit with Charlotte, but she took their conversation in a surprising direction. What makes his telling of the "proposal" visit believable is that a full reading of his diary reveals that he was simply not clever enough to make up Charlotte's words.

His account gives us an even more conflicted picture of Charlotte than the one she presented in her journal and letters. There is sharp contrast between her own terse announcement in her journal of a proposal of marriage and the dialogue in Walter's extended chronicle. Walter's portrayal, particularly her asking him to focus on her physical attributes and mention of "consummation," suggests that she failed to see how her own words and behavior might be interpreted by a man. As for Walter, fundamentally he did not engage with Charlotte's inner struggle. He heard her declare that she wanted his admiration, friendship, and love. In the language they shared, he understood that she desired him sexually. He ignored her statements of fear that with sexual consummation would come her undoing. To him, her words were a simple declaration of love and desire.

Thus the seeds of their future troubles were there from the beginning. A romantic, seeking a pure woman to marry, he wrote in his diary in the months following this encounter not only of his hopes of sexual fulfillment but also of his dreams of possessing Charlotte and making her his muse.

In 1882, when writing in her journal of good times with Walter, Charlotte typically used the words "happy evening."[31] On June 29, she wrote "I love him," and on September 17, she called him "my lover."[32]

We have come to know the resisting Charlotte, the Charlotte who felt in February 1882 that she didn't want to combine. History has portrayed the reasoning Charlotte with the strong will as the true Charlotte. But, of course, she was more complicated than that. There was also the Charlotte who yearned for love, who embraced the sexual urges of her body, the woman who loved Walter, who enjoyed happiness in his company.

What did she experience in the times that she loved Walter? Beyond instinctual urges, what were the sources that helped shape her understanding of her loving side? The feeling of happiness in love is difficult to analyze, for it seemed as "natural" in Charlotte's era as it does now. Yet examining this is central to understanding Charlotte.

Her love and happiness are perhaps easier to see if first explored in the context of her earlier relationship with Martha Luther. Let us recall what Charlotte wrote in the summer of 1881: "why in the name of heaven have we so confounded love with passion that it sounds to our century-tutored ears either wicked or absurd to name it between women. It is no longer friendship between us, it is love." Friendship, she asserted, was for the multitudes; love was for one person only. But despite her own intense feelings and the physical intimacies she shared with Martha, Charlotte did not label her "love" for Martha as "passion." Charlotte reserved that word for erotic feelings toward someone of the opposite sex. When she wrote to Martha about her decision not to marry and her dream that the two of them might live together, she described this as winning the "war between plain duties & irrepressible instincts." The engagement of a woman's instincts, her sexual self as she understood it then, could only happen with a man.

Love required intimacy, the ability to express oneself freely.[33] Charlotte won the necessary freedom for intimacy in letters when she reached twenty-one. When Walter visited Charlotte's household, if they were not alone, the two often sat and wrote letters to each other rather than speaking words that Charlotte's mother might overhear.

When Charlotte experienced love for Martha, she wrote as if her dear friend was exactly like herself. In the summer of 1881 she was constantly seeking to enlist Martha in all her enterprises—reading together, a gym class, a set of new friends, an essay club. Although letters from Martha are lost to the historical record, from Charlotte's responses we know that Martha pulled away and continually asserted that she was a different person from Charlotte's imagining. Martha got engaged, and Walter appeared at the door. And Walter, unlike Martha, relished Charlotte's deep identification with him.

What then did it feel like when Charlotte was "happy" with Walter? A poem she wrote before going to bed one evening in June 1882 is revealing. In one section, she addressed Walter directly:

> But before I go I must let you know
> That I love my love tonight.
>
> With body & heart & brain, dear love.[34]

Not mind, not soul. As Charlotte experienced her feeling for Walter, she imagined that it was her body, her animal self, that engaged with him.[35] With this man, she identified her feeling of "love" as passion. Here she connected to her instinctual self, her animal nature, what she called the woman side of herself. Charlotte typically used the word "happy" when she accepted this side.

In accepting instinct, she believed she joined the masses of womankind. In June 1882, she was surrendering to the world around her that called her to passion, marriage, and childbearing. This sharply contrasts with her January explanation to Walter that she would not "combine." At that time, she was trying to resist the commands to "Yield!" Women's traditional path to marriage and childbearing was, as she put it, spoken by the "voice of all the ages," defined as "noble, natural, and right."[36] To wed, bed, and bear was her mother's way, it was the choice of Martha Luther, it became Walter's fervent and oft-repeated wish, and it was given modern vocabulary in *Popular Science Monthly*.

During the years of Walter's courtship, Charlotte continued to read the magazine at the Providence Athenaeum, and it seemed to address her current dilemmas, in particular how she might think about love and marriage. For her, this question was inextricably linked to issues of ethical living. The April 1882 issue featured a debate that clearly caught her eye. A long piece by frequent contributor Goldwin Smith considered ethics and morality, sharply criticizing Spencer's *Data of Ethics*. This set off a lively discussion in the magazine's back pages, as Youmans cried foul, citing Smith's many errors of fact and interpretation. Youmans argued, in words that would have great resonance with Charlotte, that Spencer's great contribution was to move ethical discussion away from religion and ground it in science. The editor quoted Spencer's phrases that the "science of right conduct" had to be rooted in "the necessary consequences of the constitution of things." Youmans emphasized that Spencer's effort has demonstrated that "moral laws can not be broken with impunity, because of the inexorable causal relation between actions and results."[37]

Charlotte went on a summer excursion in Maine in July 1882, and her host lent her a copy of Spencer's *Data of Ethics*.[38] Away from Walter and home ties, Charlotte read the work slowly. At this point in her life, given her commitment to reform physiology, Spencer's words likely had a profound impact. He argued that humans, as animals, needed to ground ethical principles in their bodies as derived from evolution. A person had to satisfy first the needs of the species for air, food, warmth, and reproduction. Morality was not merely saying no to that which led an individual to excess or to conflict with the larger social good but meant saying yes to those "vital activities up to their normal limits." As Spencer put it, in his ham-fisted way, "All the animal functions, in common with all the higher functions, have, as thus understood, their imperativeness."[39]

Spencer elaborated that humans as animals were given pleasure and pain for a reason. Pleasure worked to guide the animal to appropriate action for survival. As he stated, "Every pleasure increases vitality; every pain decreases vitality. Every pleasure raises the tide of life; every pain lowers the tide of life."[40] Spencer argued against the belief that higher feelings were the critical guides. "In the first place," he wrote, "the authority of the lower feelings as guides is by no means always inferior to the authority of the higher feelings, but is often superior. Daily occur occasions on which sensations must be obeyed rather than sentiments."[41] He stated additionally that to deny sensations, such as those of cold or fatigue, was to put the body in peril. Spencer gave examples of men who did so and whose health broke down permanently. Included was a person who brought on "softening of the brain...by ceaseless mental efforts against which the feelings hourly protested."[42] Nor was it wise to delay gratification. Thus one needed to listen to the body.

Spencer's ethics required agreement with the principle that pleasure should guide humans to satisfy their needs. Most people, he wrote, accepted that "the pleasure which accompanies the taking of food, goes along with physical benefit; and that the benefit is the greater the keener the satisfaction of appetite." Similarly, Spencer argued euphemistically, sexual pleasure had its important place: "the instincts and sentiments which so over-poweringly prompt marriage, and those which find their gratification in the fostering of offspring, work out an immense surplus of benefit after deducting all evils."[43] Grounded as she was in reform physiology, these were words of profound meaning to Charlotte.

But there was more than mere yielding to female animal nature on Charlotte's part. There were periods when Charlotte believed that her passion for Walter was entwined with love. On September 22, 1882, at a time when she felt certain of her love for Walter, she wrote in an untitled poem:

And Oh! It seems so strange!
That I who lived so long alone
Should find another heart my own;
Should find the life which I had chosen
Free if friendless, strong if frozen—
Turn with unexpected change
To such radiance of beauty—

At that moment in the early autumn of 1882, she saw her resisting nature, the one that "lived so long alone" as friendless and frozen, if also free and strong. Her artist's eye likened the experience of love, the finding of "another heart" to belong to her, to envisioning the "radiance of beauty." As Charlotte continued in the poem, she clarified that the happiness she now felt blended both "joy and Duty." She ended the poem with the prayer that

> ...my living
> May deserve this wealth of giving
> Proving as a ~~noble~~ perfect woman
> Worth ~~this~~ the gladness superhuman.[44]

At this point personal happiness and obedience to natural instincts came together. She was fulfilling Spencer's obligation in *Data of Ethics* to satisfy the needs of her animal nature, listen to the commands of pleasure, and respect the authority of the lower feelings. Charlotte aspired in this moment to be the "noble"—no, the "perfect"—woman.[45] Spencer would be proud. Walter certainly was.

Once Charlotte believed that she loved Walter, she sought to merge her identity with him. This mental melding initially both met a felt need and fit her understanding of the nature of a woman's love. Early on, Walter read aloud to her the poems of Dante Gabriel Rossetti, a British artist with whom he felt a special bond. Walter admired Rossetti for his paintings and poetry and envied his opportunities and success. Rossetti's poems written for his wife, buried with her, and then exhumed and published in 1870, created a scandal because of their sexual content. For Walter, they were the perfect blend of sensuality, spirituality, and idealism. Walter gave Charlotte a book of Rossetti's poems as his first gift. It was perhaps from Rossetti that Walter came to call her "Queen" and assume the role of "King."

Rossetti's influence is strong in an untitled poem of September 8, 1882, that Charlotte wrote about Walter:

He loves me. I am throned
Highest of earth in that great heart.
We, though apart,
So near each other live that scarcely speech
Is needed to interpret each to each.[46]

Unlike Martha, Walter relished Charlotte's desire to blend her identity into his.

Yet this is hardly the whole story. There was a side of Charlotte that knew, perhaps from his critics in *Popular Science Monthly*, to turn to John Stuart Mill. His *Subjection of Women* helped her fight assumptions of innate male superiority and gave her arguments regarding the need to change law and policy to allow women property rights, suffrage, and equal access to education. Mill, however, could not help her with her feelings or alter Walter's.

Fiction reader that Charlotte was, she was aware of the novel's typical central theme, young people falling in love. As she would write in 1890, these stories produced "an endless impression that life is only meant to love."[47] Many of the books she read confirmed the primary nineteenth-century literary convention that true love conquered all, leaving largely female readers in the ecstasy of the final clinch. Some novels of her time, however, questioned the power of love and told of its dangers. She knew the emerging work of Henry James, with its skepticism about romantic love and marriage, as well as the novels of Charlotte Brontë that brought lovers to their ordained matrimonial destination. What makes Charlotte interesting is that she embodied both sides of the conversation. She wanted both to commit to Walter and to retain her self-rule.

When Charlotte was on a vacation in Maine, she read not only Spencer's *Data of Ethics* but also George Eliot's *Adam Bede*.[48] This novel has at its center a disastrous story of love and desire across the classes. A beautiful young peasant girl, Hetty Sorrel, is beloved by the carpenter Adam Bede. She is seduced, however, by the charm of a young local aristocrat and the promise of material and social gifts she believes will come her way with marriage to him. The upper-class lover, however, proves to be a careless trifler with no thought of marriage. Finding herself pregnant, the girl first agrees to marry Bede and then runs away, delivers the child, and abandons it to die in a field. Ultimately, she is brought to trial and sentenced. Her story is one of a woman betrayed by desire.

Spencer's *Data of Ethics* encouraged listening to the body's commands. Eliot's stirring novel powerfully reminded readers of the risks women faced when they did so. Eliot's life, however, promised more open possibilities. Mary Anne Evans, one of Britain's leading novelists, wrote under a man's name and famously lived with George Lewes outside of wedlock during the period of her greatest fame. Although the Eliot-Lewes relationship mirrored traditional marriage in many respects, it was childless and unsanctioned by law. To her many contemporary female admirers, Eliot loomed large as a great woman writer who had shaped her own destiny. In the summer of 1881, when writing to Martha about her decision not to marry, Charlotte wrote, "I think G. Eliot will be much to me."[49]

It seems that on Charlotte's return to Providence in the late summer of 1882, Eliot's choices were working in her mind. When Walter and Charlotte resumed their regular visiting in August, Walter wrote of her volatility: "there is no peace with her.... There is an uncertainty about what she will be in the next half hour which is not all pleasant."[50] On August 10, as the two spent the evening together, Charlotte said, "<u>Wouldn't</u> it be fun to go to a minister quietly—let no one know of it—be married according to the law and then live as if we were defying the law.... What fun to listen to the cries of friends—the warnings—the condolings etc. & then when things were at the climax quietly open the certificate." At this point, she was playing with a scenario that seemed to flout convention, living "as if we were defying the law."[51] It is likely that while said in jest, at some level a rebellion against conventional marriage was percolating more deeply in her mind.

Meanwhile, marriage and talk of marriage surrounded them. On October 4, 1882, Charlotte's brother, Thomas, far away in Utah, married. The following day, her beloved Martha wed Charles

Lane. Charlotte stood next to Martha during the ceremony and held the bridal bouquet.

Charlotte began to model for Walter in his studio; hoping to capture the likeness of his beloved, he tried to paint her portrait. In mid-October, she met Walter at the public library and reported in her journal that she went "home to supper with him," home being his parents' residence, where he lived. The next day when she went to his studio, she had a surprise. "Lo! Mother is there! An unpleasant call, with the poor picture [Charlotte's portrait] severely criticized." Later mother and daughter had a talk. "She thinks we'd better marry & come here to board. (I don't.)"[52]

Walter gave a full account of Mary Perkins's unannounced visit. As he reported it, she spoke to him in a manner that seemed hysterical, blending into her talk about Charlotte and him words on Scripture, her own life, and secrets about her husband. Mary confessed that she had previously thought Walter to be dishonorable and that Charlotte and he were behaving in an "disorderly" fashion, that their "love was Lust." But now she saw she was wrong, that "it was Love," and she was no longer opposed. However, she insisted that the two marry right away.

Mary Perkins had much to say about her daughter, love, and lust. Walter wrote that she said that "Charlotte was passionately loving: her whole sexual nature was aflame. I too was passionate. There was danger to us of the worst sort, wrecking to moral & physical well being. If we were together we would be constantly tempted to sexual intercourse." Commenting on this, Walter added in his diary: "which certainly is true." Mary feared that the couple would yield to their desire "and thus do some 'disorderly' thing." When Walter pleaded to Mary that he first needed to get out of debt, she replied that money was of no consequence and that the couple should come to live with her.[53]

With her mother's intervention, Charlotte's doubts about "combining" were put aside. Although she would not consider beginning wedded life in quarters shared with her mother, the two planned a May wedding and began to dream of going to Europe.

CHAPTER 3 ······························

A Pullback and a Proposition

hen trouble came. In early December, after a Thanksgiving visit with the Edward Everett Hale family in Boston, Charlotte came home downcast. She stated merely that the festive high jinks of the Hales—a masquerade party with playacting and dancing—had lost its appeal: "I've outgrown this kind of fun." On her return, she wrote in her journal of the regular Sunday visit, "Walter arrives. I'm not quite right with him somehow."[1] Walter reported in his diary something far more serious—Charlotte was "in a terrible state."[2]

When she wrote to Walter to explain herself, she said something profoundly important. "What ails me now I cannot say: I have lost my love as one loses a quotation familiar as the Lord's Prayer—<u>knowing</u> it to be there, but unable to find it." She remembered that she had loved him, and it was there in her letters. She hoped that would comfort him. But now, she wrote, "I am too apathetic and senseless...even to be sorry for this state of mine." She believed that it would be wrong for her to make any decision, "for I am not my true self. If I have any?"[3] She was experiencing a serious depressive episode, the first in her new life with Walter.

Bewildered by Charlotte's shocking change, Walter first interpreted it as personal rejection. During Thanksgiving, Charlotte had been among "the tall muscular Hale fellows" a contrast with himself, "poor slight me." When subsequently Charlotte told him that her love for him had unaccountably evaporated, he wrote using the language of physiology of his day, "I can see physical reasons why her love should stop—aberrations of the brain caused by bodily disturbances: but I can see no reason why if she is as well as she appears, love could stop."[4]

Walter had a disappointment, one he did not communicate to Charlotte for many months. In the back of his mind had been the hope that his rich Philadelphia patron, Charles Vaux Cresson, would give him money that would allow him to marry Charlotte and travel with her to Europe. When Mrs. Cresson wrote it was not to be, but hinting that her husband might support Walter for a year abroad were he to go alone, Walter's dream ended.

Walter began to have his own corrosive thoughts. Perhaps Charlotte was seeking to bind him to marriage, or perhaps she had found someone else. After he wrote and read aloud to her a letter alluding to these fears, Charlotte seemed to return to him.[5]

Yet all was not the same as it had been. Walter began to worry over a changed Charlotte, who at times exhibited a religious streak that frightened him. Walter reasoned that "not finding ease for her passion with me she turns to God, and cries on thine rapt things. It is all very beautiful and lonely: but it is dangerous. The steps are short between her present state and hysteria." Perhaps her mother was right to think that Charlotte's love expressed in embraces and kisses posed a danger to her health. At the end of evening, as she talked about "Duty & Right & God" and trembled and leapt into his arms, he said, "she showed signs of hysteria.... Oh how the dear girl needs marriage, even as I do!"[6] The genie was out of the bottle. From Walter's perspective, all negative messages coming from Charlotte—all her alternative blankness, anguish, emotionalism, fears, and doubts—could be resolved by sexual consummation.

Life resumed. Charlotte continued with her pupils, her reading and writing, and her gymnastic workouts. She reported more evenings when Walter came by. She did not forget, however, the time just past in which she had felt apathy and senselessness. Her remembering explains the bewildering journal entry she wrote just as 1883 dawned: "My last act in the old year was to kneel at my bedside in shame & repentance, with hot tears and self-abasement. From which I rose resolved to pray no more for a season but to work again."[7]

By mid-January, she had returned to her loving state. The two returned to calling each other King and Queen. As Charlotte became affectionate again, Walter expressed his pleasure. "I <u>know</u> that I make her happy; that she rests in me as a child might in her father; that I fill all her mind with delight and that her whole being body & soul thrills at my presence, my kiss and my touch."[8] He cherished her growing dependence. During this time, he wrote that Charlotte "is changed a vast deal. She wants to be treated more as a child now than as a woman. I could scarcely have foreseen so complete a subjugation of self—or abnegation rather."[9] At such moments, he was delighted. He believed that he was taking her from a false life of intellect and independence to a true one of love. She was the wild colt to be saddled and brought to a course of usefulness to a man. He could not see Charlotte for what she was, a deeply conflicted being whose desires for independence and achievement outside marriage could not be long suppressed.

In February, Mary Perkins made tentative plans to travel west later in the year to visit Charlotte's brother and new wife, and she offered to vacate her living quarters for Charlotte and Walter while away, enabling them to marry. Charlotte called it "a grand new arrangement to which we joyfully accede."[10]

As he observed Charlotte entering wholeheartedly in her mother's plan, Walter noted, "She acted as joyous as a child over it and was lovely to see."[11] At this point, he began to harbor doubts of his own about imminent marriage, worrying about its effect on his art and his parents. He was experiencing the reality of poverty. His paintings were not selling, and only by borrowing rent money from an artist friend was he able to keep his parents in their home. He now projected the need for marriage on Charlotte herself: "Charlotte ought to be married. She needs it much, dear girl! She is not the strongly independent creature she was a year ago. With the softening of her heart has also come a softening of physical fibre: a less intensity of physical energy and more of the flame of desire. If she cannot marry soon I fear greatly for her, for passion must have room for itself or injury comes."[12] Anticipating their future life together after their nuptials, on a Sunday in early March Walter measured their future bedroom.[13]

At this point, Charlotte was experiencing a burst of energy, one of her apparent highs. She was keeping to her usual hectic schedule of children's lessons, serious reading, writing, art work on commission, calisthenics at the gym, and social visiting. Perhaps more significantly, she was beginning to send out her poems to magazines for publication. And in contrast to Walter's focus on domestic arrangements, she took the opposite tack and began making forays to find work outside of Providence. She wrote to her uncle Edward Everett Hale for advice. She responded to an ad in the *New York Herald*. At the end of March, she wrote, "Am feeling unusually well & strong."[14]

During that month, she got an important letter from her teacher and mentor at the Society to Encourage Studies at Home, responding to Charlotte's news of her forthcoming wedding. The words the unmarried Fanny Alden wrote on March 10 were hardly encouraging. Dashing cold water on Charlotte's hope that she would have time more at her disposal in the coming year, her teacher wrote:

> Oh! Oh! Oh!
> Not that I think it will be at your husband's. But it is not in man that walketh to direct his steps; & I know that you have put your life into God's hands, & I think He will not allow you to dispose of it as you please.

She closed, "You say you expect to marry in June—very good— June 1888, I hope; you did not mention the year."[15] This contrast to the enthusiasm for marriage that immediately surrounded Charlotte must have surprised her and likely revived earlier aspirations.

Walter seldom appeared in her journal in this period. Sunday March 18, however, was one of his regular Sunday unchaperoned visits, and Charlotte related that she dressed up for him and that he arrived with a game for them to play. Then this terse entry: "then talk till 10:45 in the parlor. Tears."[16] What happened?

To learn we must turn to Walter's diary. He wrote that as they went into the parlor, Charlotte said to him, "I've had a relapse!" Walter knew from the December experience what she meant. He wrote, "Her love of me had gone for a time in that old mysterious way, and left her full of her old self—the longings after a wholly individual life—her old ambition and all that."[17]

Charlotte asked him about marriage, what it would mean in their lives. He recorded in his diary, "I stated simply that if I married her, I married her; and she must be my wife and my companion and live with me all the time."

"She had a wild theory," Walter continued, "about living in one place—a home of her 'own' and having me come and see her when the erotic tendency was at a maximum." Though examples of women living independent sexual lives existed in reality and in literature—a part of Charlotte's mental universe—her voicing of such a hope seemed completely beyond Walter's comprehension. It was abhorrent, going against all his notions of husbandly possession, and it offended his sense of propriety. After what he saw as a long struggle to gain her love and an "era of heavenly sweetness," such an idea stained "the best of my gifts and her gifts," put them "to shame," and now "flung" them in his face.

Walter thought, "There must be something very morbid in her brain." He entertained, then put away, the notion that Charlotte got some sort of perverse pleasure in setting herself apart from other women. The way he saw it was that "sensitive nerves and ready brain play as strange freaks—and I think hers are running riot with her." He waxed philosophical:

Oh this century is cruel; we are in a transition state: the new industries for women; the talk about them has set their unused minds to work, & they see awry. They must go into the world and buffet. They will come back, I think, and find love better than all. Every one knows that I believe in the utmost freedom for women but that freedom is false which makes them rebel against the ties of love and home. She thinks much of her irregularity comes from her father. It may be: but more comes from ill-digested reading of philosophical works mixed with her imagination & the tradition of what she <u>ought</u> to inherit from her parents.

He let out this cry of pain: "God alone knows how the terrible mood came again to her. . . . And she changed—changed—changed and who knows how? . . . I had been lifted away up by her masterful passion & caresses and it brought me low and stabbed me with a rugged edged knife."[18]

Charlotte's letter of explanation to Walter about that evening reveals that she was going through a deep crisis.[19] It turns out that her job search was part of a larger plan to try and find her real self by moving away from Providence and living on her own. She contrasted her state in the present to the time before she met him. "I have lost <u>power</u>. I do not feel myself so strong a person as I was before. I seem to have taken a lower seat, to have become less in some way, to have shrunk." As she explained to him later in the letter, "Since I have been with you I have lost in great measure that strong self-confidence which was my greatest happiness."

Her love for Walter had once again evaporated. She wrote, "When love comes uppermost in me you are there—none else: but there are times when love so vanishes from out of my life that I scarce remember how it felt." These words are similar to those she said after Thanksgiving. Now, however, there was an added element, since she and Walter were moving toward marriage. What was once a longed-for state now terrified her. As she put it, "a year's flourishing tenderness has vanished in a week or two; and the delight in your love is lost entirely in the horrified shrinking at confinement, restricting possession."

Charlotte felt it important to be perfectly honest in their relationship. "Change as I might[,] I showed you every change with painful fidelity.[20] Never have you held my body in your arms when my heart was not there also." Walter, however, rejected her when she pulled away. He wanted assurance of a fixed love, a steady state. This she could not give, and it distressed her that Walter could not accept her as she was: "The moment my love goes, you go, and set me coldly down, saying that you cannot come till I want you. Less than the whole of me you say you will not have."

Charlotte could not reassure Walter that she would feel love for him in a constant way. She wrote to him, "I, who am not my own to give, who find a great part of me vanishing and reappearing at uncertain intervals; can in nowise insure you the whole of me for a month's space." This was something that she had "no hold on, no control over." She was "weak and variable," and he had to accept this, for she had to be true to herself. She believed that her life was likely to be forever "checkered." As she put it, "There will be times when this frenzy for freedom boils up with force, which, ungratified, would bring misery to myself and those around me; and there will be times when the woman's heart will wake and cry with heartrending loneliness."

So what was there to do? Charlotte set out three alternatives. The first was to take Walter's way and marry him. This would mean "subduing my deeprooted desires and crushing out this Doppleganger of mine whenever it appears." Weakly, she suggested that ultimately the joy of this might outweigh the pain. The second path was to separate from Walter to pursue an independent single life. This would mean for her "subduing in turn fierce heartache when it rose." Perhaps she might gradually become contented alone, and "my sense of duty and place fulfilled would counterbalance heartaches."

The third way offered a new possibility, that "between us two can be arranged some plan by which I can live in force and freedom, and yet when my heart rises turn to you with it and know that sweetness too." She feared that Walter would never accept this. As she put it, "That this can be done I scarce hope for you must have all or nothing and would rather go ever without me, and doom me to the same separation, than to take what I can give you and be satisfied." In the meantime, she was asking for a year alone and away from him. "Let me wait, let me try my wings, give me this year."

Walter struggled to comprehend this letter. His efforts are visible on the page: his diary entry for the last day of March set up a dialogue with Charlotte, interposing elements of the copied letter with his responses. When Charlotte wrote of feeling smaller, he answered that she was listening to the side of her that sought independence in the name of working in the world. She put it as seeking "for an unselfish grandeur of soul," but to him, she was ironically "trying for unselfishness in a most remarkably selfish manner." She was going against nature, denying her womanhood. He hoped that "God would show her that her work is to be done if done well and to purpose by getting into harmony with that 'woman' instead of rebelliously trying to murder it."[21]

What about her intellectual gifts? Walter was of mixed mind. On the one hand, he saw her as a "woman of unusual power & steadfastness to what she knows," but on the other, she was scattered. As he put it, "as yet that power is not directed, not regulated, and has but small effect for that reason." Her shallow experience in the world had shown her that she was ineffective, thus her sense of being "little" came from reality. She lost power because "she has only had a chance to test the power she thought she had and found it less."

Furthermore, her efforts were misguided. Walter wrote that Charlotte was in many ways a "mere child. She has ideas of life founded on slight hints from books." Tentatively acceding to her demand for a year on her own, he hoped that in her year away from him she would find herself "more humble and less a believer in the preeminence of her own intellect." When she wrote that "she is more C.A.P. [Charlotte Anna Perkins] than a woman," Walter retorted, "I don't believe it. Sex is the paramount thing in every human being: it is first—first—middle—and last."[22]

During the several days Walter was composing this entry in his diary, he tried another tack. He splurged and bought Charlotte a large bunch of violets—which he could not afford—and left them for her on a Saturday when he knew she would not be home. He wrote, "I knew...that they would surround her with my presence—for I have always been connected in her thoughts with violets and their odor."[23]

Charlotte responded initially as he had hoped, writing in her journal, "Find Walter had been here with a lot of violets for me." Her entry for the next day, the regular Sunday visit with Walter, was simply, "We are happier."[24]

Walter reported that on the following day when he visited, he found Charlotte much subdued and able to talk. He told her that he had given up the chance to go to Europe on his patron's money, and she sobbed on his neck. (This was the first time that he told her that Charles Cresson had been willing to pay for his trip abroad but only if he went alone.) She knelt before him, placing her hands between his, a gesture of "Saxon submission," as he put it. She then spoke to him of what was troubling her.

Walter wrote down what she said, but then he—or someone else—had second thoughts. The words are covered in loops and whirls meant to hide them from any reader. What no one was to see was that Charlotte spoke to him about sex.

Whirls covering passages in Walter's diary, 1883. Schlesinger Library, Radcliffe Institute, Harvard University.

When Walter politely summarized Charlotte's words, they stand unembellished. "It is because she thinks so highly of wedlock in love that she will not enter it save with a whole soul." What follows this statement is crossed out with thick loops. With care, bright sunlight, and a powerful lamp, the writing underneath, however, is decipherable: "She is willing to give me her body—it is not that, it is that her very existence could not go with it."[25]

A similar scene was repeated several evenings later. Walter reported that as the two sat by a wood fire in the back room of Charlotte's house, she was on his lap trying again to explain herself. She spoke of "that element in her which _must_ have its way; that thing which cries on her day and night to be 'free' & an 'individual.'" These words were preceded by a passage covered up by whorls that seems to repeat her earlier statement: "that it could be possible for her to be willing to give me her body and also her love and yet was not willing to be bound to me." Walter's subsequent interpretation of Charlotte's words, however, was left standing and fully legible: "She loves me very much & very truly. Would be glad to marry me. Has reverence alone for me; would like to give me all of her body & should enjoy it."[26]

After this, there was a rupture. On Sunday, April 8, 1883, Charlotte wrote in her journal, "Walter. We have the back room & wood fire. He is not coming any more."[27] Faced with the prospect of a lover who would not be a wife, Walter said no. He demanded what he called a separation.

Charlotte took it hard but tried to suppress her feelings in line with what she had learned from psychologists such as Carpenter about the Will. She wrote in her journal on April 10, "My pain & sorrow is all behind and underneath as yet. The least line of kindred thought in poetry brings all the ache and tears, but by myself I ~~don't~~ won't think about it."[28] The strike-through and substitution are revealing. She _will_ not rather than she _does_ not. This is thought of today as repression. Charlotte saw it as a matter of willing her attention, of directing her thoughts and feelings from the painful emotion to another object.

Much of what we know about Charlotte is visible to us in this time of pullback: the person who willed herself not to give into sadness, the side of her that dreamed of independence. But there was also something new.

In March and April 1883, Charlotte summoned her courage and tried to imagine a future that combined independence and Walter. She believed that her love for Walter had dissolved as she faced the prospect of "confinement, restricting possession" in marriage. She looked squarely at conventional marriage and Walter's expectations, saw them as a trap, and pulled away.

As she creatively sought an alternative, was she proposing sexual relations outside marriage, what the era called free love? Repeating on two separate evenings her willingness to give Walter "her body" seems to intimate this. It is, of course, possible.

Free love, from the 1850s on, was an important and controversial element of the Spiritualist world that Mary Perkins joined, if only briefly, around 1874.[29] Largely forgotten or misunderstood today, Spiritualism was a large and powerful religious movement in this era. At one level, it focused on communicating with the spirits of those who had died in the belief that the soul enjoyed eternal life. At another level, it expressed a radical individualism that refused to accept the limitations of existing religious denominations or institutional arrangements, including, in many cases, marriage sanctioned by the church and state.[30]

During this time Mary Perkins moved with her children into combined living quarters with the family of Dr. Grenville Stevens. Mary's Spiritualism brought her into contact with Isabella Beecher Hooker, her ex-husband's aunt.[31] As Isabella reached out and welcomed Mary and her children into her home, she may have exposed Charlotte to free-love influences. Isabella was then a leader of the women's rights movement and one of Victoria Woodhull's most ardent supporters. Woodhull, in fact, had brought Isabella Hooker to Spiritualism.

Woodhull had rocketed to celebrity first as a stockbroker and then as an orator for women's rights. In 1872 she won enduring fame as the first woman to run for president of the United States.[32] Her free-love position, initially stated in 1871, was an important one. In it, she affirmed her own sexual nature and argued for men's and women's right to love without regard to state-recognized marriage. Taking the position espoused by many Spiritualists that romantic love was a union of souls, she stated that marriage existed when two souls "meet and realize that the love elements of their nature are harmonious, and...they blend into and make *one* purpose of life." She allowed for successive lovers, asserting that what comes can also leave, and that law should have nothing to do with it. "To love is a right *higher* than Constitutions or laws." At the same time, Woodhull argued for women's radical independence, their right to know and to do, "to be like men, permanent and independent individualities, and not their mere appendages or adjunct."[33]

A complex and elusive figure, Woodhull held many positions during her long life in and out of the public eye. Yet an adolescent girl does not look for consistency, only inspiration. Although there is no evidence that Charlotte had direct knowledge of Woodhull and her free-love ideas, the close family tie to Isabella Hooker and Spiritualism make for a tantalizing possibility. Of course, there were other sexual radicals who might have offered inspiration. Charlotte could have looked back in history to Mary Wollstonecraft and Frances Wright, who defied sexual mores and advocated women's freedom, even without noting this in her journal. These iconic heroines and Victoria Woodhull form a misty, albeit hypothetical, background.

There is, however, a clear foreground that can be tracked— George Eliot. Charlotte read *Adam Bede* alongside Spencer's *Data of Ethics,* and perhaps pushed by Spencer's emphasis on listening to the body's instincts and pulled by Eliot's unconventional life, she began to rethink marriage. At that point, she only played with an idea that reversed the arrangement of Eliot and Lewes, the fancy of marrying Walter but pretending to cohabit in an unwedded state. But some play has a serious side.

At the beginning of her pullback, Charlotte questioned Walter about marriage and gave her own thoughts about living separately and letting him visit when "the erotic tendency was at a maximum." Her letter of explanation at the end of March phrased it more delicately when it posed to Walter a third alternative to the single life or marriage on his terms. She asked "if between us two can be arranged some plan by which I can live in force and freedom, and yet when my heart rises turn to you with it and know that sweetness too." Thus another way of understanding Charlotte's words underneath the censoring whorls of ink is that she was restating this alternative, only phrasing it in a new way. The issues for her in late March and early April 1883 were twofold: how she might be both a sexual being and an independent person, and how she might coexist with a man when her feelings of love for him were variable—sometimes intense, sometimes absent.

In telling Walter she would like to give him "all of her body & should enjoy it," she recognized Walter's sexual needs and her own. But she could not belong to him as wife according to the marriage conventions of the time. In some way, she would have to come and go. Thus, whether or not the two would be united in a state-sanctioned ceremony was not the issue in Charlotte's mind. What was the issue was a way to join freedom and sexual expression. Charlotte was seeking to find a way to love passionately yet not "combine."

Yet this alternative to traditional marriage did not exist in her time in the world of middle-class Providence in which she lived. Thus she struggled with the concept and expressed it in three ways. After posing to Walter what he called in his journal her "wild theory about living in one place—a home of her 'own' and have me come and see her when the erotic tendency was at a maximum," Charlotte then phrased it more gently in a letter. And then, twice when they met, she told Walter that she was willing to give him "her body" but not "her very existence."

Walter would hear none of it. As important as sexual consummation was to him, that she be "bound" to him was his essential prerequisite. Anything less, even if sanctified by a wedding ceremony, was a violation. Walter told Charlotte that they must separate. He would not visit her again.

His reasoning for the separation went thus: "there can be no doubt that physically it is hurting me. A man can't caress the woman he loves & longs for all the time & see her often—and know that there is a barrier between him and a proper consummation without injury to himself. Hope deferred is sickening enough, but constant tantalization is worse."[34] As he sought to justify his course, he wrote, "Yes as a man I went to her, & I have loved her as a man ever since....I have sought ever to the last degree to do that which I have believed was the best for her life—that which would purify it, sanctify it, and develope it to perfect well rounded adorable womanhood."[35]

These words, critical for an understanding of him, tell us that he was familiar with the reform physiology of his day as it dealt with sex. In the decades following the Civil War, writers such as Orson Squires Fowler, James Ashton, and Edward Bliss Foote posed themselves against the more restrictive John Cowan to argue the values to health of a robust sexuality within marriage for both men and women. The flip side, expressed as well, was the danger of sexual intercourse deferred.[36]

Walter believed he knew what was best for himself—and for Charlotte. In the diary entry that followed, Walter reported that during this conflict, Charlotte, sitting on his lap, cried out to him, "When I am with you I feel '<u>little</u>,' you hurt my pride over & over." In recalling this moment the next day, Walter commented, "The dear woman's pride <u>has</u> been touched: if I mistake not it is the beginning of a womanhood sweet beyond words."[37] Walter believed that it was in Charlotte's best interest to yield to him, that in humbling herself, she was fulfilling her true destiny.

In his anger, he forgot about his commitment to the "utmost freedom for women" and felt sorry only for himself. He was an artist putting himself in the great tradition of Romantic artists,

Charles Walter Stetson, "Song Forgotten." Stetson said he aimed to "to express the loveliness of womanhood & the purity of the sexual relations." Schlesinger Library, Radcliffe Institute, Harvard University.

such as Dante Gabriel Rossetti, who lived for art and love, but without their means for having models and mistresses. He had stated that he aimed in his work "to express the loveliness of womanhood & the purity of the sexual relations," and now his woman was denying him.[38] He alternated between his own intense sexual frustration—the delaying of sexual consummation for at least another year—and rage at the abstract wrong Charlotte had inflicted. As he wrote to himself at the end of March, "It is sin—surely sin: anything that takes woman away from the beautifying and sanctifying of home and the bearing of children must be sin."[39]

Of course, something else was at work, and here, there is mystery at its heart. Charlotte, beginning in late November 1882, experienced something disturbing. Her love for Walter seemed to come and go. And she was alternately happy and miserable.

Since her midteens at least, she had known ups and downs, noting them in a letter to her father and in her journal. The loss of Martha Luther had occasioned deep sadness over an extended period. These low times, labeled sometimes grief, sometimes feeling "blue," she experienced alone. She used the word *blue* much as we do today to express feelings of generalized unhappiness or low spirits.[40] It was also occasionally the word she attached to the first day of her menstrual period.

In March 1882, as her courtship with Walter began, she contrasted her growing happiness with him with the gloom she had felt before he came into her life. "I am beginning to wonder how I ever lived through this winter, before you—; beginning to see how tired I was, how depressed and pessimistic." At this point, her feelings—"tired," "depressed," and "pessimistic"—were comprehensible to her, for they were connected to separation from her beloved friend Martha.

But half a year later, when she thought she was completely happy in her love of Walter, such feelings came again, and seemingly in a stronger form. She was mystified. "What ails me now I cannot say," she wrote to Walter. She tried to describe her sense of loss, of blankness, looking for an analogy. The words she used were powerful, likening her loss of love to forgetting the familiar words of the Lord's Prayer—"knowing it to be there, but unable to find it." Involved in a romantic relationship with a man, her mental change now had an impact not only on herself but on him. Experiencing the change in her, Walter began to use some of the language of physicians of his day. He early on spoke of "aberrations of the brain caused by bodily disturbances." This was guided by the somatic notions of medicine that attributed mental states to bodily ones. Charlotte did not at this time share this understanding.

As she underwent an even more severe episode in March 1883, she could think back to the previous occurrence. On March 18, she told Walter simply that she had a "relapse." It is hard to interpret this in twenty-first-century terms as depression, for she imagined herself at that time to be faring well. For example, on March 28 she wrote in her journal, "Am feeling unusually well & strong." She was trying to get work away from Providence, and she asked Walter to delay plans for marriage for a year. Essentially, she was seeking a pause that would give her breathing space to allow her to make a more thoughtful decision about marriage.

In the weeks of conflict that followed her demands, Charlotte tried to explain herself. She searched for language around the issue of marriage and sex. Her struggle with words was more difficult as she attempted to account for her variable mental state. Much in Charlotte's life she could understand. She knew a good deal about herself and her nature. But this experience of recurring numbness was something inexplicable. Over the course of the weeks in the spring of 1883 that she and Walter discussed this, her courage came to fail her. She began in late March with assertion. She connected her sense of blankness to the desire for freedom, both to try her wings and to consider a relationship less restrictive than traditional marriage. She then characterized herself in neutral terms, asking Walter to accept her as she was.

By late April, the wind had gone out of her sails. She wrote to Walter, "Explain the horror as you will, the facts are these: that at one time I loved you; and that now, in the same sense, I do not. Talk of psychologic phenomena! My own consciousness is simply a lack, a loss, a part of me dropped out. Not painfully so, in some ways I feel lighter & freer; but as though a side of my nature was gone....Isn't catalepsy something like this? A trance state? My heart is asleep—numb—gone. I don't feel much in any way; only think, and pray, & work."[41]

Catalepsy was a strong word to use. Both Charlotte and Walter were readers of Edgar Allan Poe. When his characters suffered from catalepsy, they were as the living dead, in danger of being buried alive. The term also used at the time for the rigid limb or body induced by hypnotism was *trance state*. What such an expression suggests is that to Charlotte at this time, her inner numbness seemed to come from the outside, out of her own control.

She felt struck down. "Thoroughly humbled I am. A woman not a woman, the most important part of whose nature as a live being, is as intermitent and unreliable as will-o-the-wisp is not healthy. So I drop that claim. I feel myself maimed, warped, imperfect, cruelly crippled." She could only ask God for his aid to "mend this crooked life."[42] At the moment of this writing, she associated her variable life—one part of which sought independence—with illness, not health. It was hideous. It was to be prayed against.

Charlotte's passage over the weeks of late March to late April was a steep downward slope. As she moved from assertion to despair, she continued to cope—she did her work and went about her daily routine—but she lost her courage. She began with the hope of a possible life for herself that joined sexual expression and independence. She ended with self-abasement. And with that she gave up her resistance to the dominant understanding of woman and female nature held by *Popular Science Monthly,* by Herbert Spencer, and, in different terms, by Walter.

CHAPTER 4 ··

To Wed and to Bed

*I*n the brief separation from Walter in the spring of 1883, Charlotte's search for paid work away from Providence continued, but it led nowhere. Despite the lacks in her formal education, she was literate and disciplined and had experience teaching private pupils and selling her art work. She tried the Young Women's Christian Association in New York but learned on May 18 that employment there was not to be. On the following day her friend Grace Channing brought her the advice of an uncle that Charlotte should seek a clerical position in Washington, likely in the federal civil service, open to women since the Civil War. Charlotte replied in her diary, "I will not, on principle."[1] One cannot know the "principle" involved, possibly opposition to political patronage, but with this declaration she ended her small efforts to live out her dream of independence away from Providence. She secured a job as a governess for a young Providence boy and planned to summer with him and his family in Maine.

All the while Charlotte wrote to Walter, typically each Sunday. On April 15, she penned the letter and then recorded in her diary, "Cry a good deal." They almost met on April 26, for Walter came by to see her, but she was out. When on May 14 Walter did call, Charlotte wrote, "O I was <u>glad</u> to see him!" Thus, the entry of May 20 is no surprise: "Walter. I have promised to marry him....Happy."[2]

His diary has a different story. When the two met on May 14, Walter told Charlotte that he was gathering enough money for passage to Europe and planned to emigrate alone. This move was calculated on his part: "The only thing that will teach her how much she loves me & what my love is—is to <u>lose</u> me." The desired effect, however, was not instantaneous. In the midst of caresses and kisses, Charlotte continued to speak of the need for self-sacrifice.[3]

What happened next did the trick. After Walter had sent sonnets to the *Atlantic Monthly* that were returned, he wrote to Charles De Kay, the editor of *Scribner's,* pretending to be a friend of the author, and asked for an evaluation. De Kay's harsh response to the "friend" was devastating. De Kay wrote that the sonnets should remain only "the amusement of vacant hours" for they were "so slight, so little above the ordinary run of verse" as to not warrant criticism; they were, in short, of "no promise." Walter's despair at this letter knew no bounds. His poems and his paintings now seemed to him worthless. He wrote to Charlotte and Mrs. Cresson asking that they both destroy his sonnets, and he burned his childhood journals. When he delivered his anguished letter to Charlotte in person, she read it and embraced him. Walter reported, "In my arms with broken voice she told how she loved me—how she had found that she <u>needed</u> me—how she <u>could</u> not live best without me—how she must have me....She promised or vowed rather to marry me. And settled it finally."[4]

Thus on May 20, 1883, Charlotte and Walter became engaged. Although they had to delay marriage for a year to gather the resources necessary to establish their own household, this time there would be no turning back. Henry James, in a book that seems uncannily to capture elements of Walter in the character Basil Ransom, ended *The Bostonians* with the young heroine Verena Tarrant giving up her public work to marry. As Verena escapes from the lecture hall to elope with Basil, her eyes filled with tears. James wrote, "It is to be feared that...these were not the last she was destined to shed."[5]

Charlotte and Walter, however, did not elope, and Charlotte was no public figure hiding from an audience but still an largely untried writer who needed to earn money. She went ahead with her job as governess, residing with the young boy and his family first in Providence and then in Maine. Her distaste toward the pupil under her charge made this move temporary, and at the end of September she returned home. She resumed her life teaching girls, painting cards and objects for sale, and exercising in the gymnasium.

The early autumn of 1883 was hardly a happy time. There are not many clues in her journal or Walter's diary, but a major state-ment exists in two new stanzas she added to the poem "In Duty Bound," which she had first written in 1881 before she and Walter met. As noted in chapter 1, the poem imagines a woman seeking to live out her ideals but hemmed in by a woman's life ordained by "natural law." As completed in 1881, it gives the striking image of the woman living in a house "with roof so darkly low" that she "cannot stand erect without a blow." In her pain, she can only wish for death.

The stanzas of 1883 add to the poem's despair:

A consciousness that if this thing endure
The common joys of life will dull the pain;
The young ideals of the grand and pure
    Die, as of course they must,
    Of long disuse and rust.

That is the worst. It takes supernal strength
To hold the attitude that makes the pain.
And they are few indeed but stoop at length
    For something less than best;
    To find, in stooping, rest.[6]

What are presumed to be comforts, the common joys of a woman's life, easing life's pains, are here the enemy. They are parts of the lesser life that cause high ideals to die. A woman of the earth cannot continue to stand against the roof of the house of her sex. She stoops, "To find, in stooping rest." The poem is a profound restatement of Charlotte's essential conflict—living as a person of high ideals within a woman's body and seeking its common joys at the cost of aspiration.

Whatever powerful emotions caused Charlotte to write the poem, she was businesslike in seeking its publication. Beginning on October 23, 1883, she sent it out successively to the *Century, Harper's,* and the *Christian Register;* they all rejected it. She was pleased when she got word that it would be published in the *Woman's Journal* and wrote, "The first step, the entering wedge. No pay, but it's a beginning."[7]

In mid-November, Walter criticized her, seeking to encourage her to adopt "a little more softened manner." With that she painted what she called a "lugubrious picture of 'The Woman Against The Wall.'" In this lost image, she portrayed "a wan creature who had traversed a desert and came, worn out, to an insurmountable wall which extended around the earth." Walter saw in it both her potential power as an artist and her unhappiness, "I know it was a literal transcript of her mind."[8] In late November, after Walter visited her in the evening, she wrote, "One of my turns of affectional paralysis."[9] Two and a half weeks later, after noting that she felt better, she added, "Have been miserable in divers ways for weeks."[10] As the year turned 1884, she gave this summary: "My clear life-governing will is dead or sleeping. I live on circumstances, and waves of misery sweep over me, resistless, unaccountable; or pale sunshine of happiness comes, as mysteriously."[11]

Then on New Year's Day she learned that Conway Brown, a young man she had had talks and walks with in Maine during the summer, had shot and killed himself. In her journal she wrote, "I can sympathize with him; mental misery is real; and in a season of physical depression might well grow unbearable." As she dwelt on the death in a letter to Walter, she noted that Conway had told her in summer "of having times of deep depression" with thoughts of suicide. Remarking on how he, an only child, might have forgotten his parents and the grief that loss of him would cause, she stated, "in such times the love of others seems as nothing; obligation nothing, duty nothing; nothing anywhere but misery that grows and grows till click!——and it is over forever." She went on to write that in such "black hours" one does not think of others—"one can-not think, one only feels, and on every side feels only pain." It is in this letter that we can begin to grasp the intensity of Charlotte's own "times of deep depression." We also learn something else. She wrote to Walter of the possibility that she might take her own life in the future if the "black hours" increased in severity. In doing so, she called her suicide the thing that Walter did "most dread."[12] By January 1884, Charlotte had talked to him about both her darkest moments and her own thoughts of taking her life.

Walter's diary did not note this. Nor did talk about her depressive episodes cause either of them to rethink their forthcoming marriage.

Lack of money did cause them to pause. Although Charlotte continued to gain income by teaching and by selling hand-decorated paper and objects, much of these earnings went to her mother for room and board and for clothing and other essentials. Her writing did not yet pay. Seeking funds beyond her own labor, Charlotte had a card to play. An aunt had bequeathed a Hartford property to Charlotte and her brother. In the late autumn of 1883, Charlotte contacted her uncle Charles Perkins to find out more about it. She then turned to her friend Caroline Hazard, from a wealthy family, in the hope she might interest her father, Rowland Hazard II, in buying it. This effort failed. Charlotte wrote in her journal, "The Hartford hope extinguished."[13] Then, at the beginning of 1884, Walter got a lucrative secret commission from an art collector who offered him $1,000 to create etchings of the masterworks in his collection. On the basis of this, Walter felt free to plan the wedding. They set a date in May.

Happiness seemed to return, at least momentarily, as Charlotte added shopping trips and sewing for her trousseau to her busy days. Her journal reveals little beyond the whirlwind of activity. An occasional comment reported unhappiness. In early March she wrote in her journal, "Am lachrymose. Heaven send that my forebodings of future pain for both be untrue." Other signs are more oblique. She turned again to Mill and read his *Liberty* and reread, now aloud to her mother, his *Subjection of Women*. She began to take Liebig's beef extract for breakfast, mentioned approvingly in *Popular Science Monthly*, an indication that she felt weak and wanted building up. It was normal in her era to turn to physical as well as emotional explanations for inner experience; for Charlotte this would not end with marriage.

One letter reveals a great deal about her state of mind. At the end of February 1884, she wrote to Grace Channing, then in Florida for her health, after Grace had congratulated her on her forthcoming nuptials. Charlotte was a bit down, thinking ill of Walter, despite herself, after criticisms of him from unspecified others had come her way. Knowing that Grace liked Walter, Charlotte wrote that it felt good to have her support. Charlotte expressed this with a curious statement: "what a comfort it is to have some person whose judgement has weight with me look favorably on the man of my——choice? hardly, I had no choice really, there was no other; the man of my acceptance say." Charlotte was clearly having second thoughts once again.

She tried to minimize what marriage would mean to her future life in order to put her doubts in perspective. She wrote to Grace that marriage for her was not, as for other women, "a goal—a duty, a hope, a long expected fate, a bewildering delight." It was rather "a concession, a digression, a thing good and necessary perhaps as matters stand, but still a means, not an end." She hoped she would find in it "a happiness to result in new strength for other things; a duty only one of others."

Grace had written that she hoped Charlotte would be "<u>very</u> happy." Charlotte answered that she really didn't expect this.

"There will be happy times I am sure, unhappy ones too, unless marriage alters my character much." Then she stepped back to make a unique and noteworthy comment found nowhere else in her personal writing: "Well, I had rather be as I am, high and low, then mediocre always. The exaltation is worth the pain."[14]

The highs certainly returned. Walter's art commission made possible a separate apartment to begin married life. As the couple found and began to decorate it and as wedding presents arrived, Charlotte's spirits soared.

On May 2, 1884, Charlotte and Walter were wed. After a short service officiated by his father, the newly married couple walked to their new home. Charlotte then described what followed. She left Walter to finish decorating their bedroom.

> The bed looks like a fairy bower with lace white silk and flowers. Make myself a crown of white roses. Wash myself again and put on a thin shift.... Go in to my husband. He [dressed in the white gown she had sewed for him] meets me joyfully; we promise to be true to each other; and he puts on the ring and the crown. Then he lifts the crown, loosens the snood, unfastens the girdle and then—and then—
>
> Oh my God! I thank thee for this heavenly happiness. O make me one with thy great life that I may best fulfill my duties to my love! to my Husband!
>
> And if I am a mother, let it be according to thy will![15]

Charlotte's decision to marry Walter was a fateful one. It meant that she accepted his entire offer. There would be the sexual consummation that both of them desired, and she pledged, at least implicitly, to be his true woman and muse and to be constant.

Walter's understanding of womanhood and marriage was held by many American men and women in the late-nineteenth century. He believed that a woman was first a woman and was created to serve a man and bear his children. Any desire on her part for independence was mere selfishness. What made his diary musings

Charlotte at the time she became Charlotte Perkins Stetson, 1884.
Schlesinger Library, Radcliffe Institute, Harvard University.

different from those of many persons in his era were their more highly charged sexual nature. He freely admitted to his sexual desires, including, both before and after marriage, thoughts of prostitutes and mistresses.[16] Moreover, he believed that sex was at the core of his painting. In March 1883, he wrote, "My aim of late years has been to express the loveliness of womanhood & the purity of the sexual relation."[17]

As an artist who sought in his paintings to give expression to and elevate the sexual, he found in the Pre-Raphaelites true visual beauty. He said he regarded the poetry of Dante Gabriel Rossetti as "utterances of my own soul." He saw himself as modern, writing in his diary, in a manner befitting the reform physiology of his day, "I do not object to the utmost nudity in art: I advocate it. I would have every child taught the principles of generation and the hygiene of the organs pertaining thereto. I would have love made as pure and natural and easy as the mating of birds <u>seems</u> to be, or the copulation of flowers."[18] Yet he was in many respects deeply conventional. And—also in the way of Rossetti—all was to be on his terms.

He sought to shape Charlotte's thoughts regarding sexuality. One example of this happened around the time of crisis in their relationship when she expressed her willingness to give Walter her body but not her soul. After she had conversed with Grace Channing's uncle about his good friend Walt Whitman, the uncle had left Charlotte a book of Whitman's poetry. She declined the gift, explaining in her journal that she did so "as I had promised Walter I would not read it."[19] A few months later, when Walter took back his prohibition, he attempted in his diary to justify his earlier ban. He had insisted, he wrote, that Charlotte not read Whitman's poems at that time because they were too earthy. Walter wanted Charlotte, before she confronted Whitman's "slaughter-house rankness," to see men as "delicate and tender" and to imagine "sexual relations" as "holy and lovely."[20] He wanted the images she would take to their wedding night to be shaped by Rossetti, not by Whitman.

Walter seemingly got his way. Both approached their first love-making with exalted expectations, and both reports confirmed ecstasy realized. Some months later, after relating the joyful walk from the ceremony to their new home, Walter wrote:

> Oh the hush of our hearts! The stillness—it had come! It had come! Waited for, ached for—and come in all the fullness we could ask—came attended by all the fortune we could wish and quite luxury where we had been willing to expect privation. Come. Come....
>
> Leaving me in this parlor she took the bedroom which is sacred always with us. I put on the wedding garment she had made for me, a stainless chiton, and took the ring she had never worn in which Ich liebe Dich is engraved as she wished, and waited.[21] There was a gliding sound and a hush of new light and she She SHE was there. Or radiance! Oh divine loveliness! How love illumines! Clad in the thinnest white, fairer than I had ever seen her her intensely dark eyes and exquisite mouth sweeter than any thought, bearing a crown of roses, wherewith I was to crown her. When we had the true ceremony, an offering to God, as the other had been a sacrifice to civil law. Simple right, unutterable, beautiful, and imperishable long as my soul lives! Oh my Love, my more than Love![22]

Charlotte had a year's engagement to prepare for this wedding night. She did more than sew their intimate clothing and choose to have the German words for "I love you" engraved on her wedding ring. In her own way she sought counsel and knowledge—not from Whitman but from professional women.

On June 4, 1883, two weeks after agreeing to marry Walter, Charlotte traveled to Boston to visit friends and to consult with Dr. Elizabeth C. Keller. During her engagement, Martha Luther had gone to see Dr. Keller as part of her preparation for marriage and had told Charlotte about her. Charlotte stated at that time,

"I am glad such women live." In February 1883, when Dr. Keller came to Providence to lecture, Charlotte attended with her mother. With her engagement, Charlotte now called on Dr. Keller for her premarital visit.[23]

A well-known and respected physician and surgeon, Keller had served as resident surgeon at the New England Hospital for Women in Roxbury since 1875 and had a successful medical practice in the Boston suburb of Jamaica Plain. She was a distinguished graduate of the Philadelphia Woman's Medical College and a frequent contributor to its annual publication *Transactions,* which was the major professional print outlet for women physicians in the United States. Reading her precise reports of patient cases and diseases in the 1880s gives a clear sense of her professionalism and her engagement in what were understood as the best practices in her era.[24] She was known in her own community as a civic leader and, unusually for a professional woman, as a wife and mother.[25]

Charlotte began a complex relationship with Dr. Keller, perhaps one the physician sustained with many of her patients. When Charlotte first visited in June 1883, Keller received her for lunch and then took her for a drive. Charlotte reported, "Good talk with her, personally and professionally." Charlotte then got help with complexion problems from Keller's associate physician. Two days later, Charlotte impulsively made a second visit, this one only personal. Charlotte recorded, "She is a little ill. I ask for her picture and get it. Then I induce her to lie down and tell her some quiet poems."[26] Nothing in this account gives insight into the content of their conversation on their drive, but behind the words "personally and professionally" likely lay advice regarding the sexual aspects of married life.

That Charlotte sought guidance regarding sex is clear from the decision she made on May 28, 1883, a week before her visit to Dr. Keller, to "Invest $1.00 in 'The Alpha' a physiological paper."[27] From this point, Charlotte began to note when its monthly issues came and when she read it. She quickly set herself up as an expert. When lunching with a friend, Charlotte took it upon herself to "enlighten her benighted mind on various matters of sexual physiology."[28] Reading the issues of the *Alpha* that Charlotte read sheds light on her thinking about sex both at the time of her marriage and in the years that followed.

Edited by Dr. Caroline B. Winslow, a homeopathic physician in Washington, the *Alpha* served, at one level, as an organ of the Moral Education Society of Washington, which Winslow headed. This group, whose beginnings lay in efforts to convey morality to children, entered the political arena as a voice against the regulation of prostitutes.[29] Winslow also used the *Alpha* to take on a number of important issues of the day and to support women's rights, including the 1884 candidacy of Belva Lockwood for president of the United States. By the early 1880s, the *Alpha*'s more important concern was a particular vision of sexuality.

Winslow's position in the sexual conversation of her time was both interesting and complicated. She inherited much of her thinking from writers of the previous generation in the conservative wing of reform physiology, such as Sylvester Graham, who urged sexual restriction and severe limits on sexual intercourse within marriage. She shared the positions and rhetoric of moral reformers who put the spotlight on sexual wrongs, especially prostitution, and of temperance advocates who targeted drunken, abusive husbands. To this mix she added newer notions derived from liberal reform physiologists, such as Edward Bliss Foote, who wrote about the positive power of sex, the importance of the sex act, and sexual magnetism.

Winslow insisted that it was because of the very power of sex, its majesty, that she stood for sexual continence in marriage. These words appeared in the *Alpha*: "The human body is God's temple upon the earth, wherein our souls should worship the Lord in the beauty of holiness. The procreative faculties should be the very holy of holies within this temple." Although the myths of ancient times contained coarse elements, "there is yet a perceptible divine truth in their worship of the expression of sex."[30]

Winslow's conclusions were, however, very different from those of Foote, who argued for the positive value of sexual intercourse in marriage. In argument and language close to that of Graham, Winslow wrote that because men's seminal fluid was the "elixir of life," it was best "to conserve and not dissipate" it. Sexual intercourse was for procreation only. "All expenditure of the seminal fluid, except for procreation, is contrary to nature, is a dissipation of the vital forces, and is consequently a moral wrong." Her conclusion: married couples should engage in sexual intercourse only a few times during their lives together.

Winslow affirmed the strength of men's sexual drive, stating that "sexual attraction is universal, the 'hunger of the heart' world wide." Given this powerful instinct, what ought men do? Winslow's advice was that men should cultivate their spiritual selves. "Man is very slow to learn this truth. He has prostituted his highest bodily functions, the reproductive, to sensuous enjoyment, and plunged himself to the lowest hell. To get out of this he must cultivate his higher nature in every possible way. The intellect must guide the affections; the reason govern the appetites."

This was old advice. What made Winslow's approach new was her strong belief in the importance of companionship between men and women rooted in what Winslow understood as magnetic forces of attraction between the sexes. She wrote that she believed it was "necessary to the best health and happiness of both men and women to not only touch one another often, but to live in the closest social relations." In contrast to others who saw sexual magnetism as "confined to the reproductive organs," Winslow perceived that it "permeates the whole body from head to foot." Thus, she concluded, "for the sweetest and best exchange of this magnetism, it is not necessary to use those organs."

Husband and wife, she advised, should live closely and affectionately but have sexual intercourse only in order to have a child. As she put it, "The wedded life should be one long 'honeymoon,' and will be when men and women are wise, when they consecrate their reproductive organs to the use nature designed them for, and elevate their love from the flesh to the spirit, from the body to the soul."

Winslow insisted that the gain for this was morality, happiness, and good health. This "finer sexual intercourse or exchange," of affection without sexual relations, is one "that brings no exhaustion or repulsion, that breeds no loathsome disease, that brings no enforced maternity, and no unwelcome children into the world, that needs no 'nest-hiding,'[31] that does away with envy and jealousy, and all brothels, that makes woman the crowned queen in the realm of love, that gives joy, strength, health and peace of mind, instead of lassitude, weakness, gloom and unrest." She concluded, "Continent men and chaste women are full of life and magnetism, and when they are wise they will know how to exchange it, greatly to the benefit of both."[32]

Within the pages of his magazine, *Dr. Foote's Health Monthly,* Foote debated Winslow.[33] Men and women, he argued, needed to exercise their magnetism in a less sublimated form through direct sexual expression, and he advised them to use "checks" (contraceptives) to avoid unwanted pregnancies. Winslow strongly disapproved. She wrote, "I would not, I could not, under any circumstances, use or recommend another to use a prevention, or advise an abortion, or assist in one, or recommend 'prudential checks,' because I believe and know them to be always wicked and injurious."[34] In the exchanges that followed, Winslow's arguments for sexual continence within marriage (excepting the intercourse necessary for pregnancy) became known as the "Alpha doctrines."

Winslow had the law on her side, while Foote was arrested and fined. The 1873 federal act for the "Suppression of Trade in, and Circulation of, Obscene Literature and Articles of Immoral Use," commonly known as the "Comstock Law," made it illegal to send contraceptive information and materials through the mail, and little "Comstock laws" passed by state legislatures made the sale of such items illegal. (These laws were not enforced, and the commerce of contraception—condoms, "womb veils" (diaphragms], and spermicides—continued, though generally hidden from view.) After 1873, it became dangerous for a writer on moral physiology to discuss contraception, advise free love, or offer clear sexual information, closing off a vital element of reform physiology. What remained available in public prints for someone like Charlotte to read was that any efforts to prevent pregnancy other than abstaining from sexual intercourse were wrong both morally and physically.[35]

The *Alpha* supported an aspect of the women's movement that objected to the concept of what were known as men's marital rights.[36] That a husband had an unlimited right under law to sexual intercourse with his wife was a source of disquiet among women, surfacing early in the women's rights movement. Elizabeth Cady Stanton reflected on the way "women flock to me with their sorrows" and openly spoke against the laws and assumptions governing marriage in the nineteenth century. When Henry Blackwell got Lucy Stone to marry him, he promised her the sole right to determine "where and how often you shall become a mother."[37]

The *Alpha* both shaped Charlotte's consciousness and became a place of opportunity for her. On November 24, 1883, she copied one of her poems and sent it to the monthly. Early the next year, Winslow accepted it for publication, informing Charlotte that she "would be glad to hear...again" from her, and it was published in February.[38] "One Girl of Many" is on its face a conventional, sympathetic narrative of a prostitute's first fall. A poor and lovely thing is offered the goods of the earth in exchange for the unmentioned sex. She takes what is proffered and moves along the path to sin, degradation, and death. What makes the poem interesting are echoes of Charlotte's own childhood. The female child is "hungry from her birth," often deeply sad with thoughts of death yet "gay at little pleasures." She is tempted by a man, in a way reminiscent of the seducer in *Adam Bede*, offering fine clothes, "shelter, protection, kindness, peace and love." Charlotte then distances herself from her subject by telling us that the girl (unlike the author) is "untaught of woman's worth" and, ignorant of "nature's laws," chooses "a stylish look" over comfort. Heredity and environment work against her. Her instinct is "debased in ages long," and nothing in her "daily sight" tells her of sexual purity or the value of marriage. The poem ends with an ironical statement of the conventional wisdom that men required regular sexual outlets:

> ...Men cannot live
> Without what these disgraceful creatures give.
> Black shame, dishonor, misery and sin;
> *And men find needed health and life therein!*[39]

The poem thus engaged the Foote-Winslow debate, if only indirectly, on the side of the Alpha doctrines.

In their conflict of April 1883, Walter made clear his sexual needs, and Charlotte offered the possibility of an unconventional marriage of independent living enlivened by sexual intercourse, when "the erotic tendency was at a maximum." He told her he would not accept this. Perhaps he or she equated, as some writers did at the time, sex outside traditional marriage with prostitution, an association that would have placed Charlotte in the position of the "girl" of the poem. But half a year had passed, and by late November 1883 she anticipated sexual relations within conventional marriage. During this time, Walter continued to convey his views, and Charlotte continued to read the *Alpha*. She was engaged, different. She could distance herself from the "girl" of the poem, who was ignorant; who knew not "of the color white"; who had seen nothing that let her "revere the title 'wife.'" By the time Charlotte copied her poem to send it off, the impact since April 1883 of the broader culture and of the *Alpha* was clear: sexual desire was sanctified by love; love was sanctified by marriage; and sexual intercourse was sanctified by imagining the creation of a child.

Thus arrived the wedding night of Charlotte and Walter's journals. Hardly spontaneous, the two carefully scripted their first sexual consummation with scene and costume. In the July 1883 issue of the *Alpha,* in an essay on healthy conception, Winslow praised what she called "a beautiful service of consecration and preparation of body and soul for the inception of an immortal being" described in John Cowan's book of reform physiology, *Science of a New Life.* His scenario of a married couple's initial act of intercourse involved walks in the open air and sex in the bright light of noon.[40] There is no indication that Charlotte read Cowan, but she did read this issue of the *Alpha,* and it may have shaped her thinking. The figures in Dante Gabriel Rossetti's paintings and poems, Walter's romantic notions and his familiarity with costuming models, and Charlotte's love of dress and theater came into play. The bed covered in "lace white silk and flowers," gowns of sheer white cloth for both husband and wife, her crown of white roses, the ceremony of the ring—this was the rite Walter and Charlotte created to purify the long-deferred act. Both in anticipation and in retrospect, the gloss the wedded couple put on their first consummated lovemaking was what made Charlotte different from the "One Girl of Many."

After Marriage, What?

C harlotte reported in her journal the day after the wedding that, after a good breakfast, "Lie on the lounge in the soft spring sunshine and am happy. Happy. Happy. Walter stays quietly at home with me, and we rest and love each other."[1] As delightful as this appears on the page, it described their only honeymoon, a single day free of work and free for lovemaking.

With that, life resumed. Walter went to paint in his studio. Charlotte continued to give lessons, visited with her mother and friends, and read, all seemingly at a quieter pace than before. There were for her a few changes from the outset. After the wedding she gave up gymnastics. Moving to their shared quarters, she took on the new tasks of organizing the housework and doing most of it herself.

Her first quarrel with Walter came a week after their wedding. Although she had always helped her mother with housekeeping, noting in her journal her specific tasks, she now found she had much more of it, and she particularly loathed dishwashing. "I suggest that he pay me for my services, and he much dislikes the idea. I am grieved at offending him, mutual misery. Bed and cry."[2]

Fourteen years later this grief and misery would be transmuted into a great work of social analysis and reform, asserting women's need for paid labor, but in the spring of 1884, these feelings only pulled her down. On May 24 she reached a low point and wrote, "Am disgusted with myself—numb—helpless. Tomorrow God helping me I will begin anew!"[3]

These early moans did not signal the onset of a depressive period, however; good times came and went. As she adjusted to her new life, Charlotte tried to find a focus. She learned that it would not be possible for her to merely live for love, for Walter was often tired.

For years there had been a wiggly line alongside a journal entry. Charlotte's symbol for the onset of menstruation, it generally appeared at four-week intervals. After the wedding, the wiggle marked May 14. On the following day, she "read Naphey[s]," a work of popular medicine focused on the female reproductive system. Walter brought her flowers.[4] The wiggle appeared again on June 12. Beside that day is the one word: "Bad." The following day, Charlotte reported, "Feel sick and remain so all day. Walter stays at home and does everything for me. Bless him!"[5] What living closely with Charlotte during her monthly flow meant to Walter, one cannot know, but it is likely that, given his exalted notions of her purity, it distressed him. On June 14, day three of her menstrual period, Charlotte was rebuffed by him. In her journal she put in parentheses "Am sad. Last night & this morning. Because I find myself too—affectionately expressive. I must keep more to myself and be asked—not borne with."[6]

On June 20, she told of a lovely day of boating and companionship when she felt happy. Beginning about ten days later, she napped more, returned to bed after her early rising in the morning, and reported digestive problems. There is no wiggly line for July. On July 31, after she threw up her breakfast, she had a visit with her mother: "Tell her my expectation." Charlotte was pregnant.[7]

The Physical Life of Woman, by George H. Napheys, M.D., read by Charlotte in mid-May, may have come at the suggestion of

Dr. Keller. Or it is possible that Mary Perkins recommended it to her daughter, for it was an older book, initially published in 1869, that in later editions came recommended by Catharine Beecher, Henry Ward Beecher, and many other worthies.[8] As was usual in such books, Napheys described the signs of pregnancy beyond cessation of the menses. He also offered practical advice about how to handle morning sickness and fatigue. He recommended lying abed in the mornings and napping whenever tired. Charlotte, who had always prided herself on early rising and strenuous days, immediately began to allow herself these indulgences.

Fearful that she was ill, on August 7 Charlotte visited Dr. Olive Herrick in Providence. Although pregnant, she was treated for a displaced uterus with an instrument and given a bitter medicine, probably to relieve constipation. Then on August 18, Charlotte traveled to Hingham without Walter to visit Martha and to see Dr. Keller. Three days later, Walter reported that he had a letter from her. "She is better. And Dr. Keller pronounces 'prognosis favorable.' "[9]

Charlotte had framed her initial lovemaking in terms of creating a child, in keeping with her era and with the *Alpha*. Walter continued to do this, writing in his diary, "In the very ecstasies of bodily marriage I have been conscious of prayers...of intense longings that the child that might come should be noble, beautiful in soul & body and a grand helper of the world."[10] Napheys encouraged such thoughts. For the well-being of the child, a couple needed to have a proper state of mind during sexual relations.[11]

Then there were the thoughts and feelings of the pregnant woman as she carried the growing being. Napheys shared with others, including Caroline Winslow and other *Alpha* writers, the belief that prenatal influences profoundly affected the mental well-being of the developing fetus. When Charlotte was at a lecture on free trade, Walter worried that her interest in political economy during the pregnancy would determine a child who leaned toward statecraft: "I would rather it had been a subject more esthetic."[12] But more than subject matter was at issue. As Napheys put it, the child could be deformed by the mother's "*habitual,* long-continued mental conditions" or by her "*violent and sudden emotion.*" It was necessary for an expectant mother to remain cheerful and calm.[13] This, however, Charlotte could not do. Her journals and Walter's diary give clear indications of her strong emotions. On September 4, she registered the first note of real trouble: "I feel unable to do anything and am mortal[l]y tired of doing nothing." It was very hot in Providence, and Charlotte wanted to sleep on the roof. "I humbly ask if I can sleep there tonight, and am told 'No, you cannot!' Serves me right for asking."[14]

Napheys stated that pregnancy could lead to a change in mood. Among the possibilities he posed this one: "The woman is rendered more susceptible, more impressible. Her character is transformed. She is no longer pleasant, confiding, gentle and gay. She becomes hasty, passionate, jealous and bitter."[15] The response of the husband and others should be to bear with her and help her to restored cheerfulness. Walter often tried to be accommodating. He remained aware, however, of Charlotte's conflicted self. In mid-September he wrote, "She bears it patiently, though she is more sensitive and easily fatigued both physically & mentally & at times despondent, especially when she has fears that all that dreamed of life of great usefulness, may be past or beyond her reach. Truly, I think, she is becoming better fitted for usefulness." As before, Walter loved her growing dependence, though now he felt somewhat put upon to sacrifice his art for the housekeeping chores he believed were rightfully hers.[16]

Charlotte stopped journal entries from mid-October until January, stating in her year-end summary that the cause was "ill health."[17] Walter's entries in October and November give a different picture, presenting highly romantic notions of her happiness. He wrote at the end of October of Charlotte's joy at "quickening": her face "beaming with goodness & love.... All the intense motherliness of her nature seems to flower." He thrilled at his role: "She is happy, happy, happy! And I—I—I, from painter that I am have made her so!"[18]

Charlotte herself registered this side as the new year came. In her annual summary, she expressed some dissatisfaction with her accomplishments and had questions about the future but wrote:

> I am a happy wife. I bear a child. I have been far from well. I do not know that I am better in any way. Unless it be better to be wider in sensation and experience, and perhaps humbler. Ambition sleeps. I make no motion but just live.
>
> And I am Happy? Every day almost finds me saying so and truly. And yet—and yet....I will see what my life counts when I am old....I should not be afraid to die now; but should hate to leave my own happiness and cause fierce pain. Yes. I am happy.[19]

She was at that moment, at least, partially accepting what she understood as the animal side of her nature, enjoying the intimacy of marriage, and living as Spencer dictated.

Then in late January, trouble struck. Charlotte described it in physical terms. "Very hot and nervous evening." After several such nights, Walter's father, a dealer in patent medicines, came with "bromide of potassium for an opiate," the frequent recourse for a distressed patient.[20] As Charlotte took what he administered, she reported that she slept at night, but in the day was "down cast." Bromide of potassium or bromide, intended to calm or quiet a patient, can have a depressing effect. A few days later, she wrote, "Am very very tired and lame at night which displeaseth and grieveth my Walter." After a respite of about a week, the trouble returned, and there was a different level of crisis. In mid-February, after a night of bromide-induced sleep, she reported, "Not well in the morning; so hysterical indeed that Walter decides to stay with me." Then, two days later, "Hot, cold, hot; restless, nervous, hysterical." Walter and a double dose of bromide helped get her through this.[21]

When Charlotte used the word *hysterical,* what did she mean? It was a powerful word that she used only a few times in reference to herself, and it was then and is today a very tricky word, for it crosses medical and vernacular discourse. Charlotte used it here colloquially to signify a time in which she completely lost control and abandoned self-restraint. It has this meaning today when one speaks of being overtaken by laughter by a joke. In the nineteenth century, people also used it in this sense—but more often in relation to sadness. Persons could weep; or they could weep hysterically—loudly, perhaps with screams, rapid movements, and beating of hands against those who attempted to constrain them or bring them out of it. Charlotte, a month before her confinement, appears to have been distraught in that way. The signs were hardly auspicious.

On March 23, 1885, Charlotte gave birth to a healthy girl. The couple named her Katharine. Early reports in Charlotte's journal describe a common experience of new mothers—initial ecstasy, then fatigue. When May 2 came around, the couple's first wedding anniversary, Charlotte wrote that she dressed up for the first time, and Walter brought her roses, but she was too tired to enjoy the day—"So I cry."[22] Charlotte experienced some pleasure and relief in early May when her mother returned from Utah, where she had been helping Thomas and his family. Mary Perkins quickly took over much of Katharine's care.

Between May 11 and early August, Charlotte made no journal entries. On August 5, she reported that she had organized her books that day, "hoping to be able to keep account of my life and expenses again. I have long been ill; weak, nerveless, forced to be idle and let things drift. Perhaps now I can pick up the broken threads again and make out some kind of a career after all."[23] Together, the failure to keep her journal and the words themselves, especially "nerveless," inform us that Charlotte had little energy and had most likely experienced a serious depressive episode.

Another hiatus in the journal followed. When Charlotte wrote again, on August 28, she reviewed the month. Two weeks earlier, Walter had asked his older friend and patron Dr. Edward Balch Knight to come by. "I had had one of my bad times when he was first sent for. The next day was bad too; highly excited, hysterical, seeming to myself wellnigh insane."[24] This was a new word to describe herself. It tells us that what Charlotte now experienced was more than a passing hysterical episode of losing control. Her outbursts felt to her as though she was approaching insanity, feared in that era as a potentially permanent condition.

Walter set down a review of his material conditions and state of mind. The "little dove cote" the couple had rented was too small to accommodate Mary Perkins, forcing the family to move to a larger, presumably more expensive dwelling. In addition, Charlotte had hired household help. By then, Walter's fortunes had declined. His etching commission was over, and a Boston show did not take his work. He was deeply in debt, unable to support either his household or assist his parents, and he was terrified about his future prospects.

He wrote that after Charlotte's mother came and took over Katharine's care, Charlotte "broke down entirely, and has been since—a nervous invalid requiring the utmost care and tender treatment, lest it should settle itself into an incurable mind disease." Walter feared that what had seemed like only temporary distress could become permanently fixed. He related Charlotte's continuing descent into illness. "There have been violent hysterical symptoms, and long periods of taciturnity, melancholy and utter loss of the desire or power to will." Dr. Keller came, sought to cheer Charlotte up, and left medicine. It was when this seemed not to have helped, in mid-August, that Walter, against Charlotte's wishes, sent for his friend Dr. Knight.[25]

According to Walter, Dr. Knight talked to Charlotte, and she told him her feelings "that her whole usefulness & real life was crushed out of her by marriage and the care of the baby." Knight then talked to Walter, who gave his understanding of "the whole case from the beginning." Knight assured Walter that he thought he could cure Charlotte. He would try "moral measures," coming twice a week to talk to her.[26]

When Dr. Knight stated that he thought that he could bring Charlotte to her right senses by talking to her, he did not mean psychotherapy in the mid-twentieth-century sense. Fifteen years older than Charlotte and Walter, Knight brought to his practice the training of an earlier time. He relied on the approach, common in the pre-Civil War era, of offering reassurance and exhortation intended to strengthen a person's will in its fight against negative emotions. From this perspective, one's inner life involved forces of rationality and emotion struggling against each other for control. A hysterical episode registered that emotion triumphed over reason. The sufferer needed to exert the will to prod and strengthen reason.

Walter had wanted to turn Charlotte's interest and engagement away from the public world and toward his private one. In the spring of 1883, he interpreted her desire to live independently and work in the world as selfishness. His diary recorded his struggles and triumphs. In the late summer of 1885, Charlotte's earlier ambitions returned in full measure. She was now his wife and the mother of his child, and his response to the return of her ambition beyond the domestic sphere was distaste. Charlotte seemed to him obsessed with her sense of mission. As he put it in August 1885, she "rushes in her mind from all our sweet life to try to go out into the world to rid it at one fell swoop of all evil, pain and the like. Strange and terrible how such ideas can take possession of one's brain."[27] Charlotte's feelings about him were unstable. At times she expressed loving feelings—but "I think at times she feels hatred of me." Heavily burdened with debt, seeking to paint and build a reputation, he wrote that he was coming to the end of his patience: "The true Charlotte is in a dreadful mist—oh, for recovery soon! I can't bear it much longer." He closed one diary entry with his own plaint. He could write no more. "I myself have grown too 'nervous.'"[28]

Walter's explanation for Charlotte's distress was different from that of his old doctor friend. Walter held a tenet of the rising medical orthodoxy at the time that the normal functions of the female reproductive system continually put women at risk both physically and emotionally. He located Charlotte's misery and hysterical outbursts in her body. "I have no doubt in my own mind," Walter wrote, "that the whole trouble is some uterine irritation and until that is cured she will be no better." Here the belief was that lesions in the womb caused "irritations." These were not felt directly as pain but acted sympathetically and indirectly on the nervous system, causing a woman to lose control over her emotions, or in the language of the day, to react hysterically. Walter urged her to return to Dr. Keller. Two days later, Walter reported with hope that Charlotte was cheered and maternal once again. "She now sees herself that her brain is not diseased in itself but that the trouble is purely local. She purposes going to see Dr. Keller as soon as she can. Dr. K. can examine her & 'treat' her if necessary."[29]

There were ups and downs over the next weeks. On August 30, Charlotte chronicled: "Every morning the same hopeless waking. Every day the same weary drag. To die mere cowardice. Retreat impossible, escape impossible. I let Walter read a letter to Martha in which I tell my grief as strongly as I can. He offers to let me go free."[30] Just as Walter would not countenance sex with Charlotte without marriage, so she could not then imagine legal separation or divorce. She saw death as the only possible escape.

There were times when Charlotte felt herself improving. On September 3, she had the pleasure of receiving the month's *Alpha* that contained her short essay "Advertising for Marriage." This short piece can be read in a number of ways. On its face, it is a defense of marriages made by long distance, by the placing of and responding to advertisements in publications such as newspapers. But the soul of the essay's argument is that a man and a woman should come together not on the basis of sexual attraction but out of their mutual sympathy with ideas. Meeting through letters rather than by chance encounter allows for a better choice. "If a man sees a fair woman before he knows her; feels the charm of her presence before he begins to understand her character; if first aroused to the necessity of judging by his strong inclination; surely he stands less chance of a cool and safe decision than one who

Charles Walter Stetson, "Evening—Mother & Child," 1886–87 (Charlotte with Katharine). Courtesy of the private collection of Christopher and Melinda Ratcliffe.

begins knowingly, learns a character from earnest letters, loves the mind before he does the body."[31] This, of course, is the opposite of what Walter had done. Charlotte was beginning to see what a wrong choice Walter had made.

At this time, Charlotte was reading Henry James's novel *The Bostonians,* then appearing as a serial in the *Century.* On September 2, she reported beginning to read what was likely the September 1885 issue. Two days later, as she finished the part labeled chapters 25–28, she wrote, "I am much displeased with 'The Bostonians.'"[32] In this segment of the novel Verena Tarrant, the vibrant young speaker for women, whose fate is at the center of the story, is visited by Basil Ransom, a handsome southerner living in New York and languishing as a lawyer. As they walk around Cambridge, he learns of Verena's triumphs at the women's convention and tells her that her work is wrongheaded, intoning, "The use of a truly amiable woman is to make some honest man happy."[33] After this meeting, kept secret from Olive Chancellor, Verena's champion and companion, Basil receives an invitation in New York to hear Verena lecture. As Basil listens to her speech, he refutes the words but finds himself falling in love with the speaker. He muses to himself that her expressions were "the veriest of delusions, and that she was meant for something divinely different,— for privacy, for him, for love."[34]

No wonder Charlotte was displeased with the novel. Basil's words were so close to Walter's that they must have cut Charlotte deeply. Ironically, however, given James's unsympathetic portrayal of the Boston women gathered around the suffrage movement, the novel may have shown Charlotte a way out and given her a focus for her mission. Although she had published a poem in the *Woman's Journal,* the official organ of the Boston-based American Woman's Suffrage Association, Charlotte had remained aloof from the movement it represented. *The Bostonians* may have nudged her to seek kindred spirits there. Soon after reading it, Charlotte made her first direct contact with the Boston leaders of the women's rights movement.

In the meantime, Charlotte's emotions descended further. On September 11, Dr. Knight prescribed "Elixir Coca." Walter stated that the physician had recommended that Charlotte take this mixture of cocaine and alcohol "once in a while if she felt dismal & growing more & more tired."[35] The next day, the two made an excursion to the pharmacy. So eager was she for relief that she came to his studio "for her Coca. Left at once."[36] It did not seem to help for a few days, but then, in the afternoon of September 14, she reported feeling better. On September 22, her journal recorded "general breakdown" in the evening, and Dr. Knight recommended that she wean Katharine.[37]

Napheys had written of "puerperal mania," defining it as "a variety of insanity which attacks some women shortly after childbirth." He warned that, although it could be only short-lived, in a few cases "the mental alienation is permanent, and the wife and mother is never restored to her sanity."[38] This is, of course, what Charlotte and Walter feared most. Along with hereditary predisposition and exhaustion, Napheys cited displacement or ulceration of the uterus as one cause. This carried a positive side, the likelihood that a definite lesion in the uterus could be fixed.[39]

On September 28, Charlotte traveled to see Dr. Keller. Walter wrote, "I hope we shall find out if there is any organic disease by it."[40] Charlotte left an account of the visit. "Am examined and speculumed and told that I am all right. Great is my satisfaction and relief. . . . Feel as if I should get well."[41] The flip side, of course, was that there was nothing to fix, and Charlotte was left without hope of a surgical cure.

At the beginning of October, Charlotte followed Dr. Knight's suggestion and began to wean Katharine, feeding her formula. Day by day, Charlotte registered in her journal that she was no better. Napheys suggested that the best hope for a victim of puerperal mania lay "in quiet lodgings, or with some sympathizing friend."[42] Perhaps this gave Charlotte the courage to propose that she travel west and stay in California with her friend Grace Channing. The whole Channing household had moved from Providence to Pasadena in an effort to protect Grace from tuberculosis. On October 8, 1885, Charlotte wrote, "We propound discuss and decide the question of Shall I travel? Yes I shall. I contemplate wintering in California. Hope dawns. To come back <u>Well!</u>"[43]

Charlotte departed for the West in mid-October, leaving Katharine in her mother's care. During this time, Walter seems to have lived in his studio and only visited his child on occasion. Charlotte stopped first to visit Thomas in Utah and then in San Francisco to see her father, now the city's librarian, before settling into the Channing household in Pasadena. There she found herself not only among kind friends but also in the grand home of one of the most prestigious residents in this enclave of eastern and midwestern Protestants in southern California. The Channings' large house stood on four acres at the highest point in the town, and their grounds included a tennis court. Grace's father embodied the aspirations of this culture-starved society. William Francis Channing was a physician, inventor, and the son of the transcendentalist minister William Ellery Channing. As the Channings' guest, Charlotte found that being a great-granddaughter of Lyman Beecher and the great-niece of Harriet Beecher Stowe mattered. The Pasadena world was primed to receive her.

Without journal entries, the record thins, but Dr. Channing testified later to Charlotte's well-being during her stay in his household. "In our large, quiet sphere," he informed, "free from the home frictions, [she] regained apparently perfect health."[44] An important letter Charlotte wrote on March 13, 1886, from Pasadena told Martha of her enhanced sense of well-being. She stated, "You can see I am not as sick as I was." The real subject of the letter was a play she had created with Grace: "twas fun! To write a play and give it ourselves and all in a real theatre, to a real audience, who laughed and clapped and enjoyed it. We enjoyed it more. It's a pretty good play. We're going to try and sell it."[45] The playbill that survives for "Changing Hands," on March 8, 1886, describes a parlor farce set in Pasadena during the real estate boom, complete with an English lord, a wealthy American widow, and two mismatched young couples. Charlotte played Sophronia Blackstone and Grace, Amelia St. John, her intimate wealthy friend.[46] From the beginning, Charlotte had high hopes that she would be able to sell the play to a big-time producer and it would be the making of her and Grace's fortunes. Later in her life, Charlotte criticized writers who wrote only for pleasure or profit. All fiction had to have a higher purpose, and she insisted that hers always had. This gloss conveniently forgot her own play-writing as a younger woman.

Five months after arriving and soon after putting on the play, Charlotte made preparations to return to Providence. On Valentine's Day, imagining her homecoming, she wrote Walter a poem declaring that whether in sunny climes or in cold and gloom, "Love holds us one with power supreme / Triumphant still."[47] More soberly, she wrote Martha that she anticipated going back home with "both joy and dread. Joy to see my darlings again; and dread of further illness under family cares." With resignation, she continued, "Well. I have chosen."[48]

After a difficult journey, Charlotte returned home. On April 3 she wrote in her journal, "Am trying to get accustomed to life here."[49] Quickly she fell back into her misery, and her journal entries ceased. In early June, Walter reported that he had left her "in tears this morning, as I have almost ever since she came home. She goes to bed crying, or at least deeply melancholy, inconsolable. I am not sure that she does not weep all night."[50] He was sinking deeper into debt, and he saw her condition as making it difficult for him to paint his way out. Walter believed that if they had money, he could rescue Charlotte with gaiety, possessions, and travel.

In mid-August, Walter summarized the two months since his last entry. He reported that Charlotte experienced "another rather prolonged attack. Dr. Keller came down to perform an operation and succeeded. Then Charlotte had a violent time & went to see Dr. Keller in great haste. Stayed over night at her house. The

Walter, 1886. Schlesinger Library, Radcliffe Institute, Harvard University.

Dr. told her that she was suffering from a disease of the nerves, that her brain was all right. It is a form of nervous prostration." The unspecified "operation" was probably a procedure designed to correct a minor uterine irregularity. Charlotte's reaction to her treatment and new diagnosis was disappointment. Walter wrote his secret thought that "she expected to hear that her brain was organically injured."[51]

The two talked about separating. Walter had written to Grace to inquire about the possibility of Charlotte gaining employment in Pasadena. While Grace advised the separation, she expressed concern that Charlotte would be ostracized by those in Pasadena who "would not understand how she could leave her family a second time."[52]

At the end of August, Charlotte returned again to journal keeping, now a signal that she was well enough to think through her days. On August 25, she wrote, "Begin to feel myself again. Am taking Buckland's Essence of Oats, with infinite good effect." Wrapped in a healthy-sounding name, Dr. Buckland's Essence of Oats was a serious narcotic that offered a combination of alcohol and morphine. Walter testified to its immediate results: "I bought the essences of Scotch oats which has had a most certain & marked effect. She has worked a good deal, been cheerful & peaceable."[53] Given his straitened finances, both Charlotte's earnings and his own freedom to paint were essential to him. After Charlotte had taken the elixir for a month, Walter remarked on her "amazing" improvement. He wrote, "She is very very greatly better and seems to me almost, yes, quite better than her old self, for she is more mature & gentle. I never saw her look better."[54] Rather than separating, they began to discuss moving somewhere together, ideally to London.

A gift from Mrs. Cresson allowed Charlotte to take a two-week vacation at Stone Lea, the grand Cresson house near the shore in Narragansett, Rhode Island. Charlotte enjoyed playing tennis there, and her athleticism returned. As she got back to work, she made decorative cards on orders from friends, bringing in a small income. Walter appreciated this, for he was now $1,000 in debt and felt his financial obligations keenly.[55]

There were, in fact, plenty of downs as well as ups. Reading *Aurora Leigh,* by Elizabeth Barrett Browning, with Walter caused this outburst in her journal, "It brings up my grief. Anything does." The slightest new demand from Katharine caused great distress. On September 19, she reported, "Get hysterical in the evening while putting K to sleep." Walter took her place and slept beside his daughter. "When I am nervous she never does sleep easily."[56]

Sometime in August or September 1886, she wrote a short sketch of twin brothers: one who grew strong, courageous, learned, and wise; the other, kept by him in a mold and denied all challenge, education, and experience. The free, tall brother denigrated the small, trapped one, telling him he was weak, stupid, and foolish. Throughout the telling comes a repeated refrain: "And the weaker brother bore it, for he loved him well." When the smaller one outgrew his mold and sought to grow strong in the struggle of life, he was cursed by the tall one. Because "he loved him well," the slighter brother reentered the mold, only to rebreak it and try again. Charlotte left the story in rough shape and its outcome unresolved, perhaps because it was too personal, too close to her own experience and her feelings about confinement in marriage.[57]

She found a more effective expression of her anger in a poem, "The Answer."[58] In this harsh poem, evolutionary nature stands in the path of human aspiration, as represented by one man building a house, another seeking to do great work, and a young woman approaching marriage. Each is destroyed in turn by Nature, indifferent to individual suffering, answering each with the same refrain. The house-builder dies of the disease lurking under his house; the reformer ends his days unremembered and unappreciated. And the woman, who anticipated "in the holy name of wife, / Great work, great pain, and greater joy in life," finds herself only doing work "as brainless slaves might do." She feels only pain and cannot remember joy.

Helpless she died, with one despairing cry,—
"I thought it good. How could I let the lie?"

The poem ends with the refrain (repeated for the third time):

And answered Nature, merciful and stern,
"I teach by killing; let the others learn."[59]

"The Answer" distilled Charlotte's powerful feelings of betrayal. She had listened to Herbert Spencer and obeyed her body's instincts, and now she was suffering. Evolutionary science and Walter's love had done her in. Yet, as with earlier work, whatever angry feelings lay behind their words, publication of them gave her pleasure. She sent it to the *Woman's Journal,* and on October 2, when the issue came with "The Answer" in a prominent place, she was delighted. Her pleasure was increased when ten days later a letter from the editor compensated her with a year's subscription to the paper.[60]

Another big moment came in late October. For days, Charlotte reported in her journal that she was copying a play, presumably "Changing Hands." On October 27, she announced to her journal:

> The great day. Succeed in getting everything well arranged and myself dressed by three o'clock. Shortly after Mr. Gillette appears. A very pleasant afternoon with him. Mother comes over to supper, radiant in her best black silk. A good supper. Read play thereafter. He is favorably impressed, but does not stop to give a full opinion, having to catch train. But he liked it.[61]

William Gillette, a great actor and stage manager and only five years older than Charlotte, was the nephew of Isabella Beecher Hooker's husband, a close neighbor of the Hookers, and a schoolmate of their son. During the difficult and uncertain years of his early career, Isabella had offered him advice and material help. The family connection explains why Charlotte called on her mother to attend the supper and why Mary Perkins appeared in her best dress. On leaving, Gillette gave his hosts three tickets to his play in Providence, which Charlotte enjoyed and thought "a deserved success."[62]

Charlotte's increased well-being and pleasure gave Walter hope. The sexual frustrations he admitted in his diary eased. In late November 1886, reflecting that Charlotte a year before had been away in Pasadena, he wrote, "Now, thank God, she is here, in my very arms nightly, in my heart daily, well, happy, hopeful, good, true, loving beyond anything she ever was before."[63] On December 13, she wrote, "Walter and I are very happy together."[64] The Christmas festivities of that year marked a high point.

At the end of the year, as she summarized 1886, Charlotte wrote one of her most intriguing journal entries. It began, "I leave behind me tonight a year of much happiness, growth, and progress; also of great misery. But the happiness and progress are real and well founded; and the misery was owing mainly to a diseased condition of the nervous system. It is past, I hope forever."

In her next paragraph, she wrote revealingly. She was now in greater harmony with her surroundings, more comfortable with friends, and able to paint and write. Yet she experienced a loss of her "self abandoning enthusiasm and fierce determination in the cause of right." Although she felt happy, she was uneasy. Was her sense of well-being for good or ill? A part of herself felt "lowered—degraded," that she had become a "traitor to my cause." But then came a doubt. What did this sense of abandoning her "cause" mean? Was it real? Or was it only "a lingering trace of the disordered period just past"? She then wrote that she would have an answer only when she was truly well.[65]

This is the question. What was health for Charlotte? Was it living comfortably within her surroundings and the limitations that required? (One might add, though she did not, was this enabled by taking morphine in the guise of Dr. Buckland's Essence of Oats?) Or was righteous discontent the real health? Although their answers differed, the nature of true health was a major issue that played out in her mind and in Walter's.[66]

Charlotte's response in the winter of 1886–87 was complicated by her full engagement with the *Woman's Journal*. Not just the mouthpiece of the American Woman's Suffrage Association, what the weekly paper carried for an avid reader and aspiring writer such as Charlotte was a wide range of articles about women who did and dared. The weekly noted the first women to enter various occupations and reported on the broad field of women's work in public as professionals, employees, and leaders of voluntary associations. These subjects were presented within the context of a clear understanding that women should have full civic rights, including suffrage. The *Woman's Journal* offered regular news of women's rights gatherings, speeches, and petitions.

On October 6, 1886, Charlotte went to her first woman suffrage convention in Boston and there heard Lucy Stone speak.[67] Charlotte then began a serious course of reading on women, including both radical formulations and books of conventional wisdom not to her taste. Normally, as she sewed in the evenings, Walter read to her. Now to such books as *Tale of Two Cities* he added Margaret Fuller's *Women of the Nineteenth Century*. Charlotte pronounced Fuller's work "fine," but he objected to her reading program. She stopped pursuing it for a while, noting when she got a library book on women in western Europe, "I had left off my course of reading for two weeks to oblige him."[68] During this time, she was writing poems and essays on a wide range of women's issues and sending her work to the *Woman's Journal*. When Alice Stone Blackwell asked Charlotte to write a regular women's column for the *People,* a Knights of Labor paper in Providence, she used it to think through issues of women and paid work.[69] After returning to gymnastics with great enthusiasm, she began to consider "teaching gymnastics next winter."[70] When she traveled to Boston, she went to both the offices of the *Woman's Journal,* noting a "nice talk" with Blackwell, and to gymnasiums, including that of Sargent of Harvard, who had established a private gymnasium for female students at the Harvard Annex.[71]

For Charlotte, one serious issue in this period was money, or lack thereof. In the cold of mid-February, she was hit by full awareness of household poverty and the need for action: "A Financial Crisis. No coal, no money. I tell Walter he <u>must</u> get it, or I will; and he does."[72] At this point, as she was doing whatever she could to bring in cash—making cards for sale and writing newspaper articles—she was angry at Walter for failing to provide for the household. Another deep concern may have been sex. One hint of this came in her journal as she was befriending a young married woman with a sickly child. After dinner with the woman and her husband, Charlotte had a talk with the young mother. Charlotte described her as "Young, girlish, inexperienced...now very sick herself....Ignorant both, and he using his 'marital rights' at her vital expense."[73] Charlotte herself some weeks later began to sleep in the spare bedroom.[74]

For Walter, however, the primary concern was the obverse. He was distressed at Charlotte's increasing engagement in women's rights. He was especially upset when she began to exchange visits with the cross-dressing Dr. Mary Walker. In February 1887, he wrote, "Charlotte of late has been so absorbed in the woman question—suffrage, other wrongs, that she has tired me dreadfully with it."[75] As an early April election for a woman suffrage amendment in Rhode Island approached, Charlotte wrote in its support and helped with advocacy mailings.[76]

Then the terrible slide began. Although Charlotte had a capable housekeeper who cared for Katharine, when the child became ill she demanded her mother's presence, during the night as well as the day. Such times seemed to unhinge Charlotte. When Kate took sick in early March, Charlotte called on her mother to help, and Mary Perkins came, but Kate continued to need her own mother. Charlotte wrote, "I give out completely in the morning, crying with weariness." Walter brought her coca, but this time it seemed to fail her, and she reported after taking it that she did "not feel brilliant." After Kate recovered, Charlotte had rapid mood swings. In late March she wrote, "Bad day. Getting back to the edge of insanity again." Nonetheless, even on that day she was able to write her column for the *People*.[77]

Charlotte's journal gave evidence that her life was veering more and more out of control. As her old friends Sam and Jim Simmons came by more often, Walter—perhaps out of jealousy or because of his own inability to comfort Charlotte adequately—could not take it. On April 5, she wrote, "Evening approaching to frenzy; but Jim Simmons arrives just as I get hysterical and calms me down finely. Walter rushes out for a walk, and Jim drawls and talks and is as pleasant as can be. After he goes Walter breaks down, and I soothe him and love him and get him to sleep." Then, the day after the woman suffrage amendment went down in defeat, Charlotte noted "Bad again." On April 9, she felt "worse," and went to Dr. Knight.[78]

In late April, Walter wrote a summary of Charlotte's condition.

> She grew weaker. She was frightened; fancied her brain was sadly diseased; went to Dr. Knight who gave her medicine that helped her, and advised her to go into the country for a while.
>
> Privately he told me that she was simply hypochrondriacal, and to his mind better than she was a year ago.[79]

During these months, Charlotte had been teaching Emily Diman, then fourteen. Her late father, J. Lewis Diman, a Brown professor, had been kind to many aspiring women in Providence. Emily's sister, May, had been one of Charlotte's closest friends before her accidental death. In the years since these deaths, Charlotte had continued a fond relationship with Emily's mother, a sympathetic listener, and she now grew close to her. On April 11, Mrs. Diman offered Charlotte $100 to use to seek help. Charlotte immediately went to a friend to inquire about the sanitarium in Clifton Springs, New York, and gave some thought to a sea voyage.[80]

Walter wrote in his diary on April 28, 1887, that Mrs. Diman "rather wanted" Charlotte "to see Weir Mitchell." The entry continues, "So Charlotte wrote to Mrs. Cresson, & Weir Mitchell was heard from."[81] Dr. S. Weir Mitchell was the natural choice. He built his successful medical practice on restoring women to health.

Born in 1829, the son of a Philadelphia physician, Mitchell had been well trained at Jefferson Medical College and in Paris. In the antebellum years, he had been known for his scientific research, particularly his work on snake poisons. The Civil War was the pivot of his career. Working as a contract surgeon, he treated soldiers' gunshot wounds, and his books, *Gunshot Wounds and Other Injuries of Nerves* and *Reflex Paralysis,* both published in 1864, gained him a lasting reputation.[82] Attempting to assess and treat so-called malingerers and return them to the battlefield, he saw their symptoms as out of their control, caused by real but unseen changes to their nervous systems. After the war, he turned to civilians who had suffered "breakdowns," becoming a specialist in what were called "nervous disorders"—at the Philadelphia Orthopedic Hospital and Infirmary for Nervous Diseases—and a popular writer on the subject. His first wife had died, leaving him two boys to rear. In 1874, he married into a wealthy and established family and took his place among his city's social elite. With his practice and popular books, he earned $64,000 a year, an enormous income in his era. Charlotte turned to him at the height of his career.

In preparation for her treatment by Mitchell, on April 13 Charlotte moved in with her mother, reporting that "Walter sups with us and sleeps & breakfasts alone in the house." She returned home to do housekeeping chores and to write in her journal. On April 19, she reported that she had received a letter from Mrs. Cresson. When she went to her own home, she was shut out: "Doors locked. No key to be found." This insult, whether by accident or design, did not deter her, and she forced her way into the house through a window. Once inside, she wrote, "Begin to write an account of myself for the doctor."[83]

Charlotte's letter to Mitchell was a long one, informing him of her condition and its possible causes. Carefully crafted, it tells a great deal about both Charlotte and her state of mind in the spring of 1887.[84] Believing in the hereditary nature of illness, Charlotte first set out the health life of her grandparents and parents. There was a great deal of illness, beginning with her famous great-grandfather, the preacher Lyman Beecher. When Charlotte recorded the internal history of her physical and mental states, she reported that she "reached womanhood in perfect health." As medical thought regarded the onset of menstruation as particularly perilous, Charlotte wanted the doctor to understand that she passed this moment safely. Then she showed herself to be the acolyte of her great-aunt Catharine Beecher and wrote, "At fifteen [I] became impressed with the truths of physiology and hygiene, and adopted 'reform-dress,' cold daily sponge bath, open window at night, gymnastics, etc., abjuring corsets, tea, coffee, late hours and all other known evils. (If one can abjure what one never has had.)" This regimen was successful, and she grew physically and mentally. As she put it, "Was never tired, did not know what the word meant, could walk indefinitely, wash, scrub, lift, row, run, do anything; and never know I had a body. As for nerves I denied their existence." She asserted that she was well physically until her marriage.

Running alongside this healthy body were her mental states, and Charlotte went on to give them due attention. She related that at age eight she began to dwell in her imagination in "visions of unattainable delights" as she went to sleep. She allowed herself particularly grand dreams only once a week, and "Once a month things still more unusual and delightful. Once a year anything I chose!" Then, when she was thirteen her mother told her that such fancies were "dangerous and wrong" and she was never again to think of them. Charlotte banished them from her thoughts. But in their stead came "a sea of Poe-like visions, carrying my dream life through a most wicked and unhealthy world."

She kept her inner world private. As she matured, she resolved that she would no longer think, only act. When she turned twenty, she finally felt free of these torments. She began to read science and philosophy and developed a personal theory of self-culture. She practiced it "till will and reason were free to act, and mind and body were strong and willing servants."

It was her belief that this was the origin of "the strain which brings me here today." This was how she explained it: "Those servants [mind and body] were so strong and so willing, and so severely disciplined withal; that they never complained under their burdens, and I over worked them steadily for eight years. They both fail me now." There was "the constant self supervision and restraint. I never <u>rested</u>."

With this, Charlotte focused on her relation to her mother, the cause of "a constant strain on the nerves." She and her mother were "utterly uncongenial—antagonistic," and living with her was an unceasing trial. About the woman who had taken full care of her baby for her absence of five months in California and on whom she now depended as she prepared to go to Philadelphia, Charlotte wrote, "The ingenious agony she unwittingly inflicts has never been equaled by any one else."[85]

At age twenty-one, living and working in Providence, she lost her dearest female friend. Never suggesting that the loss was to marriage, not death, Charlotte wrote that it was "a desperate grief to me." At this vulnerable moment, a male lover came calling, Charles Walter Stetson. Then began "two years [of] torture called courtship." Stetson broke her resistance, and she was, as she put it, "weak enough to marry him." She became pregnant soon after. During this period she "had terrible fits of remorse and depression," mirroring what she had experienced in the preceding two years. Beginning with her confinement, she "began to show 'nervousness.'...Had wild and dreadful ideas which I was powerless to check, times of excitement and times of tears."

In her narration, whatever well-being she had experienced as a young woman ended with her marriage and pregnancy. And with her daughter's birth she took a deep downward turn. She had a nurse for four weeks, then spent three weeks alone with the baby.

In an odd statement, Charlotte wrote, as if in blame, "Then my mother came and took the baby, and I have been sick ever since." Reflecting a bit later in the letter, she stated, "This agony of mind set in with the child's coming. I nursed her in slow tears. All that summer I did nothing but cry, save for times when the pain was unbearable and I grew wild hysterical, almost imbecile at times." Her doctor found no physical trouble.

Not realizing inconsistency, she described herself as being of a "very cheerful disposition" before marriage, unable to "imagine the combination of circumstance that would make me unhappy." She also wrote that her husband was "devotion itself." Her unhappiness was not caused by her "circumstances." She described her situation as living in a "lovely home" attended by a "perfect maid-servant," facing only the poverty that she had always had and did not "mind." With this she returned to her narrative.

Frightened, she weaned her daughter, borrowed money, and in October 1885 traveled alone to California. There, living with close female friends in the sunshine, she seemed to get well. She returned to Providence the following March, taking ill with bronchitis on the way home. Her distress came back. In August 1886, she began to take Dr. Buckland's Essence of Oats and seemed to return to health. Then, in March 1887, when Katharine's cold required Charlotte's personal care, the anguish returned. Nursing her child, she said, "finished" her: "I broke down in helpless tears, and since then have grown steadily worse." She now had "mental symptoms which alarm me seriously."

She would not write these symptoms but would wait to tell him. She begged Mitchell "not to laugh at me as every one else does, not to say it is 'almost as bad as a disease' as one of my friends does, not to turn me off." At this point, moving toward the close of her letter to Mitchell, Charlotte wrote a declaration of her hope. "I am an artist of sufficient merit to earn an easy living when well. I am a writer, a poet, a philosopher....I can do some good work for the world if I live." She did not want to live as an invalid. "I want to <u>work</u>, to help people, to do good." Imagining

herself under Mitchell's care, she wrote that she anticipated coming "to rest and try to get well."

Then she alluded to her fears. She began with a statement and
question: "I understand you are the first authority on nervous diseases. Are you on brain troubles too?" And then she wrote, "There
is something the matter with my head." She feared she was losing her memory. It was getting harder to write each day. "I can't
think. I can't remember, I can't grasp an idea....I fear every day
to lose memory entirely." Even now she was losing power, and
she apologized for the length and content of the letter. "I am all
alone in the house or I couldn't write this. People tire me frightfully." Then she closed on a pathetic note: "I'm running down like
a clock—could go one [sic] scribbling now indefinitely—but the
letters don't come right."

Charlotte heaped blame on her mother and praised her husband for his devotion in this letter to the doctor she hoped would
cure her. Her next-to-last entry in her journal, however, written
with the anticipation that Walter would read it, said something
quite different.

> Pain pain pain, till my mind has given way.
> O blind and cruel! Can Love hurt like this?
> You found me—you remember what.
> I leave you—O remember what, and learn to doubt your
> judgement before it seeks to mould another life as it has
> mine.
> I asked you a few days only before our marriage if you
> would take the responsibility entirely on yourself. You said
> yes. Bear it then.[86]

In the Care of S. Weir Mitchell

*B*efore leaving home, Charlotte tried to make sense of her illness, writing in her long-kept journal, "Now I am to go away for my health, and shall not try to take any responsibilities with me, even this old friend [the journal]. I am very sick with nervous prostration, and I think with some brain disease as well. No one can ever know what I have suffered in these last five years."[1] The phrase "Sick with nervous prostration" is familiar, if not fully knowable. Charlotte's depressive episodes can be tracked for many more than five years before 1887, but she only recognized those that began with Walter's courtship.

She had dealt with the experience of deep melancholy and emotional blankness before marriage by diet and exercise, not outside help. Once pregnant and experiencing "hysterical" outbursts, however, she fell into the hands of others and the drugs, treatments, and counsel they offered. To calm her during her pregnancy and protect the unborn child, Walter's father brought her bromides. Then, over the course of the next twenty-seven months, Charlotte was variously diagnosed and treated for mental distress believed to be related to her uterus or her nerves.

After Katharine's birth, Charlotte reported feeling "nerveless" or, more often, its flip side, "nervous." As she became, in her words, "excited, hysterical, seeming to myself wellnigh insane," Walter's friend, a local physician schooled in the older practice of "moral treatment," spoke to her regularly and attempted to strengthen her will against her emotions. He also gave her a prescription for coca, a mixture of alcohol and cocaine. Walter, more au courant in his thinking, saw her problem as "uterine irritation." To check out this possibility, Charlotte went for an internal examination to Dr. Keller, who found nothing the matter. With this, Charlotte determined to put herself in the care of a friend and go to California for an extended sojourn.

In August 1886, many months after her return home, Charlotte experienced an emotional episode severe enough for Dr. Keller to come to Providence to perform an unspecified gynecological procedure. When this did not calm Charlotte, Keller diagnosed her with "a disease of the nerves," telling her "that her brain was all right. It is a form of nervous prostration." In stating this, Keller was echoing the basic medical understanding of her era that emphasized the role of the nerves.

All of these diagnoses and treatments, with the exception of the Providence doctor's moral exhortations and Charlotte's travel to California, were centered in the body. In the most current medical thought of Charlotte's era, if the body could be healed, the mind would follow. This was in keeping with the new specialty of neurology. Attempting to base medicine on science, a group of American physicians, including S. Weir Mitchell, established themselves as neurologists and struggled against an older generation of medical practitioners who were responsible for mental asylums. As they established their practices, the new neurologists asserted that research on the brain and the nervous system demonstrated that mental disorders were physical disorders, with clearly traceable causes. Although the tools of their laboratory were inadequate to detect the specific causes, to register lesions on the brain or spinal cord, these physicians nonetheless sought to treat patients. Earlier doctors had primarily sought to calm the body, but the newer generation focused on the dangers of depletion. In 1869, a new diagnosis—"neurasthenia," meaning "want of strength in the nerves"—came into being, and it reached the general public in 1881 in George Beard's *American Nervousness: Its Causes and Consequences.*

Given that neurasthenia could not be seen in a laboratory, how could a diagnosis be made? Beard offered that the determination was based on the "positive symptoms" and the "exclusion" of organic causes. The symptoms of neurasthenia were, among many others, "insomnia...mental irritability...deficient mental control...hopelessness...tremulous and variable pulse and palpitation of the heart...a feeling of profound exhaustion unaccompanied by positive pain...attacks of temporary paralysis."[2] Beard himself advocated electrical treatments for neurasthenia, but the more general recourse of physicians was drugs, used as tonics or stimulants. There is no evidence that Charlotte in 1887 was aware of this understanding of neurasthenia, but Dr. Keller, who prided herself on being up-to-date, certainly was. She would have used the term "nervous prostration" to explain to Charlotte that her symptoms were signs of physical illness of the nerves, and thus treatable and curable.

Over the next months, Charlotte was kept going by the alcohol and morphine of Dr. Buckland's Essence of Oats. When she began to slide, Walter got her coca, but this time it did not seem to help. As her distress deepened, she now began to have fears again, ones Dr. Keller had previously tried to quell. Lurking in Charlotte's mind was a dread that she had "some brain disease." Thus in her preconsultation letter to Dr. Mitchell she had asked if he was the "first authority" not only on "nervous diseases" but on "brain troubles" as well. In Charlotte's era, the distinction between symptoms caused by nervous illness and insanity caused by brain disease was a basic one. Dr. Keller had made it, at least implicitly. It had been suggested in Napheys's discussion of "puerperal mania," mentioning insanity with its possible lifelong consequences.

Charlotte, spring of 1887. "This is what my 'breakdown' did to me." Schlesinger Library, Radcliffe Institute, Harvard University.

Charlotte may have known about insanity caused by brain disease from talk around her, or Dr. Keller may have explained it to her in discussing the distinction between it and a curable condition of the nerves. From her reading of *Popular Science Monthly*, Charlotte had encountered a full discussion of brain disease in 1882 in an article by one of Britain's leading neurologists on the early-eighteenth-century satirist Jonathan Swift. In a consideration of the Swift's maladies, the neurologist contrasted Swift's melancholy, his "increasing irritability of temper and mental depression," with his ultimate true insanity. Looking at evidence after his death, the physician-author concluded that Swift's brain demonstrated a "localized left-sided apoplexy or cerebral softening, which determined the symptoms of his insanity."[3] In his summary, the author stated that however great the misery of Swift's depression, so long as that was the cause of his distress, he kept his reason. The madness at the end of his life, however, was different, a result of a disease in the brain itself. Unlike his melancholy, Swift's brain disease was permanent, progressive, and the cause of his death. When Charlotte separated "nervous prostration" from "brain disease," this was the distinction she had in mind. She could recover from a case of the nerves, but not from disease of the brain.[4] This, then, was the great fear. And curiously, for Charlotte it was a kind of hope. She felt she was permanently wedded to Walter, and unless he chose to divorce her, death provided the only freedom.

Charlotte went for a weeklong stay to the home outside Philadelphia of Mary Cresson, one of Walter's portrait subjects and the wife of his patron. Prior to coming under Dr. Mitchell's care, Charlotte was required to consult with him to see if he would take her as a patient. Typically, when a potential patient came for the rest cure, Mitchell carried out an initial medical examination to see if there were any perceptible organic lesions and offered treatment only if he found none.[5]

Charlotte may have been deeply angry at Walter on her departure, but she wrote to him dutifully after she arrived in Philadelphia and had the initial consultation.[6] Walter reported in his diary, "Dr. Mitchell seems to think her case very serious, and says that separation from home for at least a year is very desirable. He also wants her to go to his sanitarium for a month." "He says that she cannot live at home...has a most unfortunate temperament with a graft of hysterical disorder of the mind." Charlotte concluded from this that she and Walter should divorce. "She prays me to divorce her and take to myself some other who can make me happy."[7]

Walter heard from Mary Cresson "that Dr. Mitchell said that Charlotte was doubtless really insane at times, and that he never had had but one other such case, and that of a lady with the same blood in her veins." Mrs. Cresson, who seems to have had possessive feelings toward Walter, was not necessarily a reliable witness. Moreover, she expressed uncertainty about the outcome. She herself had long had nervous trouble, and she called Mitchell's cure "a doubtful experiment."[8]

Charlotte entered Mitchell's care for the month of May 1887. Like other patients, she was not allowed to write letters. She could, however, dictate to a nurse. On May 7, Walter wrote in his journal that he had heard from Charlotte via the nurse that "she seems hopeful but can neither read nor write." Mary Cresson reported that Charlotte might receive two letters a week, but they had to be cheerful ones. She also reassured Walter that Charlotte was "very pleasantly placed."[9]

On May 11, Walter received a letter from Dr. Mitchell. It was typical for the doctor to write to a husband or close relation. No copy survives, but Walter reported in his diary that day that Mitchell's letter said, "it is much too soon for him to offer any valuable judgment as to Charlotte and that the case is one of 'profound interest' to him."[10]

Walter reported no more until May 26. As the month of treatment closed, he got two letters from Charlotte "in her own dear hand."[11] He wrote, "She seems stronger, but the Dr. has given his consent to her starting a gymnasium if she wishes to do so, but he thinks the best thing if we could do it would be to go to England for a year. He thinks the climate would do a great deal for her."[12]

Dr. S. Weir Mitchell, c. 1890. Schlesinger Library, Radcliffe Institute, Harvard University.

The month under Dr. Mitchell's care was a momentous event in Charlotte's life, and it has loomed large in writing about her. With the record so thin, how can we begin to understand what she experienced? While there is much we cannot know specifically, Mitchell's prominence, writings, and records reveal his likely approach to her. He wrote informatively about his treatment both for other physicians and for the public at large.

In 1887, nearing sixty, Mitchell was at peak of his fame. White-haired, handsome, with an intense gaze and charismatic presence, he was known for his charm and resourcefulness. He had a commanding bedside manner, and he was a good listener. Whether or not she knew it at the time, he was a person who had achieved success as a writer, not just as a physician: he was a poet and novelist as well as author of influential medical books.

Like his contemporary George Beard, Mitchell wrote for a wide audience and linked his understanding of nervous disorders to the stresses to the body caused by the American environment. He first came to public attention in 1869 when *Lippincott's* published his article "Wear and Tear." It asked these critical linked questions: "Are we suffering? Are we of the Atlantic coast becoming a nervous race?" The answer was, of course, yes. Mitchell then set out why Americans sickened and what could be done about it. He made a critical distinction between "wear," the normal process of tiring after exertion, and "tear," an unhealthy development that led to distress. Outdoor, physical labor brought wear, repaired when a person followed it by rest and a good night's sleep. Indoor, brain work was not experienced as tiring in the same way and thus was subject to tear. In using his brain, Mitchell wrote, a man "does not feel in the common use of it any sensation which warns him that he has taxed it enough" but instead becomes stimulated and feels wide awake. He thus abuses his brain, driving it harder for a long period of time. Only "after very long abuse" does the brain tell the man to quit, "and at this stage the warning is too often in the shape of some one of the many symptoms which indicate that the organ is already talking with the tongue of disease."[13]

For men pained by "tear," Mitchell devised the "camp cure," a vigorous outdoor vacation. When he shifted to women, he took a different tone and developed a different therapy. After writing of the young and charming American girl, he stated, "Look a little further, and especially among these New England young girls: you will be struck with a certain hardness of line in form and feature." They lacked the rosy cheeks of health. Mitchell looked into their future: "their destiny is the shawl and the sofa, neuralgia, weak backs, and hysteria—that domestic demon which has made, I am persuaded, almost as much wretchedness as the husband's dram."[14]

What was the cause? For both men and women, there were the woes of the climate, especially the harsh extremes of hot and cold. Mitchell shared with his colleagues a belief in the ill effects of American weather and air. But something more was at work, something that changed the unexcitable souls who arrived on American shores to develop a "nervous temperament." Here he singled out experience, which—unlike climate—could be changed. For men it was overwork.

For women, it was the education, or rather the miseducation, of girls. Between the ages of fourteen and eighteen, when girls needed exercise and to be outdoors, they were attempting to finish their schooling and, remaining indoors, crammed their heads with learning. Mitchell believed that the teenage girl should labor at her books only three or four hours each day. Because of her mis-spent girlhood, Mitchell declared, "To-day, the American woman is, to speak plainly, too often physically unfit for her duties as woman."[15]

Those who advised Charlotte to enter Mitchell's care most likely knew his *Fat and Blood: And How to Make Them,* pub-lished in 1877. It publicized his rest cure, brought him a broad popular audience, and underlay the tremendous growth of his practice. Mitchell first presented his new therapy in a lecture to a medical audience. To his fellow physicians, he made it clear that his treatment was an adaptation of his successful wartime work with malingerers, in which he had "learned to treat these cases by rest in bed, with porter, beef soup, and strychnia."[16] Mitchell began to apply bed rest and feeding to women who similarly were ill without visible organic cause.

Mitchell gave the dramatic story of his breakthrough case. "Mrs. B," as he called her, came to him "on a couch from a distant New England State." She had begun her adulthood with "certain overwork of the brain, a long, steady strain, backed by unusual mental force, and a certain vigor of will." She married and nursed three children, "far beyond the common time of breast-feeding." During this time, she met all "the claims of society, family, char-ity, and mental culture." Then suddenly "she gave way, lost flesh, came to weigh ninety-five pounds in place of one hundred and twenty-five pounds." She stopped menstruating, but there were no signs of disease in her uterus. The only medical problem Mitchell could find was the presence of too high a proportion of white corpuscles in her blood. As she walked across the room, her state of extreme tiredness and pain was "what you see in overworked, busy, worried men."[17]

Mitchell secluded her and put her to bed. He fed her frequently. Hoping to avoid the negatives of bed rest—weakened digestion, constipation, and lowered circulation—he saw that she received daily massage and electric treatments, both intended to give the body passive exercise.[18] The treatment was successful. The patient gained thirty pounds in two months, resumed menstruation, and by the end of the third month could "go where she pleased, and do what she pleased." Mitchell had taken a "sickly, feeble, wasted creature" and restored her. She emerged from his treatment "a handsome, wholesome, helpful woman."[19]

Three decades later, Mitchell modified his account to empha-size how difficult it had been for him to find an appropriate therapy for Mrs. B. She was an experienced patient, who turned to him only after trying "Spas...physicians of the utmost emi-nence...gynecologists" and after wearing spinal supporters. She had taken "every tonic known to the books." Mitchell's efforts were initially as futile as the earlier attempts. He "sat beside this woman day after day, hearing her pitiful story," pained that a woman with youth, wealth, and once good looks should be con-demned to "hopeless invalidism." When she let him know that because he seemed to have nothing to offer, she would be leaving his care, she plunged him into "therapeutic despair."

Mitchell asked her for another day. He then suggested full bed rest, a treatment she had tried before with negative consequences, for it made her unable to digest her food. Failure loomed when a week's trial confirmed this. Then Mitchell recalled a successful treatment with massage once given to a man, and Mrs. B. agreed. After several days, he added electricity as an additional element to stimulate the body at rest and enable digestion. Since she had done better when secluded, "I insisted on entire rest, and shut out friends, relatives, books, and letters." It worked. Mrs. B. could assimilate food and iron. She gained weight and hope, what he called a "new tonic." Her cure was permanent. She sustained her recovery: except for the natural process of aging, Mitchell declared, she had remained "what I made her."[20]

Mitchell knew at once that he had made a great discovery. By hit and miss, he had devised a therapy for a disease he could not identify and would not name. A later generation looked on Mitchell's "rest cure" as a reversion to infancy, as a milk diet synonymous with the comfort of the breast, but it was neither loving nor mild. It involved extreme rest (a nurse moved a patient who wanted to turn in bed), total seclusion (nurses and masseuses were not to talk to patients), rubbing serious enough to raise the body temperature, and feedings every two hours, consisting of malt extract, raw beef, butter, and wine. In addition, cod liver oil was inserted up the rectum, and iron was concealed in the food fed to the patient. Many patients also faced the withdrawal of the "tonics," often narcotic drugs, that they had been taking. It was a harsh regimen. But for some women, the combination broke through the cycle of insomnia, self-starvation, and drugging that had been destroying them.

Mitchell, like many of his contemporaries, was a somatist who believed that mental disorders were at base physical disorders. Mitchell's rest cure, however, despite its new somatic underpinning, drew on earlier traditions—the isolation and restorative environment of the early mental asylums and the rest and opposition to drugs favored by water-cure establishments.[21] Moreover, the treatment, far more invasive than the "camp cure" normally prescribed for men with the same symptoms, carried important gender assumptions.[22]

Mitchell saw women and men differing in pain and its relation to blood. Whereas in men, pain was "accidental," depending to large degree on the "chances of life," women were subject to pain from menstruation and bearing children. Not only did women have pain by virtue of their reproductive functions, they also experienced it more acutely. Mitchell believed that the severity of pain was inversely proportional to the thickness of the sufferer's blood. The thinner the blood, the more severe the pain. Since a woman lost blood throughout her reproductive years, she was more vulnerable than a man to pain.[23]

And Mitchell carried his sense of the differences between the sexes far beyond this distinction. Writing of a generic woman in the late 1880s, he said, "She is physiologically other than the man." Mitchell believed that many of the problems he saw in his female patients came from their failure to appreciate that difference. He was then fully aware of the campaign for women's colleges, as well as the woman's rights movement and its criticism of much of the dicta of evolutionary science's understanding of women. In this tortured sentence, Mitchell responded, "I am concerned with her now as she is, only desiring to help her in my small way to be in wiser and more healthful fashion what I believe her Maker meant her to be, and to teach her how **not** to be that with which her physiological construction and the strong ordeals of her sexual life threaten her as no contingencies of man's career threaten in like measure or like number the feeblest of the masculine sex."[24] Needless to say, he opposed woman's suffrage and had grave doubts about women's colleges. He expressed his strong opinions about women of independent spirit in his novels by presenting them either as repellent characters or as women who became submissive to their husbands once married. As one commentator who knew him well put it, "his ideal woman was the well-sheltered woman."[25]

Whether or not Charlotte knew about Mitchell's deeply traditional approach to women when she put herself in his care, that she turned to him was a sign of her profound desperation. Knowledge of his attitudes was widely available to a reader of novels and of works of popular science, and Charlotte was both. Either she did not avail herself of information or, knowing it, went ahead anyway. As a result, she placed herself in the hands of a man whose understandings about women were diametrically opposed to her own ideas, hopes, and ambition.

Although some somatic practitioners may not have revealed their beliefs to their patients, it is likely that Mitchell did. He believed that a doctor had a double task when working with a patient—to work with the mind as well as the body. As Mitchell put it, the physician's duty was only "half fulfilled when we think of the body as our only province." The other half of a physician's responsibility came when he provided counsel and gave warnings.[26] Thus it was that Mitchell's rest cure had two sides. Isolation in a secluded setting away from family not only gave a patient real rest and nutrition, it gave the attending physician an opportunity to talk to the patient at a time and in a place where she could hear him. Cut off from all home ties, attended only by a nurse and masseuse who were forbidden to speak to the patient of her ills, the patient learned that she could speak of "her aches and pains" only to her doctor. He then applied "tact to seize the proper occasions to direct the thoughts of his patients to the lapse from duties to others, and to the selfishness which a life of invalidism is apt to bring about."[27]

Through this, the doctor became privy to the secrets of women. Mitchell wrote that the physician hears confessions at the bedside, "more, indeed, than he may care to hear. To confess is, for mysterious reasons, most profoundly human, and in weak and nervous women this tendency is sometimes exaggerated to the actual distortion of facts." Women's disclosures give the physician special knowledge. He learns that "the causes of breakdowns and nervous disaster, and consequent emotional disturbances and their bitter fruit, are often to be sought in the remote past." Not only do women's utterances give him unique insight, they confer upon him special authority. An attending physician is able to understand "some of the things that are strange in daily life, and the man who does not know sick women does not know women."[28]

This might suggest that Mitchell came close to Freud—a medical practitioner with a listening ear, able to probe in a patient's deep past and thereby to heal. But Mitchell's understanding remained deep within a nineteenth-century context and shaped by his conservative attitudes about gender. He saw a woman as a being whose vulner-abilities always kept her at risk. As Mitchell wrote, he was aware as a physician of "how near to disorder and how close to misfortune she is brought by the very peculiarities of her nature."[29]

Mitchell also had a nineteenth-century sense of the role of emotion. Interestingly, this led him to rethink one basic gender difference and to argue for new approaches. By the late 1880s he came to believe that, in addition to the miseducation of girls in their teen years, there was their mistraining at home from the out-set. Girls needed the same kind of play as boys. He expressed this in words that Charlotte would have approved: "Train your girls physically, and, up to the age of adolescence, as you train your boys....To run, to climb, to swim, to ride, to play violent games, ought to be as natural to the girl as to the boy."[30] He wrote that when a boy has some little injury or accident, a mother "assumes from the beginning that the hurt boy is to be taught silent, patient endurance. What! you, a boy, to cry! Be a man!" By contrast, a girl is allowed tears, and her "little aches and complaints" are taken seriously.[31] Mothers need to teach their young daughters as they do their sons. And as they mature, girls need to develop stoic acceptance of the pain they will inevitably experience. Rough play helps. Mothers should encourage girls "to live out of doors, and to use the sports which develop the muscles and give tone and vigor." Tennis, fencing, and boxing "teach...endurance, con-tempt of little hurts, obedience to laws, control of temper."[32]

By coming to emphasize play and sports to toughen young girls, Mitchell focused on the weakness of emotional control in many of his patients. Sharing with William Carpenter a belief in the impor-tance of habits to strengthen reason and will, Mitchell wrote that at the base much of women's trouble is "unrestrained emotion and outward expressions of pain or distress...the beginnings of that loss of self-rule." This spirals to "habitual unrestraint" and then to "more and more enfeeblement of endurance" and then to "worse things."[33] That ultimate outcome was, of course, the hysterical woman.

Mitchell and other American neurologists, unlike their French contemporaries, did not typically isolate hysteria as a disease. Mitchell wrote, "Hysteria is the nosological limbo of all unnamed female maladies. It were as well called mysteria for all its name teaches us of the host of morbid states which are crowded within its hazy boundaries."[34] As a word, *hysteria* goes back deep into history. Beginning in the early modern period, as physicians observed female patients who presented symptoms with no organic cause, they grafted their observations onto ancient medical texts dealing with the movements of the womb or retention of blood and seed. One of the wisest commentators on hysteria, the seventeenth-century English physician Thomas Sydenham, wrote about hysteria's imitative ability: "Few of the maladies of miserable mortality are not imitated by it. Whatever part of the body it attacks, it will create the proper symptom of that part." It could deceive the physician into treating the symptoms rather than the underlying cause. In nineteenth-century France, as the numbers of these women seemed to increase, hysteria moved to the center of the new science of neurology. Mitchell in Philadelphia would have been aware of these developments. Jean-Martin Charcot, the great professor of nervous diseases at the University of Paris, was studying, photographing, and drawing hysterical episodes at the vast hospital of Saltpêtrière. Uniquely and mistakenly, he segregated inmates suffering from epilepsy and hysteria from others in the hospital. As the hysterical patients began to imitate the seizures and fits of the epileptic ones, they gave rise to extraordinary manifestations. Charcot's reports in the 1880s seemed to many to be the definitive statements about the course of hysteria as a disease.[35]

Mitchell seems to have been only mildly influenced by Charcot. When he wrote about hysterical women, his words were normally close to common speech. When he used the term, it was typically as an adjective for a woman completely unable to control her emotions. In employing the noun *hysteria,* he generally was simply referring to the condition of such a woman.

In one passage in the late 1880s, however, Mitchell showed some awareness of Charcot's work. But even here, Mitchell, unlike his French counterpart, retained his emphasis on the importance of self-control. He wrote of a typical woman who, for whatever precipitating cause, becomes "a ready victim of hysteria":

> The emotions so easily called into activity give rise to tears. Too weak for wholesome restraint, she yields. The little convulsive act we call crying brings uncontrollable, or what seems to her to be uncontrollable, twitching of the face. The jaw and hands get rigid, and she has a hysterical convulsion, and is on the way to worse perils. The intelligent despotism of self-control is at an end, and every new attack upon its normal prerogatives leaves her less and less able to resist.[36]

Mitchell was using the word *convulsion* initially in its technical sense, as a muscular contraction, although as he spoke of "hysterical convulsion" he suggested something of Charcot's sway.

Mitchell's larger body of writing makes it clear that as he dealt with women experiencing emotional outbursts, sometimes designated hysterical subjects, his responses to them varied. He alternated between somatic determinism, sympathetic understanding of suffering patients, and moral condemnation.

Believing that much female debility lay in the body, Mitchell saw his first task as somatic therapy. When he faced a distressed patient, such as Mrs. B., who was either in danger of developing hysterical symptoms or just beginning to have them, his goal was to arrest the decline, build up the patient, and keep the incipient symptoms from becoming habits that, if repeated, would create organic damage and become fixed. His language in describing the case of Mrs. B. was morally neutral, and it could be in other instances. On occasion, however, Mitchell gave vent to feelings of moral outrage, shedding, as did many other physicians who treated women's nervous complaints, his tone of medical neutrality. In *Fat and Blood,* for example, he stated that that the hysterical woman suffered from a form of "moral degradation." She was selfish and had lost "the healthy mastery which every human being should retain over her own emotions and wants."[37]

One description stands out. As Mitchell made an argument for the need to remove a sufferer from her family, he wrote how she destroyed those around her.

> By slow but sure degrees the healthy life is absorbed by the sick life.... The patient has pain, a tender spine, for example; she is urged to give it rest. She cannot read; the self-constituted nurse reads to her. At last light hurts her eyes; the mother remains shut up with her all day in a darkened room. A draught of air is supposed to do harm, and the doors and windows are closed, and the ingenuity of kindness is taxed to imagine new sources of like trouble, until at last the window-cracks are stuffed with cotton, the chimney stopped, and even the keyhole guarded. It is easy to see where this all leads to,—the nurse falls ill, and a new victim is found. I have seen a hysterical, anaemic girl kill in this way three generations of nurses.[38]

After a woman retreats to her sofa or bed, he continued, "Then comes the mischievous role of bromides, opium, chloral, and brandy." A woman typically experiences some problems diagnosed as uterine. She gets emotional, "and even the firmest women lose self-control at last under incessant feebleness." Women "acquire tender spines, and furnish the most lamentable examples of all the strange phenomena of hysteria."[39]

From the outset Mitchell, understood that his female patients were part of an interactive system in which they were curiously being rewarded for becoming ill. His regime was thus intended to remove patients from family members whose ministrations abetted the condition. In addition, his treatment was intentionally boring in order to provoke women to seek health. He wrote that while women might find it pleasurable "to lie abed half the day, and sew a little and read a little, and be interesting and excite sympathy," they find it "bitter medicine" to be "bidden to stay in bed a month, and neither to read, write, nor sew, and to have one nurse,—who is not a relative." They ultimately welcome the physician's order that they "rise and go about."[40] Fundamentally Mitchell's regimen was based on an understanding that many of his female patients participated in their own sickness and could be brought around to participate in its cure.

Once a woman was allowed to "rise and go about," what advice did Mitchell have for her? First of all, he understood that a woman after treatment in his clinic was not "cured" in the sense that a person is cured once a ruptured appendix has been removed. She needed to establish a continuing road to health in the year that followed.

An important element was adequate rest. He wrote, "To lie down is not enough. What she needs is undisturbed repose, and not to have to expect every few minutes to hear at her door the knocks and voices of servants or children." He suggested that the hours after meals were "very often…the most available and the more desirable as times of repose, because in the weak digestion goes on better when they are at rest."

She also should shun any "great exertion." Here he insisted, as his example, "that letter-writing, of which many women are fond, must be altogether set aside." But he found value in sewing or other handiwork. The recovering nervous woman must seek to remain calm and not worry. "We can stand an immense deal of work, and can, even if weak, bear much, if only we learn to dismiss small questions without worry or unreasonable reconsiderations." She must, above all, protect herself against the "small beginnings of nervousness." She needs to avoid tears, which are "for the nervous woman, the seed of trouble." When she feels them coming on, she should isolate herself to better fight the impulse to cry. Moreover, she should seek to "avoid all forms of emotion" during this interim period of trial and rehabilitation. "For the nervous strong emotions are bad or risky, and from violent mirth to anger all are to be sedulously set aside. Calm of mind and quiet of body are what she most needs to aid the more potent measure of the physician."

She must believe her doctor when he tells her not to think of symptoms. "To think too much about their disorders is, on the whole, one of the worst things which can happen to a man or a woman." Mitchell gave as his example a woman fearing dizziness to the degree that she feels she cannot walk. She must trust her doctor when he insists that she take walks, finding ways to distract herself by going with a friend and talking along the way.

Mitchell came to be a firm believer, by the late 1880s, in exercise for women. Following his new sense of the importance of emotional toughening, Mitchell expanded his repertoire of treatment for women to include the camp cure, once reserved for men. He wrote in *Doctor and Patient,* "I have been led to regret that I did not see when it was written that what I therein urged as desirable for men was not also in a measure attainable by many women."[41] In an informal fashion, he related a case study in which a nervous woman continued to languish under his rest cure. He said to her, "If you were a man I think I could cure you." She agreed to anything he suggested, and, as someone with seemingly unlimited means, she was able to hire men and go to a lake in the West. There she lived in a tent in isolation from letters and newspapers. The hired men fished and shot game and prepared her meals. She herself began to row, fish, and shoot. "Before August came she could walk for miles with a light gun, and could stand for hours in wait for a deer." She learned to swim and to take photographs. "In a word, she led a man's life until the snow fell in the fall and she came back to report, a thoroughly well woman."[42]

Although it took great resources for this particular cure, Mitchell knew from observation that in places like the White Mountains in New Hampshire women and men of modest means were finding ways to live on holiday cheaply in the outdoors. "Nothing so dismisses the host of little nervousnesses with which house-caged women suffer as this free life."[43] He advocated vigorous exercise for women, including "chest and arm exertion." He wrote, "Nothing is a better ally against nervousness or irritability in any one than either out-door exercise or pretty violent use of the muscles."[44]

It was with these understandings, biases, and approaches that Dr. Mitchell received into his care, treated, and counseled Charlotte.

Charlotte met with Mitchell for an initial consultation, and he recommended that she enter his sanitarium for a month. We can understand this advice now as both a key element of his basic treatment and the basis of his medical business. The additional recommendation that Charlotte should not live at home for at least a year she interpreted as a prescription for divorce. Mitchell would have conveyed no such thought. Charlotte's gloss, that she and Walter should divorce, sprang from her own wishes.

What kind of place was Mitchell's sanitarium when Charlotte entered it? Although it has normally been assumed that she was at the Philadelphia Orthopedic Hospital and Infirmary for Nervous Diseases at Seventeenth Street and Summer Street, according to hospital records, she was not.[45] Those at the hospital and infirmary whom Mitchell saw during 1887 included women and men with serious illness and debilitating symptoms, many of them lower-class patients with work-related injuries or people with nervous conditions following severe illness, such as polio, malaria, or inflammatory rheumatism. More than rest attended such patients: Mitchell and his fellow doctors prescribed for them quinine, digitalis, cannabis indica, arsenic, bromide; administered electricity; and ordered blisters and cauterization.[46]

Moreover, admission to the hospital and infirmary took effort and time that Charlotte did not expend.[47] Armed with the money to pay for a month of treatment, Charlotte went through no time-consuming process to gain admission. Mitchell met with her at the end of April, and she entered his care immediately. Finally, Mary Cresson wrote to Walter that Charlotte was "very pleasantly placed," words that do not describe a nineteenth-century hospital ward.[48]

The record is completely blank as to the existence of a private sanitarium run by Dr. Mitchell, however. In the absence of information about such a place in his papers or in any known directory, how might one learn about the setting in which Charlotte and his other private patents underwent their rest cures? Letters regarding two of his other patients from roughly Charlotte's period give a glimpse of the sanitarium setting where his private patients underwent their rest cures. The first came from Harriet Strong, writing in 1882 to her husband: "There is a Boston lady in room next to mine—one of the fussy sort. Dr. M's patient—also—she is not a favorite in the home. Nor her nurse—while <u>all</u> in the home are ready to do anything & everything" for Strong herself and her nurse. She wrote regarding her own nurse, "If she think Dr. M—does not come often eno—she goes down to his office & gives him a regular 'blowing up' wh amuses him very much." On a day when Mitchell was away, Strong also told of seeing Dr. Sinkler, "the 4th Dr. I have seen."[49] This letter provides several important bits of information. Each female patient had a separate room, not on a first floor. These rooms were perceived as being in a "home," a word used twice. Each patient had a nurse assigned to her. Mitchell had an office downstairs, and at least three other physicians were in attendance. Mitchell or one of the other doctors on duty visited patients regularly.

The second description was written by William Dean Howells after he took his daughter Winifred to Philadelphia to place her under Mitchell's care in 1888. He wrote that Winifred was put "in a sweet, airy big room, in a vast, quiet house, in a pleasant street, among the kindest people."[50] Several months later, after Winifred had gained some weight, Mitchell moved her to Merchantville, a more rural setting.[51] In her case, two homes were available for her treatment.

The actual locations of these houses seem lost to history. They appear in no city directory, business directory, or list of institutions in Philadelphia. It is likely that the perceived need for discretion, especially regarding women, dictated secrecy. So how might we imagine them? Perhaps they were like private college dormitories. At Smith College, for example, property-proud and cash-poor local women, often widows, took in college girls, providing housing and board under a supervised arrangement.[52] With each patient paying Mitchell the equivalent in today's dollars of $2,000 a month, the doctor could afford such arrangements. It is also possible that the second Mrs. Mitchell financed the houses.[53]

As the month of treatment closed, Walter got two letters from Charlotte. He learned that she was better, and that Mitchell strongly recommended a year in England, because "the climate would do a great deal for her."[54] A climate change was often advised for a neurasthenic patient, and England's air was regarded as healing to the nerves of men and women. Of course, it had long been Walter's dream to go abroad to further his painting and his reputation. Now there was the added incentive of Charlotte's health. But Walter was $1,000 in debt, and such an interlude was expensive. This was the real meaning of Mitchell's initial recommendation for Charlotte to spend a year away from home—he had meant away from the United States, not away from husband and child, as she had originally interpreted it.

Mitchell also gave Charlotte his permission to start a gymnasium, an important recommendation from him. Right before her breakdown, Charlotte had inquired about teaching at the new gymnasium in Providence. It was likely this prospect, in keeping with his new encouragement of women's vigorous physical activity, to which Mitchell gave consent.[55]

One piece of advice from the doctor can only be inferred from Charlotte's actions and from Mitchell's writings. In discussing the overeducated girl and the New England woman, Mitchell had declared, "To-day, the American woman is, to speak plainly, too often physically unfit for her duties as woman."[56] Unquestionably, Mitchell meant these words to include not only motherhood and housekeeping but a wife's duties in the marital bed. Restoring a woman to be able to live fully as a woman was the goal of his treatment. It is likely that as Charlotte left, Mitchell spoke of those duties. We do not know if he used euphemisms for sex, as he did in his writings, or spoke more directly. We only know that Charlotte left Mitchell eager for Walter's embrace.

Return to Providence

Charlotte ended her rest cure under Dr. S. Weir Mitchell at the end of May 1887. Whatever the doctor actually said to her, it is clear that she first interpreted a return to her "duties as woman" as a return to her duties of the marital bed. And perhaps, after a month away, her "erotic tendency was at a maximum." Walter reported in his diary that he had surprised Charlotte by going to New York to meet her. She was evidently returning to Providence by boat. He wrote, "We spent a long delightful night in our state room." This was followed by a two-week vacation. "Charlotte is indeed very much better; is loving and brave and trying to follow the directions of complete recovery. I have never seen her so well."[1]

Mitchell had clearly given Charlotte guidance about the way she was to conduct herself in the period ahead. How did she understand his "directions of complete recovery"? Many years later, she wrote of this in a number of contexts, and her words have been accepted as an accurate account of Mitchell's prescription. We are now in a position to examine her recollections and test them against the record.

In 1913, she wrote about Mitchell's rest cure in the *Forerunner*, the magazine she published as Charlotte Perkins Gilman. She repeated this telling, using only slightly different wording, in 1919 in a letter to William Dean Howells and in her autobiography. A note, written at the bottom of her copy of the long letter she wrote to Mitchell in 1887, contains this version:

> He kept me a month. Found nothing the matter apparently! Sent me home with this prescription: "Live as domestic a life as possible. Have your child with you all the time. Lie down an hour after each meal. Have but two hours intellectual life a day. Never touch pen, brush, or pencil again as long as you live."
> I did it, that summer, and came to the edge of insanity.[2]

The words have come down to us unquestioned. As a handwritten statement, this text below the letter to Mitchell carries a certain authenticity. However, the handwriting resembles that of Charlotte near the end of her life, suggesting that this note was not written at a time close to that of the 1887 letter.[3]

Was this remembrance a true account? There is no way to be certain, for only the two were there. However, I have shown Charlotte's capacity for misreading others—Martha's thoughts during the summer of 1881, Walter's proposal, Mitchell's suggestion of separation from home. We know that she was very ill in the spring of 1887, and this likely meant even greater distortion. When she wrote versions of this statement long after the fact, she had no personal records to rely on, for she did not return to journal keeping until 1890. Thus, this memory, filtered through the lens of time, was unaided.

"Have your child with you all the time." Given Mitchell's feelings about maternal duty, it is likely that he disapproved of Charlotte having left Katharine for many months when she was a baby and wanted to discourage any separation of mother and child in the future. Yet Mitchell explicitly urged recovering women to have uninterrupted periods of isolation each day for rest, protected from the demands of children and servants. Could Charlotte have misinterpreted his statement to her that she have her child with her (and not leave her for months at a time) as an unlikely command to keep continual companionship? Since she turned his suggestion of a removal from Providence into a divorce from Walter, this is possible.

"Have but two hours intellectual life a day." Mitchell was facing a woman who had written to him in her own words of her hysterical outbursts, her deep distress, and the tonic she had taken containing morphine. She had stated that she feared brain disease. Given his understandings of mind work and his strong belief that a woman should avoid tears and emotional outpourings, Mitchell probably recommended a limiting of intellectual activity as he prepared Charlotte to return home and continue to build up strength. Thus, it is likely that Mitchell gave this recommendation for the short term of continuing recovery.

"Never touch pen, brush, or pencil again as long as you live." Of course, this is the most controversial element. "Pen, brush, or pencil"—it is quite possible that Mitchell urged Charlotte not to draw or write during the time of convalescence, just as he generally told women to avoid letter writing. "As long as you live" is a different story. He believed that if a woman built up her strength, she could return to a full and active life. Mitchell was capable of speaking in strong language, but nothing in his writings or in his dealings with other patients suggests the life sentence that Charlotte recalled.[4] His advocacy of a year in England is the strongest piece of evidence that he saw Charlotte as a woman on the road to recovery but not yet recovered. She had only been with him for a single month. In accord with his writings, he likely advised her that she needed at least a year of modified activity to restore her strength.

In her discussions of Mitchell's prescription, years later, Charlotte never mentioned that he had agreed to her opening a gymnasium. Perhaps she forgot it. What it signaled is important. Mitchell did not insist that Charlotte return to total domesticity.

He valued physical exercise, and he saw a relationship between a woman's being nervous and being "house-caged." Her working in a gymnasium suited his belief that "Nothing is a better ally against nervousness or irritability in any one than either outdoor exercise or pretty violent use of the muscles."

Forgetting is sometimes as important as remembering. In this case, never referring to the gymnasium strengthens the likelihood that in the quarter century after her month of the rest cure, Charlotte Perkins Gilman recalled the other elements of Mitchell's advice through a veil of distortion.

Unquestionably, in the months after returning from the rest cure and the ensuing vacation, Charlotte moved on a steeply downward slope. Walter did not see it initially. In the period immediately following her homecoming, he continued to report her health and sweetness, in words such as "Charlotte was tender last evening, tho' a little tired" and "Charlotte continues _very_ much better."[5]

Walter told of the return of their sexual life with expressions of his gratification. We have Charlotte's side only secondhand. Although there was no direct mention of sex, there was what has come to be called among scholars "genital proof." In Walter's diary entry of September 10, he stated, "Charlotte did not feel quite so well this morning. She thinks she is going to have another child. I do not."[6]

By the time Walter wrote this, his hopes for Charlotte becoming a loving wife were over. Toward the end of June, she had taken a sharp downward turn. On June 30, Walter reported that when he returned to their apartment in the afternoon, "Charlotte was in the depths of melancholia again, with talk of pistols & chloroform." Charlotte was using her era's terms to talk of suicide, raising the ante.[7] Walter tried to distract her—to get her out of the house, take her on walks or for a ride on the horsecars, and bring her into contact with others. In mid-July, he reported, "Charlotte had only two or three spells of morbidity." Later than evening, Walter gave Charlotte eggnog before she went to bed and then reported, "Love this morning." His sexual pleasure quickly turned to gall, for immediately afterward she had "a flow of the tide of her distemper" and spoke of insanity. His response this time was not patience but anger. He reported that he "took the name of God."[8]

During July, amid Walter's reports of Charlotte's ups and downs were also accounts that she had in company, played card games, dressed up as Martha Washington, and gave a reading. All this suggested that she was re-engaging with the world. What Walter didn't know was that behind this return an inner change was taking place.

He learned of it in early August 1887. With bitterness, he wrote, "Charlotte has been better but she thinks she is so not from any change in her but because she has a new plan for her and my salvation!" Charlotte had made previous inquiries about selling the Hartford property she and her brother had inherited, and she had now returned to this project with a new seriousness. Walter wrote that if she could sell it, then she, along with mother, brother, daughter, and maid, would, as he put it, "emigrate to Pasadena & lead a happy life." Charlotte also made plans for Walter. He was to take off for Europe to paint and "regain lost enthusiasm." She had thought it all out. Walter wrote, "I may keep a mistress there, if she be clean so my generous wife says!" Charlotte's hope was that they both would regain their strength and, in Walter's ironic paraphrase, would "meet again on Pasadena's happy shore and live joyfully ever after."[9]

What Charlotte wrote to her close friend Grace Channing in Pasadena a few months later adds a great deal of information. The two women were currently thinking through arrangements to spend the next summer together and continue collaborating on their play. Writing in a moment of elation, Charlotte began, "I am so much better! First there was the great lift of my western plan." Her next sentence jumps from the page: "Then I decided to cast off Dr. Mitchell bodily, and do exactly what I pleased." After the summer's terrible downward slide, Charlotte now rejected Mitchell's directives for a period of gradual recovery.

What was doing what she pleased? "Then I laid plans for more sociability this winter, and am carrying them out. And then Sam Simmons suddenly presented himself as a sympathizing friend and is helping me out amazingly." As she offered this list, the repetition of the word *then* is important: first the plan, then the rejection of Mitchell, then the scheme for sociability, then renewing an earlier friendship. Important here is what happened after this series. Charlotte wrote of her pleasure with playing whist and chess and the mental stimulation it gave her. "This is mental exercise at once easy and pleasant; and I can feel my brain crystallizing into some sort of shape under the genial influence."

Coupled to this was her most important statement: "What underlies the change is this decision: I have given up trying to assimilate with Walter: have accepted my life as I did that with Mother, as a thing to be endured and resisted, not a thing I must agree with; have determined to be myself as far as I can in spite of circumstances. It is astonishing how my whole nature responds." Essentially, Charlotte was stating that she had determined to be Charlotte, to not combine. She continued, "The other life is impossible, that's all."

This called for no apparent alteration on the surface but rather a hidden transformation. She continued to live with Walter in their home but separately, inviting in her own company and suiting herself. But that was not all. "What pleases me most is that when I leave Walter entirely out of my calculations, and make no attempt to fulfill my wifely duties toward him; why strait way his various excellences become visible again and he becomes a loved companion instead of a nightmare husband. And under that arrangement a certain approximation to **Alpha** doctrines becomes possible, as my health improves and conscience does not gnaw unceasingly."[10]

This was a code Grace could understand. "Wifely duties" meant sexual intercourse. As noted, the "Alpha doctrines" of the 1880s preached sexual continence in marriage. Prior to Charlotte's determination to approximate "Alpha doctrines," Walter had been a "nightmare husband." Thus he must have made constant demands for sexual intercourse that were distasteful to her.

The genie is out of the bottle. Charlotte no longer lived under the marital requirement of regular sexual relations with Walter. A little care is necessary here. Charlotte's words—"a certain approximation to Alpha doctrines"—do not state that she embraced a totally sexless marriage. Rather, they suggest that she would no longer treat sex as an obligation or, as she put it, she would "make no attempt to fulfill my wifely duties toward him." If sex happened, it would be her choice. Under this new arrangement, she could accept Walter's presence. Until she had the money to leave him for California, Charlotte was going to attempt to enact her version of marriage, the one Walter rejected in April 1883.

He would have rejected it again in 1887 if he had had a choice. But Charlotte did not give him that, and while it cannot be said that she consciously used illness to get her way, her state of mind did not allow him to refuse her terms. At the times Charlotte was "loving," Walter voiced his pleasure. For example, in late February 1888, he wrote, "Charlotte has been unusually loving since yesterday morning. Ah it is so sweet & helpful to have her loving. I confess that when she is not so for such long times it almost drives me to seek pleasure and comfort in other women."[11] Thus Charlotte's suggestion of a clean mistress did not come out of nowhere.

More often, Walter used his diary to voice his unhappiness. He expressed his dissatisfaction with their sex life many times, but the clearest moment came in June 1888 when Charlotte was away. He had spent the previous evening with a Providence judge and wondered if the man was "rigidly continent" or kept a mistress. Walter went on to say that he himself had slept poorly. He wrote, "I never was made to be a 'continent' man. I should be healthier, happier and more useful if my creative instincts could have fuller play. I am young yet. There is a fullness of life in my sexual nature that is now cramped thwarted and made contemptible." He mused that had he lived in an earlier time, he would have kept mistresses, but he was a man of his era, with Puritan forebears, a nervous sensibility, and a respect for womankind. As such, he was "in a state far from blessed." He rephrased this: given "the circumstances of my married life," it would be appropriate, he believed, to keep a mistress, but he loved and respected Charlotte too much. "But it is certain that I need more of that sort of thing than there is any way of my getting." He worried that his unsatisfied state would lead him to break down and "revel in some demoralizing nauseous excess." In the meantime, he was not able to sleep or work well "because of the disquiet and unsatisfied longings."[12]

When Charlotte wrote to Grace in November 1887, the two women already had part of a plan. Continuing in her recovery mode, Charlotte told Grace that she had been able to return to sewing and housework. "By next summer I shall be able to aid you in taking the world by storm. Hm! We will be the leading dramatists of the age!"[13] They planned to share a house together in summer 1888 and continue writing plays.

One must take this ambition very seriously, for Charlotte did. It was part of both women's scheme to make money to live independently. As Charlotte continued, "My dear girl, a good play is a paying thing. If we can write one we can write two. If we can write one in one year we can write another in another year. Yea verily. Our names shall be long in the land." Given her relationship with William Gillette, the actor and producer, Charlotte's dream of selling the play was not mere fantasy. Charlotte concluded, "Dr. Mitchell be————!"[14] Not only failing to fulfill wifely duties but also living a dramatist's life was a violation of Mitchell's prescription. Charlotte threw him off body and soul.

All the while, Charlotte and Walter went on together. Charlotte did not leave for California until autumn 1888. According to Walter's accounts, she sought regular entertainment at whist parties. What neither of them ever mentioned was that during this time she was likely writing a series of essays designed to accompany forty-nine art prints by European painters, *Gems of Art for Home and Fireside*. Immediately prior to the breakdown that led her to Mitchell, she had gone to the Providence publisher J. A. and R. A. Reid, only to report that she had failed to get work. At some point, however, the firm commissioned her to contribute to this art book. She is listed on the title page, uncharacteristically, as Mrs. Charles Walter Stetson.[15]

In her material for each print, Charlotte typically focused on the subject matter being illustrated, but sometimes she included material about the painter and his reputation and occasionally considered aesthetic elements of the painting itself. This allowed her to state her prejudices and predispositions—opposition to religious asceticism, awareness of the class structure and its inequities, belief in the civilizing power of culture, appreciation for the emotional sources of music, love of cats, and admiration for aristocratic beauty, especially of the Norman English type. She may have projected her own story onto a painting of Tennyson's Enid, pictured in the print as leaving home to marry with "dim forebodings of an unknown future that may bring joy or pain, she knows not which. Well it is that she does not know of the trials and struggles in store for her tender, loving heart, the cruel suspicion of her husband, and the harsh trials she had to pass through."[16]

Cultivated references abound. One reads the author as a literary person who could quote Shelley and Tennyson, could retell Roman history, and agreed with (and possibly even penned) these lines on the artistic and literary value of the romantic past:

> Gloomy castle on towering hill,
> Maiden imprisoned against her will,
> Lovelorn lady with noble knight,
> Gay young gallant and damsel bright,
> Priest and page and fool and king,
> Haunted mansion and magic ring,
> Ghost and wizard and palmer slow,
> That wonderful world of long ago.[17]

Although she was clearly working on commission, no record has been found that Charlotte got paid for her writing for *Gems of Art.* It is also possible that Walter was her silent collaborator (and the explanation for why her authorial name was Mrs. Charles Walter Stetson). Some months later, Walter wrote, "I have done a good deal of writing for the Reids and get $62.00 for it. I could make ten dollars an evening at it, which is good pay for my odd hours."[18] Money was needed, for despite the fact that Walter got some important commissions, the household remained in debt. Mary Perkins, unable to afford separate living quarters, moved in with them.

Charlotte had planned that Walter would go to Europe in May, and she to a country place with Grace for the summer. Walter had no resources for his trip.[19] But in early June 1888, Grace Channing arrived from California, and Charlotte departed with her for Bristol, Rhode Island, taking Kate and a maid in tow. Grace had rented an old farmhouse near the shore not far from family friends. The two women began in earnest to revise their "Changing Hands," working hard on it each day.

In Grace's voluminous letters home, she wrote much about Charlotte. Initially she was shocked when, on arrival in Providence, she saw her friend. "Charlotte is, I think looking far more ill than I ever saw her, so white and thin and wan, but <u>exceedingly beautiful</u>—more so than of old." Though he appeared even more youthful, Walter, too, was "sad and tired, for "all these years of illness and worry are telling upon him sorely."[20]

Grace wrote often about the development of the play and the collaboration. Each evening, she and Charlotte discussed where they wanted the story to go and then all the next morning worked together to devise dialogue. With Charlotte too weak to write, it fell to Grace to transcribe their work. Over the summer weeks in Bristol, the two discarded some of the secondary characters, tightened the drama, and gave more free play to the comedic characters. Grace's Amelia emerged as a daffy widow, and Charlotte's Sophronia as a rather scolding bluestocking.

Over the previous months, Walter had been hoping that Charlotte's resolution to leave him would disappear. She occasionally fed that hope after "some extraordinarily loving moment," when she would suggest that she might be able to stay with him after all. All that vanished when he got Charlotte's letter from Bristol after her first week of absence, telling him that she was happy and did not miss him. "The fogs and mists," she wrote, "are rolling away; I begin to feel alive and self-respecting. Oh the difference! You are very dear to me my love; but there is no disguising the fact that my health and work lie not with you but away from you."[21]

A few days later, Walter came to Bristol for a planned visit, and Grace wrote to her mother about what it was like to see the couple in distress. "They just prey upon one another. He makes Charlotte absolutely sick—she gets so exhausted and depressed—before night yesterday there were great circles under her eyes and she was white as a ghost, purely from the mental fatigue. This morning she is lying down, fit for nothing! And he grows as bitter and cynical in five minutes with her." Grace did not take sides. She wrote of her warm feelings for both of them: "they are both charming, lovable, gifted people." If they could separate, she believed, both would recover.[22]

Charlotte and Grace renamed the play "Noblesse Oblige." Grace believed that its central purpose was to set up a clear contrast between European and American types. She wrote home, "Charlotte and I feel very enthusiastic and quite sure we are about to produce the only great Comedy of the age!...We expect to make the Anglo-American studies of Howells and James pale before this and those great luminaries shake in their shoes."[23]

Two manuscript copies of "Noblesse Oblige" exist, of varying lengths. The shorter is in Charlotte's hand and bears on last page the notation "Finished copy, Tues. Aug. 7th, 1888."[24] With many elements of amusement—coincidence, star-crossed lovers, fortunes landing in the right places, and true love vindicated at last— the play was meant to be light fun. It did carry one serious note, however.[25] Both young women are engaged to men they no longer wish to marry. In the end, both are allowed to follow their hearts. Eleanor, the beauty with the leading role, is even allowed to break two engagements, including one with the English lord, to fulfill the higher obligation of true love. As Grace wrote to her mother, "I hope that moral is <u>im</u>moral enough to save the play!"[26]

From the beginning of the summer, Charlotte repeatedly wrote to William Gillette, trying to engage him in their enterprise. The women waited anxiously for him to respond, hoping he would guide them in revision. Grace wrote home in late June that while his acceptance of their play was important to her, as it would justify the added expense to the Channing family of this eastern sojourn, for Charlotte it was, by contrast, a much more serious matter. At this point, Charlotte was pinning all her hopes on Gillette taking the play, for this would give her enough money to send Walter abroad and herself to California with Kate. In late August, failing to hear from Gillette, the two women decided to telegraph him that they were coming to New York to read the play to him.

After a series of misadventures, Gillette arrived at the theater and for a long afternoon paced and made comments as he listened to the reading. He liked the work, especially its novelty and the quality of the writing. He encouraged Charlotte and Grace to think that he might produce it, if backers could be found. When the women asked if they might speak about it to others, Gillette gave them permission to do so. Grace wrote home and instructed her mother to say "simply that Gillette has taken it and intends to bring it out if possible." She could add that Grace and Charlotte were "about to write a second—under his direct encouragement and advice." In Grace's mind, Gillette's aegis provided a necessary justification for Charlotte's impending move to Pasadena.[27]

Just when it felt like the two women had a chance for their play to be performed in New York, fate intervened. On September 1, Gillette's wife died suddenly. No money ever came from Gillette, and the plays Charlotte and Grace wrote were never produced in a commercial theater.

Charlotte desperately needed money to move to California. Jane Augusta Senter, Grace's good friend from Pasadena, who had traveled east with her, came for a long visit to Bristol. The women schemed that Augusta's family might loan Charlotte the needed funds. Augusta's mother, the widow of the mayor of Cleveland, was as well connected as one could be in Pasadena, but prominence did not turn out to yield cash. When on September 1 Charlotte learned that money from that source would not be forthcoming, an old and true friend came to the rescue. Caroline Hazard had long been Charlotte's quiet benefactor, giving gifts and arranging sizeable commissions for her artistic works. In mid-September 1888, her wealthy father, Rowland Hazard II, purchased Charlotte's Hartford property and anticipated the settlement by loaning her the money immediately.[28] Caroline's influence would have been consistent with her many kindnesses to Charlotte in the past, and it also anticipates her future role in fostering independent women as president of Wellesley College.

By September 22, 1888, Charlotte had packed all her worldly goods to ship to Pasadena. All the Hazard money she received went to settle debts and meet the expenses of shipping and moving. There was none left over for Walter to travel to Europe, and none to settle herself in California.[29] Charlotte and Katharine began their journey almost immediately, staying first with Mrs. Cresson in her great house on the Rhode Island shore and then traveling west where, as Charlotte wrote to Grace, she hoped to find "rest and hope and health and joy."[30]

To "The Yellow Wall-Paper"

"Rest and hope and health and joy" is a tall order, one hard to live out in the best of circumstances. The real experience of Pasadena proved for Charlotte to be much more complicated—and much more creative.

How would Charlotte live when she arrived with her three-year-old daughter and a household helper in Pasadena in the autumn of 1888? She had, in Grace's words, "embarked without resources," spending all the money from the Hartford property to pay her debts and transport goods and persons. Grace warned her parents, "she literally has nothing to start with."[1] By nothing, Grace meant cash, for Charlotte brought with her nine wooden packing cases containing furniture and household goods. Grace's family helped with the transition. Someone, possibly Mary Cresson, loaned Charlotte $100, and this tided her over while she got her bearings.

Charlotte immediately found a small cottage to rent at the corner of Orange Grove and Colorado. The house was across the road from Carmelita, a large house and gardens owned by the

2

in it all and grows visibly. Miss
Murphy remarked every morning what a
beautiful day it was till she got tired.
She likes the place very much and the
people. The Channings have been
kind as one they can, have helped in
every possible way, and put me into
the house bodily with all my goods.
Its very cosy here. I have had it
beautifully papered with paper at 12cts
and 7½cts a roll, and the lovely familiar
things look well in it. There is a
pretty piazza in front with an orange
tree at each end and two great
rose vines in front.
The roof is dull
red and house
white washed or yellow
washed some time since, a very nice color.
There is a straight path to the front
— hitching post with lots of flowers on
each side. Two lemon verbenas of
great size one over six feet high, are
on either side of the path.
My packing box kitchen is visible in the
rear. I've got a cunning little wood
stove, and prosper finely in my
cooking. Miss Murphy is

Charlotte's sketch of her cottage in a letter to Walter's mother,
1888. Charles Walter Stetson Letters, Bancroft Library, University
of California, Berkeley.

naturalist Jeanne Carr and her husband, two of Pasadena's most distinguished residents, and was within easy walking distance of the Channings' home. Charlotte's little house had a cellar and four rooms that she immediately had papered and whitewashed. Using her wood packing boxes, a carpenter constructed a small kitchen at the back of the house, and Charlotte installed a little woodstove for cooking.

Within a week, she moved in with Katharine and the Providence seamstress who had come to assist with domestic chores. What Charlotte really appreciated about the house were the surrounding flowers and its porch, what she called her "best parlor," where she and Kate spent their days. A letter described Kate as "swinging there in a hammock while I sit in a wicker rocker and write."[2]

At the outset, Charlotte was encouraged about her prospects in Pasadena. She did not keep a journal in her first fifteen months there, but in a descriptive letter to Walter's mother she wrote, "I get up at half past six and fly about at my work as briskly as you please. Shall go to painting as soon as I get settled, in two days more perhaps." She anticipated a good market for her art work, "of all kinds, nice or cheap."[3]

Whatever Charlotte initially felt on her departure from Providence, her marriage to Walter was not really over. In early December, he organized a sale of his paintings in Providence and made enough money to travel to California.[4] When he arrived, he found that Charlotte's new life had begun. He immediately took the measure of Charlotte's Pasadena world, peopled by the sociable Channings and by many others who came on visits throughout the day, invited the Stetsons over, or joined them for walks in the arroyo. In his words, he and Charlotte received invitations to many "swell" affairs, such as concerts and the Valley Hunt Ball, and were asked to take part in civic activities.

In February 1889, the great event was a weeklong benefit to raise money for a handsome building for the public library. Dr. Channing was on the library board and drew on the talents of both newcomers. Walter helped organize a loan exhibition of paintings and took charge of the "Feast of Lanterns" pageant. Charlotte acted in a play, *Ici On Parle Francais,* and read the "Pied Piper of Hamlin" before an audience on Children's Day. Of course, all of this involved preparation and meetings with others. Walter wrote to his mother about how busy Charlotte was, "with house-work, reading, writing[,] giving drawing lessons and taking lessons in French." He added, "I think she is trying to do to[o] much."[5]

Among those who provided company in Pasadena were former Providence residents. Walter wrote about Mrs. Mitchell, the wife of Providence's Dr. Mitchell, who often came by to play whist. In the spring of 1889, Charlotte formed a class on "modern litera-ture, its causes and effects." Mrs. Mitchell was among the dozen women students, each paying $5 for ten sessions, and often hosted the class meetings. Others relocating from New England appeared at their doorstep. Jeanne Carr, across the way, took in boarders, including the two Misses Hill from Worcester, Massachusetts, who came to call.

Charlotte became quickly connected with the economic and cultural elite then forming in 1880s Pasadena. She may have lived in a small cottage, but around her were some of the great homes of the prominent. Amateur theatricals brought her into working and social relations with fellow drama enthusiasts, such as the land developer Charles Scharff. Once Charlotte began to teach or tutor young people, their parents sought her out. These included some of the most powerful movers and shakers of the growing region, including James F. Crank, a founder of the Los Angeles and San Gabriel Valley Railroad, and Willis Masters, postmaster and pres-ident of the Union Publishing Company and the Pasadena Board of Trade. Some of these associations came from Grace's particu-larly well-connected friend Augusta, whose sister was married to Masters. Delia Masters, their daughter, became one of Charlotte's regular pupils.[6] A goodly number of persons in Charlotte's larger social world were charter members of the Valley Hunt Club, then and now one of the prime markers of local social status.

Walter reflected on Charlotte's new life in a letter to his mother. As he was writing, Charles Scharff came to call. Walter commented, "There is almost always somebody here. Everybody seems to like to come, and Charlotte has a very long list of disciples among the young women. They simply adore her. Not only the young women but the older ones also." Walter summarized, "She is doing lots of good work and making no end of friends without any effort."[7] What Charlotte found in Pasadena was less a place for "rest" than a welcoming one that appreciated her verve, talent, and ambition. It did not hurt that Charlotte carried the Beecher heritage. Her presence promised to add to the aspiring town's cultural resources. And of course, behind it all were the Channings with their impeccable eastern credentials, grand house, and ever-present kindness.

Charlotte became involved in writing for new magazines that carried her beyond Pasadena. Beginning in the summer of 1889, she worked for the *Pacific Review,* launched in Los Angeles. Walter wrote that she had promised to be a "regular contributor." She wrote a review of Tolstoy's novella *The Death of Ivan Ilyich.* The review also published one of Grace's poems, and Walter submitted a poem of his own and a notice of Grace and Charlotte's play. He was the women's courier, traveling several times to the magazine's offices in Los Angeles. In August, he wrote his parents about Charlotte's and his roles, "I believe she has become a sort of associate editor of it: at any rate she is to furnish three pages of matter every month and to oversee the things that are to be put in it. I am supposed to illustrate it." They all hoped that they would be paid for the work.[8]

By November, those hopes had died. But Charlotte was involved in a new and potentially more promising venture, the *Californian.* Charles Frederick Holder, Pasadena's leading writer and naturalist, planned a monthly illustrated magazine and engaged the help of the Channings and the Stetsons. Charlotte was involved in this undertaking from the outset. As Walter wrote home, all were optimistic about this endeavor, "even Dr. Channing who is the most cautious of men. It has quite waked him up and he is busy writing

Charlotte on the steps of her cottage, Pasadena, c. 1890. Schlesinger Library, Radcliffe Institute, Harvard University.

an article for it called the Romance of the Telephone." Walter reported on Charlotte: "It seems that the more work of this sort Charlotte has to do, the better she is. She thinks herself well now, and if <u>She</u> thinks so she must be."⁹

In its anticipatory flyer, the *Californian* promised to present the work of all those around Charlotte, as well as Holder and Charles Dudley Warner. Walter was to provide illustrations, and there were to be literary contributions by Edward Everett Hale,

Frederick Perkins, Grace Channing, Dr. William F. Channing, and Charlotte herself. Raising the money for the undertaking, however, proved difficult—Pasadena supporters had more aspiration than capital. When the magazine finally appeared in October 1891, it was published in San Francisco and was Holder's alone, although on occasion it published pieces by Grace and Charlotte.

Lack of money was a constant source of anxiety. Walter got very few commissions and had a hard time collecting fees when he did. Charlotte had great difficulty earning enough to support herself and Katharine. What little she gathered came from private art teaching and her women's class and from decorating cards and objects. In the second year in Pasadena, she offered the literature class with a different subject, biographies of women. Her financial dream still revolved around making a theatrical hit. Although the earlier high hopes for Gillette's patronage had faded, she remained optimistic about finding a producer to stage her joint work with Grace.

Charlotte's connection to the Channings gave her support, access to Pasadena's elite, and Grace's company. It took a different turn after Walter arrived at the end of December, however, for he was appreciated quite on his own. Immediately, the Channings offered Walter studio space in their house. Their hospitality increased, and by the spring of 1889 the Stetson household was dining communally with them.

Whatever hopes for reconciliation with Charlotte that Walter brought to Pasadena eroded during his year there. Gradually, he readjusted his sights and focused on Grace. She had always liked him and defended him to her family, and now an opportunity for her arose. William Channing seemed to encourage Walter's attentions to his daughter. In letters home to his parents in Providence, Walter told of a number of long rides he took alone with Grace in the Channing wagon. In March 1889 he wrote, "Yesterday Dr. Channing came over and asked me if I would take Miss Grace and the buggy out to the poppy fields. He wanted me to see a big field near at hand in full sunlight and he wanted her to have the ride, as she was feeling rather miserably and ought not to sit up in her room to write all day. I was

Charlotte taking the air under a white umbrella, Long Beach, California, c. 1890. Schlesinger Library, Radcliffe Institute, Harvard University.

only too glad to go."[10] Several times, when Dr. Channing needed his large container of sherry refilled, he asked Walter to take Grace to the winery. Walter painted and repainted her portrait. When she visited at the Stetson cottage, he often walked her home. During the summer, as Charlotte went to Long Beach with Kate, Walter joined Grace and her mother in Laguna.

Over the course of a year, Walter shifted his affections from Charlotte to Grace. One can see this indirectly in his words, as

Grace Channing at the time Charlotte and Walter were in Pasadena, 1888. Schlesinger Library, Radcliffe Institute, Harvard University.

he wrote of the way Grace's unspecified illnesses became a matter of grave concern to him. The Channing family had moved to California to protect the health of Grace and her sister Mary. In December 1889, when Mary, married and living in Seattle, fell sick, Dr. Channing traveled to attend her. Walter was left in charge of Grace, who was still "very ill." Dr. Channing had left instructions that Grace, who had little appetite, must eat every two hours. Walter told his parents of his skill in pleasing Grace: "From long practice I have learned how to concoct nice little dishes of a sort to surprise. By that means she has done very well at eating.... Besides I know better what she likes, or how she likes it, than they do, so I have, I flatter my self, been of some use. I like to do it."[11]

Charles Walter Stetson, portrait of Grace Channing, c. 1889. Schlesinger Library, Radcliffe Institute, Harvard University.

Walter's portrait of Grace from these months provides visual evidence of his feelings. Posed in an open position with her hand behind her head, she wears a passion flower tucked between her breasts and is surrounded by a passion vine with an open flower and buds. Walter wrote in his record book, "I have done in it all that my love combined with my present skill can do" and noted that the painting was never to be sold.[12] At the end of October, preparing for a later return to Providence, Walter made his breach with Charlotte clear to his mother, writing "No, Kate & Charlotte will not return with me."[13]

In early January 1890, Walter received word that his mother was dying and immediately left for Providence. Given the costs of travel and his penury, his journey back east meant he was there to stay. Although the Channings had attempted to promote his work and gain him portrait clients, Walter had never gained a financial footing in California. By this point, however, he and Grace had reached some sort of understanding about their future together. Although as parents of Katharine, Charlotte and Walter continued to write regularly to each other, with his departure, her physical and emotional separation from him was now complete.

All the while, Charlotte's and Grace's close friendship and collaboration continued unabated, seemingly unaffected by Walter's shifting allegiance. During the year of Walter's stay in Pasadena, the two women worked together on their plays. Walter acted as their assistant, transcribing several of their works in his beautiful hand. In June, he took one of their plays to Los Angeles and arranged for three typewritten copies to be made to send out to theatrical managers. He participated in evenings of play-reading. He wrote home, "Miss Channing has been here for a final revision of their last play. I have just come from walking home with her in the starlight. Last night we read the play called 'Noblesse Oblige,' to Dr. Channing, Mr. Scharff and Harold [Grace's brother]. Mr. Scharff is an amateur actor and a very intelligent and educated man. They all seemed to enjoy it much indeed, as I'm sure they ought."[14]

Charlotte and Grace had great hope for the success of their work. They anticipated a May visit from Gillette and the possibility of his producing the play in San Francisco. In August they sent it out to E. A. Sothern, an actor, and Mr. Daly, a manager in New York.[15]

Charlotte wrote Martha that in addition to playwriting and teaching her class, she had also written some poems. She admitted that life remained difficult. "The weakness of brain that has so devastated my life for the past five years still holds very largely." The gains of the last year were "large and deep," but, as she put it, she had no surplus: any little thing "will undo me."[16]

Her letters to Martha provide a window into Charlotte's consciousness during this period. She renewed their correspondence while Walter was in Pasadena, perhaps in the wake of his growing attachment to Grace. About that, Charlotte only wrote, "He and Grace are great friends, which gives me sincere delight." Perhaps anticipating Grace's possible defection, Charlotte reassured Martha: "No one has ever taken your place, heart's dearest. No one has ever given me the happiness that you did, the peace, the rest, the everpresent joy. I do not forget." Yet Charlotte was careful to be clear in telling Martha how different the present moment was from the summer of 1881. "I do not forget" was immediately followed by "Neither do I remember, for the immediate past is still so vital a horror, and all the antecedent years so lonely and drear, that I never look back if I can avoid it."[17]

As their correspondence continued into 1890, Charlotte sought to convey to Martha that she was a different person from the young woman of 1881. "You knew and loved me once. You do not know me now, and I am not at all sure that you would love me if you did. What you cling to so tenderly is a sweet memory, a lovely past; as many a man or woman cherishes a lost love." While transformations in Martha may have been gradual, Charlotte saw herself as growing and changing "wildly, darkly, strangely, beyond a mother's recognition, beyond my own. The girl you knew, the woman you loved died in some years past, died in long slow unutterable pain." Again she wrote, "I doubt if most people have as much happiness in all their lives as I had then. I do not forget. But neither do I remember, because it hurts."[18] Along with Charlotte's new life in California came bursts of energy, taking her in new and frightening directions, and a willful forgetting.

Although Charlotte described her life to Martha, over a year after moving to Pasadena, as "unstable, rootless and windblown," her journal, which she resumed in 1890, conveys a different picture. The life she built in Pasadena had much of the structure of her earlier days before marriage: she had private drawing pupils, she wrote, she socialized. On many days she reported that she was tired. Her troubles were not really over, but they were diminishing in strength.

A letter to her distant cousin and friend Marian Whitney in the spring of 1890 attempted a portrait of her state of health. "A large part of the time I fizzle out," she wrote, which meant idle days, "gloomy because the illness of six years hovers gently in the background, and extra weariness brings melancholy in its train." She then corrected herself: "Melancholia I should say—which is a different thing." By this shift, Charlotte seems to have been trying to make it clear that her state of mind went beyond sadness—she was suffering in a more profound way from a pathological condition clinically recognized in the medicine literature of her time.[19] Is this depiction to be believed? Yes and no. It is stated within a larger letter much of which rings false; but it seems a fair, albeit revised, interpretation of the severe trouble that was then ebbing.[20] Charlotte was changing, but in ways she could not yet recognize.

She was now finally free of Walter. As she approached the age of thirty in Pasadena, her situation was very different from her experience as a young single woman in Providence. She now had both prestige and an emerging literary vocation. She had developed a meaningful place in a town that hungered for culture and roots.

Important new interests came to absorb her and take her in new directions. Edward Bellamy's utopian novel *Looking Backward* sparked a broad interest in reform among middle-class readers and led to a raft of Nationalist clubs devoted to bringing about his vision. California proved particularly fertile ground for Bellamy's socialist fantasy of a peaceful revolution leading to national ownership of industry, economic and gender equality, and freedom for women—liberated from private domestic labor—to engage fully in the public sphere. Charlotte joined the local Pasadena branch.

Beginning in the spring of 1890, as Charlotte Stetson, Gilman began to lecture to Nationalist audiences and write for the movement's magazines, distilling and applying to human society her knowledge about physiology, instinct, and habit—ideas acquired many years before from *Popular Science Monthly*. Fired up by anger at her own poverty and hope in a socialist future, she found words in her often repeated lecture "On Human Nature" to inspire listeners to rise up against the "tyranny of money." She addressed her hearers as descendants of the first colonists and the fighters of the American Revolution. In her call to arms, she declared that just as the first settlers had struggled for religious freedom and the revolutionary heroes had fought for political freedom, now was the time to strive for "economic freedom." As she talked about revolutionary forebears, she used the refrain "We come from those men!" At the end of her talk, she exhorted, "We are those men!"[21] She found her voice and received warm response. Lecturing emerged as a way of gaining influence and a source of needed income.[22]

Freed from Walter, her writing took a new turn. Charlotte began to allow herself to express more of the anger that raged inside her. In several poems, published in the *Woman's Journal,* she told variants of the same story, the contrast in marriage between male power and female powerlessness. "Wedded Bliss" contrasted the successive mating of an eagle with a hen, of a lion with a sheep, of a salmon with a clam.[23] In each case, the weak and passive animal ironically takes pleasure in the achievement of the strong, active one.

"O come and be my mate!" said the Eagle to the Hen;
I love to soar, but then
I want my mate to rest

Forever in the nest!"
Said the hen, "I cannot fly,
I have no wish to try,
But I joy to see my mate careering through the sky!"
They wed, and cried, "Ah, this is Love, my own!"
And the Hen sat, the Eagle soared, alone.

A poem, "Reassurance," posits that deep in the historical past, man and woman were equal. Then man conquered woman for his pleasure, forced her to love him, bound her to him, and kept her weak, "lest she be strong to flee."[24]

Charlotte set one clever piece of writing, "The Quarrel," in neither nature nor the primordial ooze but in the present.[25] Looking on the page like a poem, the piece presented a dramatic dialogue between "He" and "She." Each of its five scenes appears as a stanza, and all the scenes except the last one begin with the same two lines. The first segment sets the pattern.

HE: I like you!
SHE: And I like you! (*They embrace.*)
HE: I want more of you!
SHE: You've had enough!
HE: But I want more!
SHE: You can't have it!
HE: I'll take it! I'm the biggest!
SHE: You sha'n't! (*They fight.*)

As the pattern of embracing and fighting continues, "He" makes successive demands of "She," first of her labor, then of her freedom. He will force her to stay within the house; he will require her to do as he pleases.

The final exchange seems particularly important:

HE: Keep behind me! Don't push so!
SHE: Oh! you hurt! I want to get out!
HE: You mean, you want to get ahead!
SHE: I don't! I want to get even!

The double meaning of "even" gives this outburst a sharp edge. What follows these lines breaks the pattern of the stanza-scenes: a tirade by "He" that captures essential elements of the ideology of true womanhood enhanced by evolutionary science. It is a remarkable speech that demonstrates how Gilman penetrated the sentimental and scientific rhetoric of her era to find brute force at its core.

HE: Horrors! You don't belong even! You weren't made even! You can't get even! You are a fool—I mean an angel! Here, go back! You're a slave—I mean a queen! Get behind, I tell you! Heavens and earth, woman! Don't you understand? You were divinely ordained to stay behind; you were naturally evolved to stay behind; you look much better behind; you are far happier behind; you are more—ahem—convenient behind; you are constitutionally incapacitated for anything but staying behind; it is absolutely impossible for you to get out from behind; and therefore I will fight till I die to keep you behind! But if you'll only stay behind and keep quiet, we'll be good friends. See?

SHE: I want to get out!

HE: You sha'n't!

SHE: I will!

HE: I'm the strongest, and I'll keep you behind!

SHE: We'll see about that! (*They fight—awfully.*)

Some of the words "He" speaks are sentiments Walter articulated. Some of the action telescopes Charlotte's version of her courtship and marriage with him. Some of the language—"I want to get out!"—looks to the future. As does the cry "I want to get even."

As Grace and Charlotte continued their collaboration on plays, their second effort, "A Pretty Idiot," was, in Charlotte's words, "trembling on the verge of success."[26] The two began writing a new drama based on a colonial theme. The relationship between the women was shifting. Not only was Grace taking Charlotte's place in Walter's life, she was gaining a literary reputation. In March 1890, she had a story published in *New England Magazine,* "A Strange Dinner Party," for which Walter provided the illustrations. Charlotte wrote to Martha, "Grace is rapidly sailing into public recognition. The press is glibly passing her on as 'a young writer of promise' etc, and she is printing pretty fast too."[27]

Charlotte never expressed in writing a word of jealousy for Grace's literary success, but it fed Charlotte's ambition and pushed her to attempt publishable fiction. She wrote to Martha, "I hope to follow soon in her wake." And she did. In early March, she began reworking a story written initially in 1886 and sent it to *New England Magazine.*[28] Charlotte told Martha, "I've sent a story there too, my one ghost story, which I think I read you once. It now figures as 'The Giant Wistaria,' and has a prelude."[29]

In turning to writing short stories, Charlotte was following her father's path, for he had published several volumes of them in the late 1870s. In his day, the short story was largely a maligned genre, and Frederick Perkins wrote its strongest defense after Poe. In his preface to *Devil-Puzzlers* (1877), he argued that the short story was not merely for the youth who was preparing to write a novel; it was a true art form in its own sake. Intense, designed to be read at one sitting, "a short story, in short, is to a long one what a diamond is to a mountain." Among its masters he regarded the American writers Poe and Hawthorne as fit to join Europeans such as Hoffmann, Goethe, and Novalis. A short story could be compared with the lyric poem. It "is the product of a faculty lofty, unique and rare.... a thing of power or beauty or fantastic pleasure.... the visible, appreciable embodiment of the knowledge, wisdom, brightness and love which are in the writers' soul." It carries the "signs and certificates of immortality and fame."[30] Although Frederick Perkins was unable to fulfill this mission with his own stories, his daughter was able to do so.

With such strong words behind her, Charlotte could imagine her short story as deeply serious. In the new prelude, she portrayed a distraught young woman in colonial New England, with a cross of red stone around her neck, standing beside a newly planted wisteria vine. Because she has given birth to a child out of wedlock, to the shame of her parents, her father has condemned her to abandon the child, return to England, and enter into an arranged marriage with the unrefined male cousin she has previously shunned. In the second scene, set a century later, the wisteria vine has grown enormous, and the property is now invaded by lighthearted summer residents, a newly married couple accompanied by friends. The party initially delights in the possibility that the house is haunted, imagines the vine as a "writhing body," hears sounds in the night, and even sees the specter of a woman with a red cross. The pleasure of the summer visitors turns to horror as they discover the skeleton of a child and ultimately the bones and cross of its mother "in the strangling grasp of the roots of the great wistaria." Not simply a ghost story, the work offers a clear indictment of a cruel father's power to rule a daughter in a society that damned an unmarried mother.

At the time she was reworking "The Giant Wistaria," Charlotte became businesslike about writing as a profession. One can see this in the record book of her manuscripts that she began to keep.[31] Under the heading of each month, she listed each piece she sent out for publication and where she sent it. For example, under the very first heading, March 1890, she wrote: "11, 'The Giant Wistaria' to N. E. Magazine, via Walter."[32] At the end of the record book, Charlotte listed possible publishers in what appears to be a ranking order. The *New England Magazine* was not on that list, but Grace was publishing there, and Charlotte's uncle Edward Everett Hale had just turned over its editorship to a younger associate.[33] The *New England Magazine* quickly accepted "The Giant Wistaria" and later sent real money in exchange—$14.

And then Charlotte had her first real taste of fame. A poem, "Similar Cases," published in April in the *Nationalist,* the leading Bellamy organ, attracted favorable attention. This lighthearted but utterly serious poem is an evolutionary tale. The Eohippus, forerunner to the horse, dreams of future glory, but is laughed at by the aristocracy of the early Eocene world.

> Said they, "You always were as small
> And mean as now we see,
> And that's conclusive evidence
> That you're always going to be."

So, too, are an unusual ape and a talented Neolithic man, each drawing the derision of his seemingly more highly placed fellows. *Nationalist* readers understood the poem as a comic parable of their own time. Bellamy's utopian dreams of a cooperative human nature were mocked by conservative opponents, just as evolving species were mocked by ones who at the time seemed more powerful but became biological anachronisms. Women seeking rights could read the poem as foretelling their bright future, currently condemned by the reigning sexual ideology.

"Similar Cases" occasioned a letter of praise from William Dean Howells, regarded as the doyen of American letters. Howells wrote, "I've been wishing ever since I just read it—and I've read it many times with unfailing joy—to thank you for your poem in the April Nationalist. We have had nothing since the Bigelow Papers half so good in a good cause as Similar Cases." His words lifted Charlotte's spirits, and she replied instantly. "Among all the pleasant things I had hoped for in my work this particular gratification was never imagined. And the best part of it is that there is not a man in American whose praise in literature I would rather win!" she averred. Charlotte felt she now had entered the literary firmament.[34]

Then after a very hot day in late August, after she wrote in her journal, "Work hard & achieve nothing!" comes this sentence: "Finish copy of Yellow Wallpaper in the evening." She knew it was good. Four days later, on August 28, she sent it to Howells.[35]

By then, another social movement was pushing Charlotte into the public arena. On July 27, she wrote to Martha, "Now I am helping to organize a Social Purity society here with good success.

I may get to be a dangerous person to know, so you had better hedge a little, hadn't you."[36]

On June 17, 1890, a man had attempted to rape a fifteen-year-old Pasadena girl as she was walking in the neighborhood of relatives in South Pasadena. He asked her to give him blackberries from her basket and, when she refused, struck her, dragged her through a hedge, and threatened to kill her if she resisted. Her screams brought neighbors to her aid and the police on the trail of the assaulter. Within a week of this incident, Charlotte spearheaded an effort to organize a public meeting to discuss social purity, focusing on sexuality education for girls and women. In her call to the meeting she emphasized the importance of arousing public opinion and giving girls "knowledge for their protection." Urging both men and women to attend, she wrote: "The question is too serious for neglect, too awful to be treated lightly, too common to be ignored."[37]

On June 26, 1890, Charlotte addressed the Pasadena public meeting, calling her talk "Causes and Cures." It was the first of what would be her many speeches on social purity in the next months. By the time she wrote to Martha, she had worked with Pasadena physician Dr. Kate S. Black to form a social purity society in Pasadena and was giving a regular set of lectures to its women's study group. She was, at the same time, speaking before Nationalist club groups in Southern California, with likely overlap in the two audiences.

Charlotte's own engagement in sexual discourse can be tracked to May 1884, when, immediately after becoming engaged to Walter, she had subscribed to the *Alpha*. When the Moral Education Society, the organization behind the *Alpha*, had merged into the emerging Purity Society, which was focused more sharply on anti-prostitution efforts, the *Alpha* had ceased publication in 1889. Charlotte, however, had been shaped by the earlier association's purpose and the message of the *Alpha*.

The basic theme of "Causes and Cures" was the need for sexual knowledge. Oddly, however, in a speech about saying the words, Charlotte was so reticent that she never directly addressed the attempted rape. Instead, she emphasized eradicating ignorance and the importance of women teaching children proper respect for womankind, a clear reflection of *Alpha* views. To this she added a strong new argument against social conventions, which allows a glimpse into her own growing sense of social unrest.

> In the subtlest and most civilized form we suffer under it in those delicate but rigid conventions of society which hamper and confine our daily lives and crush out all happy human intercourse between men and women because of our unspoken fear of this very thing!...
>
> We suffer individually in body and mind and soul. In wasting illness and hideous disease, in tortures of remorse and shame and fear, in that slow ruin of the mind that comes to those [who] fall most low.[38]

For some who joined the social purity effort, there was a strong desire, at least rhetorically, to deny the sexual self, especially in women. Charlotte took the opposite position. Armed by Herbert Spencer and the *Alpha*, she affirmed the power of sex and love. She stated, "Naturalists do tell us that there is in the universe a force of 'sexual attraction.' " Common to all life, it was not a power to oppose.

> And it is because we have tried to oppose it by centuries of wrong idea—wretched falsehoods of celibacy and asceticism— because we have overdeveloped it by centuries of other wrong idea—wretched falsehoods of license and excess—because we have hedged it about with lies, and bound it down with laws, and smothered it with shame and loathing—; that the highest holiest force in nature, our most perfect happiness and joy, this link between God and man—becomes a thing we blush to mention to each other!"

Although often polluted, the sexual instinct was like a clear stream that "brings health and strength and joy." It was a "veritable river of life—this current which embraces all humanity!"[39]

This strong affirmation of sexual love may have been why Charlotte referred to herself as "a dangerous person," perhaps one Martha might choose to "hedge" on knowing. It is intriguing that in her very next sentence in her letter to Martha—suggesting some kind of link—Charlotte then wrote, "When my awful story 'The Yellow Wallpaper' comes out, you must try and read it."[40]

What caused the association? Not sex, at least not directly. Indirectly perhaps, for beginning at least in 1887 she had found she could live with Walter, once a "nightmare husband," only under "a certain approximation to Alpha doctrines" that countered his persistent sexual demands. Moreover, Charlotte likely experienced these two expressions, the talk and the story, as assertions of a new self, the self suddenly changed, as she had earlier written to Martha, "wildly, darkly, strangely."

When, in this July letter, she turned to "The Yellow Wall-Paper," Charlotte gave important information about the story:

> Walter says he has read it <u>four</u> times, and thinks it the most ghastly tale he ever read. Says it beats Poe and Doré! But that's only a husband's opinion.
>
> I read the thing to three women here however, and I never saw such squirms! Daylight too. It's a simple tale, but highly unpleasant.

Squirms were a high compliment, as Martha knew. When, in 1879, Charlotte had read to her mother Edward Bulwer-Lyttons *The Haunted and the Haunter: House and Brain,* she had noted in her journal, "We were both permeated with cold chills. I like it." She had then reread it to Martha and commented, "Mutual and creepy admiration."[41]

Charlotte likely wrote "The Yellow Wall-Paper," on June 6 and 7, 1890, five months after Walter had returned to Providence.[42] The two continued to write to each other regularly, and he assisted in fostering her work. Walter's copy of the story has surfaced with these words in his hand, "This story seems to me a masterpiece! I've read it a half dozen times, first and last, and each time it fairly makes me shudder."[43]

In her record book of manuscripts, Charlotte logged on June 14 that she sent "The Yellow Wall-Paper" to *Scribner's*. It is likely that she was referring to it (and to "The Giant Wistaria") when she wrote her journal entry of June 17, 1890: "Read two ghost stories at Mrs. Mitchells"—probably to several members of her adult women's class. Charlotte had just received Howells's letter the previous day. Perhaps his praise emboldened her to try the story out on her captive audience.

When Charlotte wrote to Martha in late July, she was facing the bittersweet end of her idyll with Grace in Pasadena. Accompanied by her mother, Grace intended to follow Walter and travel east, leaving Charlotte in Pasadena. Charlotte entertained some hope that she might join Grace briefly in New York after New Year's (perhaps with the money from her soon to be well-placed story). And she allowed herself to imagine going to visit Martha in Hingham: "Talk! & I shall bring coca tablets!"

The letter to Martha conveyed Charlotte's soaring ambitions for "The Yellow Wall-Paper." Her professional writer's long list of publishing outlets was headed by the *Atlantic Monthly*, the *Century*, *Scribner's*, and *Harper's*.[44] Not telling Martha that she had already sent the story to *Scribner's*, Charlotte wrote, "If none of the big things will take it I mean to try the New York Ledger. Have you seen that in its new form? Kipling and Stevenson etc. etc. write for that now, so I guess I can." She was already imagining herself in the world of the serious popular writers of the time.

Flush with the triumphs of writing and speaking before enthusiastic audiences, Charlotte was riding high in late July, bragging about all her successes. She expressed in the same breath how she had risked talking about sex in public and how she had broken through to write a very good "ghastly tale." She believed she held the makings of a literary and commercial success in her hands.

"The Yellow Wall-Paper"

L et us imagine Charlotte in Pasadena on June 6, 1890, an extraordinarily hot day, as she sat down to write a story, an ambitious and paying story, in the manner of Edgar Allan Poe. She drew on all her resources—her personal experiences, her educated knowledge of design, and her broad reading, which included familiarity with the haunted-house tales of Bulwer-Lytton, Poe, and Dickens. Whatever her intentions may have been at the outset, the story moved beyond them to engage her at a very deep level. What she had willfully attempted to forget she allowed herself now, perhaps unwittingly, to remember—the "unutterable pain."[1]

To bring to mind the suffering she was recalling, we need to return to the agonized cry at the end of her long letter to Dr. Mitchell in April 1887, before she entered treatment: "There is something the matter with my head.... It is harder to write every day.... I can't think. I can't remember, I can't grasp an idea.... I fear every day to lose memory entirely.... I am all alone in the house or I couldn't write this. People tire me frightfully.... I'm running down like a clock—could go one [*sic*] scribbling now indefinitely—but the letters don't come right."[2]

Three years later, Gilman set her story in a house leased for the summer.[3] The 1888 summer in Bristol, Rhode Island, was still fresh in her mind, but in her story she elaborated a grand version of a country house to give it gothic possibilities. The old farmhouse became one of the "ancestral halls....A colonial mansion, a hereditary estate."[4] She allowed herself to think of a woman who was, as she herself had once felt she was, on the verge of insanity. Perhaps recalling Bertha Mason, the mad wife in Charlotte Brontë's *Jane Eyre,* Gilman placed her character in an upper room of the house, isolated, attended only by John, her physician-husband, and Jennie, her sister-in-law.[5] Gilman left it ambiguous whether this nursery "playroom and gymnasium" with its barred windows had been inhabited by other suffering women in the past. Gilman worked within the horror genre of Romantic fiction and followed its ghostly template, but by domesticating her tale and grounding it in realistic details, she enhanced its uncanny effect and opened up a world of suggestion and potential interpretation.[6]

Most important, Gilman allowed her primary character to speak in her own voice.[7] The story is an inner tale, written as diary entries in the first person by a woman in distress. Perhaps without intending it, Gilman drew on her own utterances in her journals, beloved volumes that she kept with her at all times. They contained a record of her own unstable voice, and in them she could track her swings of mood and insight from month to month or find alternative feelings and perspectives even in the same entry. The most telling example is what Charlotte wrote on the last evening of 1886, as she summed up the year: "I leave behind me tonight a year of much happiness growth and progress; also of great misery." She was then reflecting on the span of time that began in Pasadena, after she left Walter and Katharine, and now ended in Providence. "But the happiness and progress are real and well founded; and the misery was owing mainly to a diseased condition of the nervous system. It is past, I hope forever." She then wondered: had she lost her "self abandoning enthusiasm and fierce determination in the cause of right"? Was she, as she put it, a "traitor to my cause"? Or was her feeling of self-betrayal only "a lingering trace of the disordered period just past"?[8] It is this kind of uncertainty that underlies "The Yellow Wall-Paper." Charlotte's own earlier wavering voice finds its way into what the fictional narrator tells what is said about her and what she says about herself.

What is new in the story is that now the fictive narrator's voice is clearly inflected at the outset by the doubts and uncertainties of powerlessness.[9] What gives "The Yellow Wall-Paper" its impelling force is the way the author places the narrator's voice within a world that denies her the ability to define herself and to live by her own lights. She is in a conventional nineteenth-century marriage under the dominion of her husband, who has total command of the kingdom of their house. While in a political arena domination and submission can be limited, allowing a realm of privacy in which escape is possible, in this sphere the rule of the husband is total, extending to life's most intimate areas. In the months preceding the writing of this story, in the poetry and prose of "Wedded Bliss," "Reassurance," and "The Quarrel," Gilman had riveted on male dominance and female subordination in love and marriage. Now in "The Yellow Wall-Paper," the reader experiences male supremacy in marriage through the consciousness of the wife narrating the tale. That she is experiencing mental distress makes her more vulnerable—and, ironically, more acutely aware.[10]

Initially, the character is perceived by others around her to be only mildly ill. In the first passage, Gilman drew on the distinction—important in her era—between nervous illness and insanity, understood as brain disease.[11] She put these words in the narrator's voice, but as quoted elements, with only slight comment:

If a physician of high standing, and one's own husband, assures friends and relatives that there is really nothing the matter with one but temporary nervous depression,—a slight hysterical tendency,—what is one to do? My brother is also a physician and also of high standing, and he says the same thing. (39)

For a "temporary nervous depression" with symptoms such as fatigue, agitation, crying, and hysterical outbursts, the prescription in the story is rest, air, absence of stimulation, and a ban on writing. In addition, the husband offers doses of moral treatment. "He says no one but myself can help me out of it, that I must use my will and self-control and not let any silly fancies run away with me" (45).

All of this is home cure, prescribed by a husband (and brother). But beyond it lies the larger world of the nerve specialists. Gilman has John speak in the authoritative voice not only of husband but of physician, a voice that likely drew its inspiration from the male doctors Charlotte consulted, including Mitchell, whose name she invokes.[12] The narrator quotes her husband and follows this with her own comment:

> John says if I don't pick up faster he shall send me to Weir Mitchell in the Fall.
> But I don't want to go there at all. I had a friend who was in his hands once, and she says he is just like John and my brother only more so! (44)

John gives her a "schedule prescription for each hour in the day" and insists on bed rest in the nursery where the air is good (40). Jennie, her domestic sister-in-law, takes care of the house, and there is Mary, a servant, to care for the baby. The narrator is not allowed to see company or to write.

Many have equated this treatment with that of S. Weir Mitchell, but it was not his regimen. It has, in fact, many elements that Mitchell opposed, such as being surrounded by family members. Much of the time the central character is unsupervised, left alone for long periods unobserved. She takes all manner of sedatives and tonics and alcohol. The voice of John, her doctor-husband, is not simply that of Mitchell but combines his with that of a more traditional dispenser of moral treatment, a man perhaps like Dr. Knight of Providence. As the story unfolds, John's statements also contain echoes of Walter's views and of the prohibitions against fantasies that Mary Perkins laid on Charlotte in girlhood. The experience of the narrator does recall, however, Charlotte's own fears about Mitchell before meeting him, when she begged him in her letter "not to laugh at me as every one else does, not to say it is 'almost as bad as a disease' as one of my friends does, not to turn me off."[13]

The fictive narrator does not respond well to her husband's regimen, particularly its proscription against writing. She sets down her own judgments, now in a declarative mode.

> Personally, I disagree with their ideas.
> Personally, I believe that congenial work with excitement and change would do me good" (39).

With the very act of writing, she resists her husband's dominion. Elsewhere, the fictional journal contains humorous asides that counter John's will, mock his authority. "John is a physician, and *perhaps...perhaps* that is one reason I do not get well faster" (39).[14]

She tries to write, at least at the beginning (and, of course, there is this account, a series of twelve journal entries), but as she proceeds, she states that writing has come to exhaust her. She adds that this is because of the opposition she faces and thus the need to write only in secret. (39). She states her own and her husband's position.

> I sometimes fancy that in my condition if I had less opposition and more society and stimulus—but John says the very worst thing I can do is to think about my condition, and I confess it always makes me feel badly.
> So I will let it alone, and write about the house. (39–40)

And thus, the protagonist wills herself to shift her attention away from her own infirmities and toward the house. As she turns to describe it, she begins with its beauty and isolation, its handsome garden. Then she takes up its history, some legal trouble resulting in its being uninhabited for years that causes her to remark, "That spoils my ghostliness, I am afraid, but I don't care—there is something strange about the house—I can feel it." She relates telling this to John, but he refuses to accept her sense of things and attributes her feeling about the house to a physical cause: "he said what I felt was a *draught,* and shut the window" (40). He thus reduces her interior life of feeling and imagination to physical phenomena and bodily reaction. For much of her own life, Charlotte herself had coped with her own inner self in this way. Moreover, as a reader of Poe and of Bulwer-Lytton's *The Haunted and the Haunter,* she knew the narrative tradition of the rational scientist confronting the supernatural.

The fictional narrator confesses that she now gets "unreasonably angry" at her husband. Since she had not previously been "so sensitive," she explains that she thinks this emotion is "due to this nervous condition" (40). When Charlotte was experiencing trouble during her pregnancy and following Kate's birth, she used this language about herself, and Dr. Keller reinforced it. Now her character describes the moral treatment at her husband's hands, using perhaps the words that Knight and Mitchell addressed to Charlotte: "John says if I feel so I shall neglect proper self-control; so I take pains to control myself—before him at least, and that makes me very tired" (40).

At this point, the narrator turns her attention to the room she inhabits and its hideous wallpaper. In the work she never claimed, *Gems of Art for the Home and Fireside,* Gilman had demonstrated her awareness of the prevailing aesthetic principles that were believed to govern good art. She drew on this knowledge to imagine an arabesque design on the wallpaper in a color that is "repellant, almost revolting; a smouldering unclean yellow" (41).[15] She likely began with a memory of Poe's "Ligeia," for he had set much of it in a room with a tapestry of "arabesque figures" against a yellow background.

After a break in the story, the narrator takes it up two weeks later and tells the reader more about her condition. Although she repeats that her case is "not serious," she adds:

> But these nervous troubles are dreadfully depressing.
> John doesn't know how much I really suffer. He knows there is no *reason* to suffer, and that satisfies him. Of course it is only nervous. It does weigh on me so not to do my duty in any way. I meant to be such a help to John, such a real rest and comfort, and here I am a comparative burden already! Nobody would believe what an effort it is to do what little I am able. To dress and entertain and order things. (41)

These passages could be out of Charlotte's own diary, with its shifts in her own voice as she tried to live out Walter's conception—and her own—of the good wife. So could this brief comment about her "dear baby," with the exception of the child's gender: "And yet I can *not* be with him, it makes me so nervous" (41).

John is presented complexly, but always through the narrator's eyes and ears. He is a man of the daylight—rational, practical, materialistic, and unimaginative. At times he is authoritative, at times demeaning. The narrator insists with repetitions that her husband "loves" her; but she sometimes follows with aspects of her situation or behavior that he "hates"—when she is sick, for example, or when she is writing.[16] At one moment, she tells the reader how she tried to get John to repaper the upstairs room where she lived, a room he shared with her at night. He initially agreed but then decided that a change was a mistake, saying "nothing was worse for a nervous patient than to give way to such fancies" (41). She then asked to live in the pretty rooms downstairs. John's response: "he took me in his arms and called me a blessed little goose." He further belittled her request by saying that if she wished, he would live in the cellar (42). His withering sweet talk resolved the issue. She stays upstairs in the nursery.

Gradually she begins to enjoy the view from the window. She starts to "fancy" that she sees people walking in the beautiful garden. Her husband then offers moral treatment again. "John has cautioned me not to give way to fancy in the least. He says that with my imaginative power and habit of story making, a nervous weakness like mine is sure to lead to all manner of excited fancies, and that I ought to use my will and good sense to check the tendency. So I try" (42). When Charlotte wrote to Mitchell, she related that when she was thirteen, her mother told her that her fancies were "dangerous and wrong" and she was never again to think of them. She revealed to Mitchell that she obeyed, but what took the place of fancies were "a sea of Poe-like visions, carrying my dream life through a most wicked and unhealthy world." Now in her story Charlotte revisited this prohibition and its profound effects.

The character offers a verbal counter to the proscription against fantasy. What if giving way to fancy were helpful? "I think sometimes that if I were only well enough to write a little it would relieve the press of ideas and rest me." What if she had people around her to offer encouragement and criticism of her writing? She thinks of her cousins, Henry and Julia, forbidden to visit until she is well. John says "he would as soon put fireworks in my pillowcase as to let me have those stimulating people about now" (42).

As she returns to the wallpaper, it now comes alive. Here the reader experiences the beginning of the narrator's descent into madness. "There is a recurrent spot where the pattern lolls like a broken neck, and two bulbous eyes stare at you upside down.... Up and down and sideways they crawl, and those absurd unblinking eyes are everywhere" (42). She then describes her earlier fancies as a child when the inanimate objects of her bedroom seemed to her alive at night.

With that there is an interruption, as reality intervenes:

There comes John's sister—such a dear girl as she is, and so careful of me! I mustn't let her find me writing.

She is a perfect—, an enthusiastic—, housekeeper, and hopes for no better profession. I verily believe she thinks it is the writing which made me sick! (43)

The chronicler tells the reader that she writes only when Jennie is out and visible from the window. As this passage comes to a close, the reader learns for the first time that the narrator is beginning to see a figure sulking behind the pattern in the wall paper.

Following another break, the story resumes after the Fourth of July. The narrator is getting worse. John makes the suggestion that he may need to send her to Dr. Mitchell. "I cry at nothing and cry most of the time" (44). We know that Charlotte herself suffered in this way.

The wallpaper becomes an increasing source of fascination. As the narrator lies on the bed, she follows the pattern. "It is as good as gymnastics, I assure you" (44). She describes the visual movements and considers the flawed principles of design. She describes the paper in many different ways, its "interminable grotesques" (45), now like "wallowing sea-weeds in full chase" (44), now like "an terminable string of toadstools, budding and sprouting in endless convolutions" (47). She begins to have trouble writing, even to the point of saying, "I don't feel able." Yet she continues to feel that writing is important. "I *must* say what I feel and think in some way—it is such a relief" (45). She is lying down more. John is feeding her cod liver oil and a diet of rare meat and wine and ale to build her up, as advised by Mitchell and others to increase fat and blood. (John also gives her tonics, which Mitchell did not allow during the rest cure.) She tries to persuade John to allow her to visit her cousins, but "I did not make out a very good case for myself, for I was crying before I had finished." It is hard for her to think. "Just this nervous weakness, I suppose" (45). He carries her upstairs to bed "in his strong arms," reads to her, says endearing things, and exhorts her to use self-control. At night, they share the room.

She relates that although "It is so hard to talk with John about my case, because he is so wise, and because he loves me so," she has tried to do so (46). In the moonlight, she has seen the figure who "seemed to shake the pattern, just as if she wanted to get out (46)." At the point of writing, Gilman may have been recalling the "Quarrel," written only months before—the "She" voicing the demand "I want to get out!"

The narrator's movement out of bed to feel the wallpaper awakens John, and she tells him that she wants to leave the house. He gives her practical reasons why they must stay and then tells her she is improving: "you really are better, dear, whether you can see it or not." He adds, "I am a doctor, dear, and I know." When she replies that he is wrong, he gives her a hug and answers in his demeaning fashion, "Bless her little heart!...she shall be as sick as she pleases!" (46)

When she tries to explain that she may be better only "in body," he cuts her off. "My darling...I beg of you, for my sake and our child's sake, as well as for your own, that you will never for one instant let *that* idea enter your mind. There is nothing so dangerous, so fascinating, to a temperament like yours. It is a false and foolish fancy" (47). One must exercise will to banish the wrong ideas. This, we know, Charlotte believed and continued to believe. Is this dangerous idea, this "false and foolish fancy," a fear of insanity? We know that Charlotte herself was once deeply afraid of brain disease.

When John thinks she has gone to sleep, the narrator looks at the wallpaper. At this point there is another break. As she resumes writing, she shifts to considering only the wallpaper and her reactions to it. In the moonlight, the light of gothic possibility, the pattern becomes bars, and behind them she begins to see a woman.[17] During the day the woman is quiet. More breaks occur in the narrative, at closer intervals. Jennie complains that there are stains, "yellow smooches," on the clothing of her brother and sister-in-law. As John suggests that his wife is improving despite the wallpaper, she laughs. "I had no intention of telling him it was *because* of the wall-paper!" She fears that he might take her away before "I have found it out" (48). One week remains of their stay.

Each short section picks up on a facet of the wallpaper. Its color is now a "sickly penetrating suggestive yellow," and its lingering smell is like "the *color* of the paper" (49). It is possible that Charlotte's varied and continuing use of drugs, such as cocaine, enabled her to blend sight and smell here, and that in writing this story she was able to recall in her imagination a wide range of drug-induced experiences of wallpaper or other objects that seemed to come alive. Or it may have been only that she was building on literary memory animated by the haunted-house stories of other writers.[18]

The reader learns of a low yellow streak going around the room near the baseboard, a "long straight even smooch, as if it had been rubbed over and over" (49). Later discussion of the protagonist's yellow-stained clothing suggests that she has caused the smooch, or at least contributed to it, with her catlike creeping.[19] The narrator sees the pattern move, and she believes that the woman—or women—in the wallpaper are shaking it or disturbing it by crawling. She now thinks that the wallpaper-woman breaks free during the day and creeps in the garden and out into the country, "creeping as fast as a cloud shadow in a high wind" (50).[20] She tells of her own creeping in the nursery bedroom, locking its door in the daytime, causing the reader to see her growing identification with the wallpaper-woman. She now says that she wishes John would sleep away from her at night, for "I don't want anybody to get that woman out at night but me" (50).

Two days before their departure from the house, the narrator is struggling to tear the paper from the walls. Once the passively submissive wife, she is now an active force, and her language is direct and clear.[21] She overhears her sister-in-law give a good report of her days, that she sleeps a lot. On the next-to-last night of the stay, John does not come back to the house. Throughout the night, as the woman in the wallpaper begins "to crawl and shake the pattern," the protagonist helps her. "I pulled and she shook, I shook and she pulled, and before morning we had peeled off yards of that paper" (51).

The mood of the story grows ominous; the narrator's language suggests violence.[22] The next day, when Jennie sees the wall, she suggests that she wouldn't mind removing the wallpaper herself. The central character responds, now fiercely, even dangerously. "But I am here, and no person touches this paper but me—not *alive!*" (51). She locks the door to her room and throws the key outside. She has a rope to tie up the wallpaper-woman if she attempts to escape. With the furniture now out of the room, except for the bedstead, the narrator finds herself unable to reach high enough to remove the top section of the paper. After trying and failing to move the bed, she states, "and then I got so angry I bit off a little piece at one corner—but it hurt my teeth" (52). The pattern that remains mocks her, "All those strangled heads and bulbous eyes and waddling fungus growths just shriek with derision!" She is so angry that she wants to jump out of the window but cannot because of the bars. She is aware that there are many women outside, creeping fast. "I wonder if they all came out of that wall paper as I did?" (52)

She is now fully the woman she imagines she has freed from the paper. She is the one secured by the rope. "I suppose I shall have to get back behind the pattern when it comes night, and that is hard!" In the meantime, she is enjoying creeping around the room "smoothly on the floor" where her shoulder "just fits in that long smooch around the wall, so I can not lose my way" (52).

John is at the door. Unable to open it, he calls for an axe. She tells him repeatedly, "very gently and slowly," that she cannot come out and that the key is outside near the door. As he finds her, John cries out, "For God's sake what are you doing!" She continues creeping, looking at him over her shoulder. " 'I've got out at last,' said I, 'in spite of you and Jane! And I've pulled off most of the paper, so you can't put me back!' " As he faints in her path, she continues to move forward in such a way, she observes in the last line of the story, "that I had to creep over him!" (53).[23]

Charlotte knew immediately that she had created a powerful story. She would try for "the big things," publications at the top of her list, but if they did not take it, she would send it to the new venture that was publishing noted authors of her day. As she mailed "The Yellow Wall-Paper" to Howells, her ambitions for the story soared.

Although Charlotte began writing "The Yellow Wall-Paper" as one of her many efforts to gain a living, as the story unfolded, it took on a life quite unforeseen. It emerged out of the white heat of creativity as a deep probing of her own experience and her deepest feelings. She used all the resources available to her to imagine a woman in psychic trouble and to do so in the woman's own unstable voice. As she wrote, Charlotte allowed herself to journey farther and deeper into her imagination. As the woman's calls for help went unheeded, Charlotte stayed with her character as she descended into madness. Charlotte would not let herself remember. And then she did.

CHAPTER 10 ••••••••••••••••••••••

Beyond "The Yellow Wall-Paper"

S ending "The Yellow Wall-Paper" to William Dean
Howells on August 28, 1890, was an important
moment for Charlotte Perkins Gilman, but it proved
to be only a step toward the publication of the story.
The well-connected Howells put it in the hands of
Horace Scudder, editor of the *Atlantic Monthly*. In declining to
publish it, Scudder wrote, "I could not forgive myself if I made
others as miserable as I have made myself!" After Scudder's rejection, on October 26, Gilman sent the story to Henry Austin.[1]

Austin had been editor of the *Nationalist* when "Similar
Cases" was published in April, but by the autumn of 1890 he
was a literary agent associated with Edward Everett Hale. Curiously, when Gilman sent Hale a set of poems in October 1890,
in her manuscript log she identified this familiar figure in her
life as "Traveller Literary Syndicate," the title she used for Austin. Hale had revived the *New England Magazine,* which had
recently taken "The Giant Wistaria." It is likely that Austin
moved the story along to the magazine's current editor, Edwin
Mead. Howells later claimed credit for placing the story, and he
may well have encouraged Mead, who was his protégé. But in

the incestuous world of late nineteenth-century literary Boston, Gilman had her own strong connections with the *New England Magazine*.[2]

"The Yellow Wall-Paper" was published in its January 1892 issue. A letter, probably from a physician, summarized the work in the *Boston Evening Transcript* as "a sad story of a young wife passing through the gradations from slight mental derangement to raving lunacy." Echoing Scudder's sentiments, the letter writer stated that the story was "difficult to lay aside," for its "somewhat sensational style" held the reader "in morbid fascination to the end." Moreover, it was questionable wisdom to allow such a work to appear "in print." Since the story could bring pain to those touched by insanity and danger to those struggling against a hereditary predisposition for the disease, the writer asked whether it should be "allowed to pass without protest, without severest censure."[3]

Gilman was never offered money for "The Yellow Wall-Paper," and as far as is known, she never had a chance to review the editorial changes made in the first and later editions.[4] By the time of its first printing, her interests and work lay elsewhere.

In the summer of 1890, after Charlotte had written "The Yellow Wall-Paper," Grace traveled east with her mother and under her chaperonage spent time with Walter in Providence. Charlotte was not able at that time to visit either Grace or Martha in the East. Later, Grace went abroad with a female friend to await at a distance Walter's divorce and her future. Once Grace left Pasadena, Charlotte's life there changed. Their active collaboration was effectively over, as well as their almost daily intimacy. Charlotte was left with Kate, her pupils, Dr. Channing, and a wide social circle. With his wife and daughter away, Dr. Channing came by Charlotte's cottage more and more often, but she now experienced his constant visiting as a chore and a bore. She still had her work in social purity circles and play readings, rehearsals, and performances, but with Grace's departure, much of the joy of her life in

Pasadena evaporated. More and more, her diary entries tell of her fatigue and her poverty.

Writing to Grace after her arrival in Europe in early December, Charlotte tried to express to her what the loss of her presence meant. "Do you know I think I suffer more in giving you up than in Walter—for you were all joy to me....I know I was getting very near to you and now that dreadful angel has come and swallowed you and I am nowhere." She then ventured even further. "It is awful to be a man inside and not be able to marry the women you love! When Martha married it cracked my heart a good deal— your loss will finish it."[5] These are unexpected words from her in 1890, harkening back to her younger feelings for Martha Luther but conveying greater self-knowledge.

The intense feelings Charlotte revealed to Grace anticipated her next step. In mid-September 1891, Charlotte moved with Kate to Oakland. She believed that she had a better chance there for remunerative work as a writer. Perhaps more important in propelling the move was that she was becoming emotionally involved with Adelina Knapp, whom she called Delle, a reporter in the Bay area who lent her money for the move and promised support. That this relationship was clearly passionate was something Charlotte avowed a few years later.

The period from 1891 to 1894 in Oakland was rough for Charlotte by every measure. Her literary aspirations and desire for love got mired in poverty, responsibility for others, and personal turmoil. Charlotte and Delle moved into a boardinghouse together, along with Kate. In February 1892, Charlotte became the effective operator of this boardinghouse for nine, in charge of housekeeping and cooking. Mary Perkins moved in with Charlotte, who nursed her during her terminal illness. Charlotte initiated divorce proceedings in 1892, prompting vicious stories in the San Francisco papers. In the rhetoric of the day, she was held up for public ridicule as a "new woman" giving up her higher calling of wifehood and motherhood for the lesser life of the public arena. It was a time of immense strain.

Charles Walter Stetson, "To Charlotte—In Memoriam" (portrait of Charlotte in the Pre-Raphaelite manner), 1891. Schlesinger Library, Radcliffe Institute, Harvard University.

Mary Perkins died in March 1893. In the intervening period, Charlotte had made contact with her father, who lived across the bay from Oakland in San Francisco. He never visited her or his dying ex-wife until the day after her death, when he came to see Charlotte and began to help her out with a small monthly allowance. Despite all her many efforts—writing, lecturing, keeping the boardinghouse—Charlotte could not support herself and her child. Her relationship with Delle soured and ended with terrible outbursts and bad feelings. Some years later, when Charlotte was contemplating marriage with a man, she wrote to him that it possible that her earlier letters to Delle might surface, letters "most fully owning the really passionate love I had for her." If these letters were given to the press (as had hers to Walter), she continued, there might be stories with the headlines "Revelations of a Peculiar Past! Mrs. Stetson's Love Affair with a Woman. Is this 'Friendship!'" The many words here—*passionate, peculiar, love affair*—are keys that informed her fiancé (and that confirm today) that this was, in the language of our era, a lesbian relationship.[6]

The divorce was denied in 1892 in Providence, so Charlotte filed in California. When it was granted there in 1894, there was more hostile publicity; but then it was over. Walter and Grace made plans to marry immediately. Charlotte took advantage of her father's trip to the East Coast to send Kate to them. Now living alone for the first time, Charlotte moved to San Francisco, edited the *Impress,* a publication of the Pacific Coast Women's Press Association, and reestablished herself with new friends. When the paper folded, she declared herself free and of no address. In the next years, she tried Hull House, went on long lecture tours, worked for Bellamy-style socialism, visited friends and associates, and wrote.

In the next two and a half decades, she found success as a public intellectual, building an extraordinary career. Her lectures took her to cities all across the country, great and small. In 1898, she published *Women and Economics: A Study of the Economic Relation between Men and Women as a Factor in Social Relations,* and it brought her immediate and lasting fame both in the United States and abroad. Its central argument was that unlike all other animals, only in the human species does the female depend on the male for food. The exchange of food for sex lay at the heart of marriage and explained women's subordination to men and the overdevelopment of human female sexual characteristics. Gilman saw women's domestic labor as mired in tradition, holding down the human species. To counter this drag, women—freed from household tasks—need to enter the world of paid work with its discipline and higher morality. Although Gilman saw the economic relation between men and women as the central issue, she became a strong advocate and speaker for women's suffrage.[7]

The publisher of *Women and Economics* reissued "The Yellow Wall-Paper" in 1899 in a stand-alone volume. Contrary to what was once believed, the story at that time evoked significant comment for what it said about marriage and women's lives. Howells later included it in his *Great Modern American Stories,* which came out in 1920, commenting, "I shiver over it as much as I did when I first read it in manuscript, though I agree with the editor of *The Atlantic* of the time that it was too terribly good to be printed."[8]

Other books followed in a steady stream from Gilman's pen. In the early 1900s, she published *Concerning Children* (1900), *The Home: Its Work and Influence* (1903), and *Human Work* (1904). She elaborated her scheme of kitchenless houses and collective childcare to free women from domestic chores so that they could engage in the labor of the public world. Gilman was a regular columnist in periodicals and newspapers and for a time served as editor of the *Woman's Journal.* In 1909, she established the *Forerunner,* the magazine that served as a major vehicle for her writing until 1916. Much of her fiction was initially serialized in it, including *Herland: A Feminist Utopian Novel.* In 1911, she published *The Man-made World or Our Androcentric Culture.* After *His Religion and Hers: A Study of the Faith of Our Fathers and the Work of Our Mothers* (1923), she wrote her autobiography, *The*

Living of Charlotte Perkins Gilman (issued posthumously) and continued to publish articles until her death in 1935. Gilman's remarkable body of work established her both as the preeminent theorist of the women's movement of the early twentieth century and a bridge to feminism's second wave.

And what of Charlotte's private life?

It changed in a surprising and wonderful way, one that, to put it simply, created a framework for her great public accomplishments. With "The Yellow Wall-Paper," Charlotte lanced some of the wounds of the past. Beginning in 1897, she faced the scars that remained and—at last—moved beyond them.

She paid a visit in New York to her first cousin, George Houghton Gilman, seven years her junior, in March 1897. They had been friends as children, meeting on festive occasions at the home of Edward Everett Hale and carrying on a lively and affectionate correspondence. The son of one of Frederick's well-placed sisters, Houghton had advantages Charlotte envied—a loving mother, a beautiful home in Norwich, Connecticut, and a fine education. On his father's side, Houghton was a nephew of the president of Johns Hopkins University and had graduated from that institution. He had then gone to law school at Columbia and at age twenty-nine had begun a legal practice in New York City. Cultured, an enthusiast of mathematics, and a gentle soul, he appealed to Charlotte. In 1897, she saw in this boy grown into a man a physical beauty not apparent in his photographs. She liked him. He connected her to the family she had largely lost, and he remembered her in her wholehearted girlhood, before the clouds of depression had gathered. As she once put it, "One thing that makes me hold you very near is that you knew <u>me</u>—me before I died"; this knowledge he had of her, she believed, helped her keep faith with herself.[9]

Charlotte and Houghton began spending Sundays and some evenings together, seeing the sights in New York, dining, and going to the theater. At this point in her life she had a base in New York but traveled west and south to lecture and write for many months

"Cousin Charlotte, Here's looking at you. George Houghton Gilman, April 1897." Schlesinger Library, Radcliffe Institute, Harvard University.

at a time. When away and not lecturing, she lived as a kind of writer-in-residence in the households of others, and she sojourned occasionally in a number of reform communities of the like-minded. When distant from Houghton, she wrote him long letters almost daily, and he kept them. Living a peripatetic life, Charlotte savored but did not save his letters. She began their correspondence in the guise of the older cousin simply enjoying the friendship of one seven years younger. As her letters slid into love letters, they developed into remarkable explorations of her consciousness. She wanted Houghton to know exactly who she was, to have no illusions about his older and increasingly famous cousin. In these letters, she sought to be absolutely frank with him.

Charlotte's letters to Houghton give a window on her mental state and offer insight into how she thought about the years between 1881 and 1890. She still had ups and downs, and her first depressive episode after remeeting Houghton in March 1897 came in June of that year. As she tried to explain to him what she was experiencing, she wrote that she had before been "buoyant" but now woke up "tired" and felt her own weight. He thought she was describing a spell of dizziness. No, she wrote, it was that she was unhappy: "things are grey, and I have no strength and get tired easy, and my head isn't clear. That's the mischief. I lose my grip mentally." In subsequent letters, she clarified that when she spoke of darkness she was talking about "her mental atmosphere that darkens—not the scenery. . . . I am simply low spirited and weak." Her condition in 1897 was not that of 1887, however. "This little waft of the last few weeks," she wrote, "was only a shade of pale blue over the landscape—a thing I could reason around and see through. At its long worst it meant pitch blackness—unillumined and unilluminable."[10]

As Charlotte became more depressed over the next weeks, she tried to explain that there was no way Houghton could help her. "You see nobody <u>can</u> be near me when I've fallen through a hole; I <u>have</u> to be alone because I've gone there! And I have to be miserable because that is the condition." At this point, after many such episodes, she believed that she would come back, that although she had to withdraw for the summer, she was likely to return "companionable and smiling, in the Fall." Perhaps in response to Houghton, she wrote that while summer heat did affect her, it did not explain her state. She believed that her "brain-sinking melancholy business is a good honest disease," one that she had experienced on and off since 1883.[11]

As Charlotte recovered, she began to let Houghton increasingly into her intellectual and political world. She was thinking out *Women and Economics* and used him as a sounding board. She asked him to help her with research. He differed from her in his personal style—his restraint and gentleness—and in his politics. While she was a self-proclaimed socialist who believed in collective stewardship, he was focused on the individual, and his taste ran to mathematics and the arts. Shocked that he did not know who Jane Addams was, she wrote "Not know Hull House & Jane Addams! Behold the deficiencies of a college education!" He was to immediately get *Hull House Maps and Papers,* and she would enlighten him further on her return.[12]

They were together in August. When Walter, Grace, and Katharine traveled to New York on their way to Europe, their visit and the time with Kate evoked in Charlotte complicated feelings. After Charlotte and Houghton talked at length, she sighed with relief at his acceptance of her. Houghton was neither "alienated nor a scoffer" but "patient and kind and sympathetic." She had been able to cry in his presence, and he had not rejected her. She saw the possibility that if she accepted his friendship and was "not ashamed to be plaintive and weepful occasionally," she might "come into a far healthier state of mind."[13]

She began her great book *Women and Economics* in September, writing rapidly, at one point thirty-five hundred words in three hours. As her confidence mounted, so did her expressions of the pleasure Houghton gave her. She found him just right, and she enjoyed it that he liked her for herself, devoting a full morning to a letter, writing to her merely for his own pleasure. When

Charlotte's carte de visite as lecturer, 1899. Schlesinger Library, Radcliffe Institute, Harvard University.

Houghton spoke about not doing anything to deserve her regard, she wrote to him that what she cared about was nothing that he did, only what he was.[14]

In mid-September, Charlotte visited Martha in Hingham and then went into Boston, where she was courted now by those eager to publish her work, and saw Alice Stone Blackwell at the offices of the *Woman's Journal*. She was soaring.[15] But soon afterward, she began a pullback. As in 1883, she needed to withdraw. Trying to explain to Houghton why she had been so unpleasant to him when they had last been together, she used words that revealed what today would be called problems of intimacy. She put it this way: "as soon as any one comes near me and takes hold, I wobble awfully." She had grown fond of Houghton, and at moments "I don't like it. It makes me unreasonable. It makes me feel—where I don't want to feel; and think, where I don't want to think." Being with him sometimes brought out the worst in her. Feelings of wanting to be cared for made her have the urge to bolt, and she became nastier and nastier. She used this letter to suggest to Houghton that he cut her off.[16]

He remained, and she was left to explain and explain again. After a subsequent act that made her ashamed—it seems she had asked him to kiss her—she had turned cold. What was this about? In her explanation to him, she turned not to brain disease but, unexpectedly, to feeling. All throughout her life, she wrote, she had suffered from lack of love, "from mother up." Excepting Martha, she had never had "a satisfied love." All her relations with others had gone wrong, "like a stopped sneeze!" "When the will-strength, or brain-strength, or whatever it is that keeps me happy and steady and brave, gives out, up hop all these buried things, dead and alive." What she felt was not a grief that she could bear but "a choked thwarted fiercely unreconciled feeling." She had only been able to go to sleep the night before, "after a long time of sniveling and sobbing and thrashing around," by her old trick, refusing to think. She believed that she had grabbed onto him; and she seemed to be trying to back out. But something was different from the past—she was writing this explanation because she wanted to be with him.[17]

Houghton stayed with her. She had now bared the worst, let him know the "wreck" that she was. She wrote to him that after this, she no longer saw him as the younger cousin toward whom she felt responsibility. He was now a trusted one, like a doctor or a nurse. He settled, "not as the advancing and receding vision that I have been plunging at and away from; but solid like a post."[18] By the turn to 1898, he was no longer "Cousin" but "Sweetheart," "Heart's Dearest," "Love."

Houghton had the capacity to reassure her. He was steady, he was kind, he accepted her just as she was—spontaneous, changeable, loving, even rejecting. She could let him know her darkest secrets. She could convey a dream during sleep of returning to Walter. She could be candid about the intensity of the love she had once felt for Martha. She could warn him that there might someday be revelations of the sexual side of her relationship to Adelina Knapp. Houghton seemed to accept whatever she told him, even when it was of her recognition of his limits as well as his strengths. With him, Charlotte could begin to heal the wounds of the past.

Because Houghton left no diary and Charlotte destroyed his letters, we can only see his side through her eyes. Her writings relate that his motto was "Deeds not words," that he was deeply involved in her work, and that he went over the draft of *Women and Economics* page by page.[19] As Charlotte traveled, he was trying to establish himself as a breadwinning lawyer and was a member of the National Guard. She began to associate him with playfulness, with the recovery of her youthful exuberance.

From the reflected light of Charlotte's letters, Houghton seems to have had some conflicts about the sexual side of his nature. Away again in the spring of 1898, Charlotte responded warmly to a letter of love in which he expressed his hunger for her. In answer, she tried to talk to him about sex as she now understood it. She referred to his statement, meant by him disparagingly, that his lust represented his "animal side." "Good gracious man!" she wrote, "What did you expect? To love my astral body?" As she remembered the look in his eyes, "the pressure of your loving arms—your beautiful strong body," she denied that this feeling was animalistic and promised that when they were together, "I shall make it my business to see that you do not have that hungry feeling any more!" What he was experiencing was human love, and his sexual feelings were "perfectly natural and right."[20]

By August 1898, Charlotte would call Houghton "Husband," in anticipation of the marriage that would come almost two years later in 1900. When it did, it was the unconventional arrangement Charlotte had proposed to Walter in 1883. As she wrote to Houghton in September 1898, "as you value my life, my sanity, my love; use your clear mind and strong will to work out such a plan of living as shall leave me free to move as move I must." She asked him to help her to "stand against my own sex instinct and life habits" to not become entangled in "home duties."[21] Houghton relished her professional attainments and growing reputation. He accepted the need for her to travel and be apart from him. He also accepted the fact that Charlotte had depressive episodes during which she needed to withdraw.

All of this was difficult to work out, especially in Charlotte's head. At moments Houghton's very steadiness upset her and caused her momentary doubts. She had to work through her feelings about the disparity in their positions in the world. She reflected on the way the world would see their marriage, contrasting that to the way they themselves saw and experienced it. "My public will think I have married a quiet inconspicuous young man and wonder why I should do it." On the other side, "Your public will think that you have married a cold queer rebellious unnatural sex-failure…and marvel at your foolishness." But she and Houghton had a secret, a private joke. Inside her public front to the world dwelt Ashteroth, the Palestinian fertility goddess. And Houghton? "Behind those soft pure eyes and that snowy shirt front," he was "not at all afraid of Ashteroth, but rather glad to have her in his arms!"[22]

About a year before they wed, Charlotte did something quite extraordinary. She replayed 1883 over several letters, only this time she saw herself as Walter and turned Houghton into Charlotte. She warned him that a marriage that was good for her might harm him. They should have a year of "complete separation," she insisted, away from each other with no communication between them. He should be free not to marry her, and she urged this. In this strange reenactment, in which Charlotte was tutoring Walter to take her role, she argued Walter's words: "A marriage that has no common purpose—even in the maintaining a household—where one party reserves the right to go away and stay away whenever she sees fit—it isn't a real marriage at all."[23] Charlotte offered the whole scenario, even adding the new element that a childless marriage was wrong. Steady and sure, Houghton bought none of it. He saw her epistolary explosion as a simple conflict between her head and heart and recognized that she was exhausted from work. He wrote to her of the need to establish a better balance in her life and told her that when they were married they would play together after their daily work time. Charlotte replied with her relief, and the moment passed.[24]

In the winter before her June 1900 marriage, Charlotte went to California to confront Walter and Grace, then back from Europe for a visit. Her mission was to get Katharine back, and she asked for a year's custody as a trial. The couple she found disturbed her in many ways. Walter had grown unattractive. Grace, who had had a miscarriage, was burdened with grief. The bedrock was slipping from under their feet, as Dr. Channing had lost all his property, including his Pasadena house, and its foreclosure was pending. Initially, Walter and Grace were quite hostile to her. Charlotte wrote to Houghton, "I gather a deep bitterness of feeling as to my 'free' life for these years—and my selfish unloading of Katharine upon them....They feel that I have shirked a duty as long as it was inconvenient and now wish to assume a pleasure."[25] They fought to keep Katharine with them. Then fourteen, Katharine "wisely refused to choose," but she did express a desire to go to Italy with Walter and Grace.[26]

Over the course of the next few weeks, Charlotte and Grace reconciled. In their talks, Charlotte told Grace of her impending marriage. Grace raised the question of the sexual side of married life. As Charlotte put it to Houghton, "Grace's only question seemed to be whether I was going to stand 'the relation'—(my great plea before having been that I couldn't, you know!)" With this, we return to the hidden side of Charlotte's alienation from Walter—his expectation and demand for regular sexual intercourse in their marriage that had turned him into "a nightmare husband." Charlotte reassured Houghton, "Well—circumstances alter cases, that's all I can say."[27]

As she prepared for marriage, she thought of the clothes she might buy, including lovely silky things to wear in private around him. Two premarital consultations with physicians in Chicago offered different prospects for their future. She trusted the advice of Dr. McCracken, but she did not allow him, as a man, to give her an internal examination. He advised strongly against having a child, for he saw the chances of degeneracy as high, given that Charlotte and Houghton were cousins. When she visited a female physician, Dr. Lowe, she had a pelvic exam. Dr. Lowe was positive about her bearing a child but said that she would have to have a treatment to reposition her uterus in order to become pregnant. Charlotte's response: "Happy thought—take no precautions—take no treatment—all runs smoothly and naturally and nothing happens!!! There's an easy way out of the difficulty!"[28] If there was no procedure, there was no need for contraception.

Charlotte's marriage to Houghton on June 11, 1900, began a new phase in her life. The couple initially settled in an apartment on the Upper West Side in New York City. Katharine joined them, and in the last years of her girlhood she divided her time between her mother's and her father's households. Ultimately Katharine became an artist, married the artist F. Tolles Chamberlin, had two children, and resided in Pasadena. After living in New York for many years, Charlotte and Houghton moved to his childhood home in Norwich, Connecticut. She continued to have cycles of

Charlotte's and Houghton's New Year's greeting, 1909; inscription included these words: "The tintype man and his picture machine" snapped a photo of the "city swells" "And gave us a regular country pair / A simpering maid and a Reuben's stare." Schlesinger Library, Radcliffe Institute, Harvard University.

highs and lows, and late in life reflected on her journals with their "page after page of those dismal 'downs' with the cheerfully welcomed 'ups.' "[29] Over time, however, the intensity of her depressive episodes slackened.

Charlotte found much happiness in her life with Houghton. Essentially, the "wild unrest" of her two strong natures calmed. As Charlotte Perkins Gilman, she came to accept that her two spirits—one calling her to work, the other to love—need not be at war. Both could rule in her breast.

Looking at the long span of Charlotte Perkins Gilman's life and the relatively good years of her second marriage prompts the question: What was the matter with Charlotte in the 1880s?

Dr. Elizabeth Keller called her trouble "nervous prostration." The one bit of diagnosis from S. Weir Mitchell, coming through in Walter's diary, was that she had "a most unfortunate temperament with a graft of hysterical disorder of the mind." Charlotte wrote of "unutterable pain" and later of "melancholia." A decade later, she wrote to Houghton of the "mental atmosphere that darkens" that had been at its worst "pitch blackness—unillumined and unilluminable."

How might we understand this? Did Charlotte suffer, in today's terms, from depression? Scholars writing about mental illness in the past debate whether it is better to use contemporary medical knowledge to name illnesses of other eras or to hold back and accept the language of the past.[30] A strong case can be made for using present-day terminology for mental disorders, exactly as one does for physical ones: if a person exhibited the symptoms of tuberculosis, even when there was no concept of the disease, that person had tuberculosis. Although debate continues over the mind and brain connection, with strong voices continuing to uphold the value of psychoanalysis and talk-based therapies, there is significant commitment in today's insurance-driven psychiatric community to a belief that brain chemistry is the chief cause of the sustained depressed feelings today called depression.[31] This is seemingly proven by the amelioratory effect of contemporary medications—if a type of medication alleviates key mental symptoms, the thinking goes, then the patient has the mental disease.[32]

We are not able to offer Charlotte Prozac as a test for depression. Instead, we must rely on the words she and her contemporaries wrote. To go by the *Diagnostic and Statistical Manual,* published by the American Psychiatric Association, she certainly did have some of the symptoms of what it has labeled the mood disorder depression (since the revision of the third edition). She had a sustained "depressed mood," a "markedly diminished interest or pleasure" in daily activities, "fatigue or loss of energy," "feelings of worthlessness," "diminished ability to think or concentrate," and "recurrent thoughts of death."[33] Yet one of the problems with some mental illnesses is that they, more elusively than physical illnesses, present themselves in the symptom language of their time and place.[34] These symptoms can be highly gendered. Depression in our current world is overwhelmingly experienced by females, as was hysteria in the nineteenth century in the United States.[35] Moreover, although depression today, like hysteria in the past, can be considered an independent variable, to be treated with rest or drugs, it manifests itself within the web of a life profoundly shaped by and entangled in human relationships. Its symptoms lie largely in the realm of emotions.

From adolescence onward, Charlotte had periods of feeling blue or low, something her mother accepted or simply had to tolerate. As Charlotte became intimate with Walter, she experienced these depressive times differently. During them, she had no feeling toward him and could not respond to him with affection, and he reacted powerfully to this absence. As marriage approached, Charlotte became frightened of its demands for constancy and sought, unsuccessfully, a freer arrangement. After she married and became pregnant, her times of despondency and the frantic unhappiness she sometimes called hysteria became more severe. With Katharine's birth, Charlotte moved by stages toward what her era called "nervous prostration," complete inability to function. She was in this state in April 1887, when she sought Dr. S. Weir Mitchell's help. She recovered under Mitchell's care in May 1887, as she had earlier in Pasadena in the fall and winter of 1885–86, and as she did there again, beginning in 1888. After her separation from Walter in 1890, she continued to have times of distress, but they gradually lessened in their severity, and they diminished markedly in the many years of her second marriage. In view of this chronology, one must conclude that, despite the insistence in her era and our own that depression is a disease of the brain, emotional factors were clearly an element intensifying Charlotte's pain. Recurrent depressive episodes may have been chronic, but Charlotte was worse when she was with Walter and better without him. My best judgment is that Charlotte had an innate or inherited predisposition to what we currently call depression but that this tendency was heightened by the psychological distress of her courtship and marriage to Walter.

Time and place matter. Intertwined inextricably with Charlotte's mental and emotional state was the dominant ideology of her era, constantly invoked by Walter. Buttressing religious and cultural imperatives, the science of her time affirmed that mentally and physically weaker women and stronger men were naturally fitted to their distinct tasks in human evolution, and individual women and men needed to adjust to these gendered roles. This way of seeing the world and its prescriptions fit neatly with the blocking of women's full participation in the polity in the nineteenth century. When Charlotte entered marriage and experienced the rest cure, male voices reminded her of her fundamental duty to home and family and told her that health and happiness lay therein.

But for Charlotte, independent action, work in the world, gaining a living, and securing public recognition were the road to well-being. Ironically, it may have been Charlotte's experience of serious mental illness that enabled her to open her eyes fully to the destructive force of the ideology of separate spheres.[36] She had the intelligence, powers of verbal expression, and imagination for this mighty task. But only with the deep pain of depressive episodes did she understand the larger forces arrayed against her and the need to fight for her life by challenging the accepted truths of natural law. As Charlotte battled her way out of the darkness and pain that threatened to destroy her, she separated from her husband and came to act in the world as a writer and lecturer. She plumbed the sources of her own agony to forge a new understanding of the relation of the sexes and to light new paths for new women.

Nothing Charlotte Perkins Gilman wrote was ever so intense, so personal, so vivid as "The Yellow Wall-Paper." Later, as a reformer promoting causes, Gilman disguised this deeply emotional tale by stating that it was written in protest against S. Weir Mitchell and his methods.[37] Although at one level the story rejected certain elements of his rest cure, it was much more than that. It was a deep exploration of the misery she had long felt, an expression of her pent-up rage.

Long after the fact, Gilman stated in the *Forerunner* of October 1913 that she had written "The Yellow Wall-Paper" in order to present her treatment by S. Weir Mitchell and to get him to alter his rest cure. When she repeated this tale with slight variations in 1919 to William Dean Howells, she added at the end, "Triumph!"[38] She left a handwritten statement at the bottom of her copy of her letter to Mitchell and a typewritten note in her papers to the same effect. In her autobiography, she altered the wording only slightly: "To save others I wrote *The Yellow Wallpaper*."[39] This explanation has been accepted by most of those who have written about her and the story.

It is, however, misleading.[40] By the time she wrote these statements, she was committed to fiction that served moral and political ends.[41] But on August 28, 1890, the Charlotte who sent "The Yellow Wall-Paper" to William Dean Howells saw fiction differently. It was a path to insight. It was also, as her parlor farces testify, a means to earn money and establish herself in the literary firmament.

What "The Yellow Wall-Paper" really depicted was not Mitchell's treatment but the combination of the many forces that shaped her illness and her perception of its causes. More profound than her month under the Philadelphia physician's care were the eight years of Walter's presence and the six years of marriage to him.

The strength of "The Yellow Wall-Paper" is that it distilled, compressed, and dramatized the destructive power of nineteenth-century marriage and the ideal of true womanhood. It put American culture's dominant way of understanding and treating "nervous" women into a single husband and his compliant sister, backed by Dr. Mitchell. It framed the story as the internal dialogue of a troubled woman, demonstrating the ability of the new scientific discourse to control not only a woman's actions but her very thoughts. It revealed how these thoughts, festering in isolation under the rules of enforced rest imposed by a domineering husband, drove her mad.

Charlotte knew, as her character suspected, that stimulation was good, that writing allowed her to release her thoughts. Her narrator says, "I must say what I feel and think in some way—it is such a relief!"

The relief, of course, does not come for the wife in the nursery room. She is not free. She imagines jumping out of the window. She ties herself by a rope to the bed. She methodically creeps along the wall. She is mad. When Charlotte feared insanity, saw it as brain disease, she believed that it—unlike nervous prostration— was a land of no return.

Where relief likely came was to the author of the tale. The struggle of "The Yellow Wall-Paper" is inside the narrator, as it was, at some level, inside Charlotte. The ending's imagined revenge against the husband suggests that in large part "The Yellow Wall-Paper" was a cri de coeur against Walter and the traditional marriage he had demanded. Only once before had Charlotte expressed her rage against him directly in writing. In 1887, as Charlotte closed her journal before traveling to Mitchell's rest cure, she wrote for Walter's eyes: "You found me—you remember what. I leave you—O remember what, and learn to doubt your judgement before it seeks to mould another life as it has mine." As the "She" in the "Quarrel," Charlotte had got "out," and now in "The Yellow Wall-Paper" she got "even."

What about Dr. S. Weir Mitchell? With his authoritative presence, he provided a convenient model for the husband of her tale, and his fame made him an appropriate stand-in.[42] Whatever rage against Walter boiled inside Charlotte, it had to remain disguised to the outside world forever. For as Walter rebounded, he came to love Grace, and he married her once his divorce from Charlotte became final. Walter and Grace took custody of Katharine for much of her remaining childhood. As Grace continued to be Charlotte's beloved friend, both struggled to keep all amicable. When Charlotte married again years later, this time to a man who accepted her just as she was and who married her on her terms, Katharine joined them for a while. In her autobiography written decades after Walter's death and near the end of her own life, Charlotte lavished praise on her first husband, including his kind and patient care during her breakdown. After Houghton died, as Charlotte faced the cancer she knew was terminal and elected to choose the time of her own death, she moved to Pasadena to be near Katharine and to call Grace to her side.

Katharine and Grace would live long after Charlotte's death, and they need never know who or what the physician-husband John represented in "The Yellow Wall-Paper." And given Charlotte's powers of willful forgetting, perhaps Mitchell, the stand-in, came in her own mind to take over Walter's leading role.

Gilman wrote "The Yellow Wall-Paper" early in her literary career. A lifetime of books, articles, stories, and poems were to come. For her personally, the great short story was an important step along the way. It remains a marvelous, compelling work. And it is a reminder of the deep struggle it took for Charlotte to become Charlotte Perkins Gilman, the brilliant public intellectual.

The following names are abbreviated throughout the notes: Charlotte Perkins Gilman (CPG), Martha Luther Lane (MLL), Charles Walter Stetson (CWS), Rebecca Steere Stetson (RSS), George Houghton Gilman (GHG), and Grace Ellery Channing (GEC).

To convey the feel of the handwritten documents, I have chosen to retain the underlining rather than shift them to italics. When I am quoting from printed material, for consistency's sake I have silently changed italicized words that appear there to the likely underlining of the original manuscript documents.

Gilman often left out commas and apostrophes; where they are needed for clarification, I have added them in brackets.

Introduction

1. CPG, untitled poem, first line "O God I wish to do," 1 Apr. 1883, loose scrap in vol. 18, CPG Papers (177, Mf-1), Schlesinger Library, Radcliffe Institute, Harvard University, Cambridge, Mass.,

2. The stanza in manuscript ends with a semi-colon. In what follows, she asked if she had the right, given her conflicted nature, to bring a child into the world.

3. Women's names can be tricky, especially for Gilman. She began life as Charlotte Anna Perkins, became Charlotte Perkins Stetson, or simply Charlotte Stetson, on her marriage to Charles Walter Stetson, and only assumed the name by which we know her, Charlotte Perkins Gilman with her second marriage in 1900. In this book, I follow the practice of Ronald Steel, in *Walter Lippmann and the American Century* (Boston: Little Brown, 1980), of using the first name as I treat familial and personal life, the primary subject of this book, reserving the last name, in this case Gilman, for professional work and later reputation.

4. CPG, "Why I Wrote the Yellow Wallpaper," *Forerunner* 4 (October 1913): 271; CPG, *The Living of Charlotte Perkins Gilman: An Autobiography* (New York: Appleton-Century, 1935), 95–96, 121.

5. I am indebted to the following works: CPG, *Living of Charlotte Perkins Gilman;* Mary Armfield Hill, *Charlotte Perkins Gilman: The Making of a Radical Feminist, 1860–1896* (Philadelphia: Temple University Press, 1980); Gary Scharnshorst, *Charlotte Perkins Gilman* (Boston: Twayne, 1985); Ann J. Lane, *To Herland and Beyond: The Life and Work of Charlotte Perkins Gilman* (New York: Pantheon, 1990); Denise D. Knight, editor's introductions in CPG, *The Diaries of Charlotte Perkins Gilman,* 2 vols. (Charlottesville: University Press of Virginia, 1994). I had the pleasure of reading Judith A. Allen, *The Feminism of Charlotte Perkins Gilman: Sexualities, Histories, Progressivism* (Chicago: University of Chicago Press, 2009) after I had drafted the manuscript; and it provided information for revision. Given the focus of my study, I am especially grateful for the bibliography of Gilman's works and the articles by Gary Scharnhorst and for the many detailed studies by Denise D. Knight.

6. CPG to CWS, transcribed in CWS diary, 2 Apr. 1883, in CWS, *Endure: The Diaries of Charles Walter Stetson,* ed. Mary Armfield Hill (Philadelphia: Temple University Press, 1985), 153.

Chapter 1

1. CPG journal, 1 Jan. 1879, vol. 15, CPG Papers (177, Mf-1), Schlesinger Library, Radcliffe Institute, Harvard University, Cambridge, Mass. Charlotte made a distinction between the diary she had kept for three years, with its "set space," and her new journal with its open spaces, commenting, "It feels good."

2. Material for this biographical sketch comes from Mary Armfield Hill, *Charlotte Perkins Gilman: The Making of a Radical Feminist, 1860–1896* (Philadelphia: Temple University Press, 1980); Gary Scharnshorst, *Charlotte Perkins Gilman* (Boston: Twayne, 1985); Ann J. Lane, *To Herland and Beyond: The Life and Work of Charlotte Perkins Gilman* (New York: Pantheon, 1990); Denise D. Knight, editor's introductions in CPG, *The Diaries of Charlotte Perkins Gilman,* 2 vols. (Charlottesville: University Press of Virginia, 1994); CPG, *The Living of Charlotte Perkins Gilman: An*

Autobiography (New York: Appleton-Century, 1935); and CPG to S. Weir Mitchell, copy, 19 Apr. 1887, Zona Gale Papers, Wisconsin Historical Society Archives, Madison, copy in CPG Papers (A/ G487c), Schlesinger Library.

3. Frederic Beecher Perkins, ed., *The Best Reading: Hints on the Selection of Books, on the Formation of Libraries, Public and Private, on Courses of Reading, etc. With a Classified Bibliography for Easy Reference* (New York: Putnam, 1877) (Perkins sometimes used the spelling "Frederic," as here).

4. She notes receiving these bundles on the following dates: CPG journal, 17 Jan. 1877, 26 Feb. 1877, vol. 27; 5 Mar. 1878, vol. 28.

5. Charlotte Anna Perkins to Frederick Beecher Perkins, n.d. [c. 1875], in *The Selected Letters of Charlotte Perkins Gilman,* ed. Denise D. Knight and Jennifer S. Tuttle (Tuscaloosa: University of Alabama Press, 2009), 5.

6. Hill, *Gilman,* 52.

7. Hill, *Gilman,* 60–61.

8. Manning Street near Ives.

9. Offered by manufacturers, these were small colored advertising cards whose place was usurped in the early 1900s by magazine advertisements.

10. Although I have used Gilman's autobiography, *The Living of Charlotte Perkins Gilman,* I have read it with a critical eye, often as a source to be interrogated. Whenever possible I have relied on Gilman's writings at the time, and they often contain contradictory information. Hill found this to be true as well (*Gilman,* 45).

11. Carroll Smith-Rosenberg, "The Female World of Love and Ritual: Relations between Women in Nineteenth-century America," *Signs* 1 (1975): 1–29; Lillian Faderman, *Surpassing the Love of Men: Romantic Friendship and Love between Women from the Renaissance to the Present* (New York: Morrow, 1981).

12. CPG to MLL, 15 Aug. 1881, CPG Letters, MSS 437, box 1, Rhode Island Historical Society, Providence, RI. .

13. CPG to MLL, 29 July 1881, CPG Letters.

14. CPG to MLL, 24 July 1881, CPG Letters. I have written of smashes and twosomes in several contexts, notably *Alma Mater: Design and Experience in the Women's Colleges from Their Nineteenth-century Beginnings to the 1930s* (New York: Knopf, 1984), and *The Power and Passion of M. Carey Thomas* (New York: Knopf, 1994).

15. In the margin at this point, she likened herself to her father.

16. CPG to MLL, 24 July 1881.

17. CPG to MLL, 24 July 1881.
18. CPG to MLL, 8 Aug. 1881, CPG Letters. Charlotte stated later that these kisses, however, were not on the lips. The limit she placed on herself became clear after she visited Reeta Clark in fall 1882 and wrote her the following poem ("Reserved," Oct. 27, 1882, loose scrap in front of CPG journal, vol. 18):

> My lips are my lover's.
> This hand you may hold;
> It is proud of your pressing. This girdle enfold
> With your strong loving arm. To my cheek lay your own
> And kiss as it likes you all else, this alone
> I reserve for my lover.

She reassured Charles Walter Stetson of this in October 1882, after she attended Martha's wedding. She had not liked it that after the ceremony Martha allowed many others to kiss her. Walter reported that Charlotte said to him, "No one else has kissed my lips, dear," CWS diary, 7 Oct. 1882, 2 vols., 1:271, box 1, CWS Papers, 93-M76, Schlesinger Library.
19. CPG to MLL, 8 Aug. 1881, CPG Letters.
20. CPG to MLL, 15 Aug. 1881, CPG Letters.
21. CPG to MLL, 15 Aug. 1889, CPG Letters.
22. CPG to MLL, 20 Jan. 1890, CPG Letters.
23. CPG to MLL, 29 July 1881, CPG Letters.
24. CPG to MLL, 29 July 1881, CPG Letters. Charlotte may have given Charles the nickname "Halicarnassus" (the Greek city in Asia Minor that was the birthplace of Herodotus) from her reading of ancient history or from the character Halicarnassus in Mary Abigail Dodge, [Gail Hamilton, pseudo.] *Country Living and Country Thinking* (Boston: Ticknor and Fields, 1863).
25. CPG to MLL, 23 Aug. 1881, CPG Letters.
26. By March 1883, her income from teaching was substantial: $8.50 a week (CPG to Charlotte Hedge, 26 Mar. 1882, in *Selected Letters*, 31).
27. CPG to S. Weir Mitchell, copy, 19 Apr. 1887, Zona Gale Papers, Wisconsin Historical Society Archives, Madison, copy in CPG Papers (A/G487c), Schlesinger Library, Radcliffe Institute, Harvard University, Cambridge, Mass.
28. CPG to Sam Simmons, in CPG, *Diaries*, 2:860–62.
29. CPG to Sam Simmons, in CPG, *Diaries*, 2:860–62.

30. CPG, *Diaries*, 2:862–63. I am grateful to the careful exposition of the poem by Denise D. Knight, " 'But O My Heart': The Private Poetry of Charlotte Perkins Gilman," in *Charlotte Perkins Gilman: Optimist Reformer*, ed. Jill Rudd and Val Gough (Iowa City: University of Iowa Press, 1999), 271–75.

31. CPG journal, frontispiece, vol. 18.

32. Helen Lefkowitz Horowitz, *Rereading Sex: Battles over Sexual Knowledge and Suppression in Nineteenth-century America* (New York: Knopf, 2002), chap. 5.

33. Mary J. Studley, *What Our Girls Ought to Know* (New York: M. L. Holbrook, 1878), offers an expansion of her health admonitions.

34. On Catharine Beecher, see Kathryn Kish Sklar, *Catharine Beecher: A Study in American Domesticity* (New Haven: Yale University Press, 1973); quotation, misspelling Catharine Beecher's name, from CPG to MLL, 13 Aug. 1881, CPG Letters.

35. Jane Lancaster, "I Could Easily Have Been an Acrobat," *American Transcendental Quarterly* 8 (Mar. 1994): 33–52, provides an excellent discussion of Blaikie and Brooks and the importance of athleticism in Gilman's life.

36. William Blaikie, *How to Get Strong and How to Stay So* (New York: Harper, 1884), 42, 49–50.

37. Blaikie, *How to Get Strong*, 57.

38. Quoted in Lancaster, "I Could Easily Have Been an Acrobat," 43.

39. CPG to MLL, 1, 13 Aug. 1881.

40. These words are Gilman's from an article in the *Providence Journal*, May 23, 1883, quoted in Lancaster, "I Could Easily Have Been an Acrobat," 45.

41. CPG journal, 13 Jan. 1883, vol. 18.

42. CPG journal, 2 Jan. 1884, vol. 19.

43. CPG, *Living of Charlotte Perkins Gilman*, 37.

44. Sally Schwager, " 'Harvard Women': A History of the Founding of Radcliffe College" (Ed. D. diss., Graduate School of Education, Harvard University, 1982), 30–78; Jean Strouse, *Alice James: A Biography* (Cambridge, Mass.: Harvard University Press, 1980), 170–76.

45. The Gilman Papers include essays and reports from her teacher, A. Fanny Alden, of Hingham, Massachusetts (CPG Papers (177), folder 160). Although her journal never mentions either the correspondence course or working with a teacher, it mentions social visits with Alden.

46. By contrast, on the way home she went to the Athenaeum and "dipped into" *Punch, Harper's,* and *London Illustrated* (CPG to MLL, 8 Aug. 1881).

47. Charlotte noted in her journal some of the many times she read *Popular Science Monthly* at the Public Library or the Athenaeum. Although it is likely that she missed some of her library visits, got copies of the magazine elsewhere, or read back issues at the library, I have paid particular attention to the issues she noted reading: Mar. 1881; Aug. 1881; Apr. 1882; Mar. 1883; Apr. 1883; Nov. 1883; Mar. 1884; July 1884.

48. "Prospectus," *Popular Science Monthly* 1 (1872), inside front cover.

49. Holmes quoted in John Fiske, *Edward Livingston Youmans, Interpreter of Science for the People: A Sketch of His Life: with Selections from His Published Writings and Extracts from his Correspondence with Spencer, Huxley, Tyndall and Others* (New York: Appleton, 1894), 315.

50. Cynthia E. Russett, *Darwin in America: The Intellectual Response, 1865–1912* (San Francisco: Freeman, 1976), 16–17; Richard Hofstadter, *Social Darwinism in American Thought* (New York: Braziller, 1959). It was possible for readers like Charlotte to accept Spencer's science without his politics, in his case advocacy of strict laissez-faire principles.

51. Philip Davis, *1830–1880: The Victorians,* Oxford English Literary History 8, ed. Jonathan Bate (Oxford: Oxford University Press, 2002), 71. Barry Werth has offered an engaging new reading of Spencer's influence in America in *Banquet at Delmonico's: Great Minds, the Gilded Age, and the Triumph of Evolution in America* (New York: Random House, 2009).

52. Herbert Spencer, "Psychology of the Sexes," *Popular Science Monthly* 4 (Nov. 1873): 30–38, quotation from 34.

53. Spencer, "Psychology of the Sexes," 32.

54. Spencer, "Psychology of the Sexes," 33–35.

55. In 1898 she reblended this mix with Spencer and put forth her own scheme in her extraordinarily powerful and influential *Women and Economics.*

56. Helen Lefkowitz Horowitz, *The Power and Passion of M. Carey Thomas* (New York: Knopf, 1984).

57. CPG, "In Duty Bound," poem, 1881, folder 197, CPG Papers (177).

58. In addition, Charles Walter Stetson mentions Carpenter's *Principles of Mental Physiology* (1877), CWS diary, Aug. 21, 1884.

59. William B. Carpenter, *Principles of Mental Physiology, with Their Applications to the Training and Discipline of the Mind and the Study of Its Morbid Conditions* (New York: Appleton, 1878), 27.
60. Carpenter, *Principles of Mental Physiology*, 27.
61. Carpenter, *Principles of Mental Physiology*, 147.
62. Carpenter, *Principles of Mental Physiology*, 331; I have deleted Carpenter's cross-reference here.
63. CPG journal, 1882, frontispiece, vol. 18.

Chapter 2

1. CPG journal, 12, 22 Jan. 1882, vol. 18, CPG Papers (177, Mf-1), Schlesinger Library, Radcliffe Institute, Harvard University, Cambridge, Mass.
2. CPG to CWS, 26 Jan.1882, in CWS, *Endure: The Diaries of Charles Walter Stetson,* ed. Mary Armfield Hill (Philadelphia: Temple University Press, 1985), 28–30; quotations from 28–29.
3. Rebecca M. Ryan, "The Sex Right: A Legal History of the Marital Rape Exemption," *Law and Social Inquiry* 20 (1995): 943–45; Blackstone quotation from 944–45.
4. Nancy F. Cott, *Public Vows: A History of Marriage and the Nation* (Cambridge, Mass.: Harvard University Press, 2000), 11–12, 47–54; Françoise Basch, "Women's Rights and the Wrongs of Marriage in Mid-nineteenth-century America," *History Workshop Journal* 22 (fall 1986): 23.
5. See, for example, Anna Garlin Spencer, "The Legal Position of Married Women," *Popular Science Monthly* 18 (Mar. 1881): 643–54.
6. Helen Lefkowitz Horowitz, *Campus Life: Undergraduate Cultures from the End of the Eighteenth Century to the Present* (New York: Knopf, 1987), 193–98.
7. CPG to CWS, 26 Jan. 1882, in CWS, *Endure*, 28–30; quotation from 29. Since her great sorrow had come with the loss of a female friend, this final statement is a bit strange.
8. CPG journal, 29 Jan. 1882, vol. 18.
9. CPG journal, 31 Jan. 1882, vol. 18.
10. CPG, *Diaries*, 2:867–68.
11. The existence of a small number of letters from Gilman to Charles Walter Stetson, mainly written in early 1882, in the CPG Papers at the Schlesinger Library is curious. Some, perhaps all, are drafts, and this may explain why they remain in her papers.

12. CPG to CWS, 21 Feb. 1882, letter no. 1 (Charlotte wrote two letters or drafts of letters to Walter on this day), folder 39, CPG Papers (177, Mf-1).

13. CPG to CWS, 21 Feb. 1882, letter no. 2, CPG Papers.

14. CPG to CWS, 22 Feb. 1882, no. 1a, a continuation of letter no. 1 of 21 Feb. 1882, CPG Papers.

15. CPG to CWS, 20 Feb. 1882, CPG Papers.

16. CPG to CWS, 20 Feb. 1882.

17. She edited here her own first penning: "sapped by the underlying possibility of mistake and presumption."

18. CPG to CWS, 20 Feb. 1882.

19. CPG to CWS, 21 Feb. 1882, no. 1, CPG Papers.

20. CPG journal, 24 Feb. 1882, vol. 18; Charlotte noted that she finished reading the book on 6 Mar. 1882.

21. CPG journal, 2 Mar. 1882, vol. 18.

22. CPG to CWS, 6 Mar. 1882, CPG Papers.

23. CPG to CWS, 9 May 1882, in CWS, *Endure,* 71.

24. CPG journal, 29 June 1882, vol. 18.

25. Although long excerpts of the CWS diary have been published in CWS, *Endure,* the original manuscript in the Schlesinger Library adds significant unedited detail.

26. There are many diary entries that express this, including 22 Apr. 1882, in CWS, *Endure,* 67. After writing this I had the pleasure of reading Judith A. Allen, *The Feminism of Charlotte Perkins Gilman: Sexualities, Histories, Progressivism* (Chicago: University of Chicago Press, 2009), 27–28.

27. CWS diary, 14 Jan. 1882, in CWS, *Endure,* 25.

28. CWS diary, 26 Jan. 1882, in CWS, *Endure,* 26, 27.

29. CWS diary, 29 Jan. 1882, in CWS, *Endure,* 30. By "sugar plum" Charlotte meant a compliment.

30. CWS diary, 29 Jan.1882, in CWS, *Endure,* 30–35.

31. For example, CPG journal, 10 Sept., 19 Nov., 17 Dec. 1882, vol. 18.

32. CPG journal, 29 June, 17 Sept. 1882, vol. 18.

33. Karen Lystra, *Searching the Heart: Women, Men, and Romantic Love in Nineteenth-century America* (New York: Oxford University Press, 1989), chap. 2.

34. Untitled poem in entry labeled "Prov. June 15, 1882, 9:20 P.M.," loose scrap in front of CPG journal, 1882, vol. 18.

35. Here I must part company with the otherwise intelligent understanding of CPG's notions of physiology and mental illness posited by Jane F. Thrailkill, "Doctoring the Yellow Wallpaper,"

English Literary History 69 (2002): 525–66. Gilman did not use "brain" and "mind" interchangeably (although she may not have always been consistent): she understood "mind" as the activity of the physical organ "brain."

36. CPG to CWS, 26 Jan. 1882, in CWS, *Endure,* 28–30.

37. CPG journal, 20 Apr. 1882, vol. 18, noted that she went to the Athenaeum to read the new *Popular Science Monthly.* Goldwin Smith, "Has Science Yet Found a New Basis for Morality?" *Popular Science Monthly* 20 (Apr. 1882): 753–78. Goldwin Smith was a British intellectual who moved to North America. [E. L. Youmans], "Editor's Table: Goldwin Smith on Scientific Morality," *Popular Science Monthly* 20 (Apr. 1882): 844–47; quotations from 845, 847.

38. She was the guest of Kate Bucklin, one of her wealthier Providence friends. According to CPG journal, Kate loaned Charlotte her copy of Spencer's *Data of Ethics* on 11 July 1882, and Charlotte read it in the weeks that followed.

39. Herbert Spencer, *The Data of Ethics* (New York: Appleton, 1879), 76.

40. Spencer, *Data of Ethics,* 87.

41. Spencer, *Data of Ethics,* 110. Charlotte had already been exposed to this understanding in an article by Felix L. Oswald, M.D., "Physical Education," *Popular Science Monthly* 19 (Aug. 1881): 450–59, that paraphrased Spencer's judgments in making a case of the importance of play and physical recreation, something that she, an enthusiastic gymnast, believed in fully, It would also be reinforced by another article by the same author, "The Remedies of Nature: The Alcohol-Habit (Concluded)," *Popular Science Monthly* 24 (Nov. 1883): 45–53; she read this issue in Providence's Public Library on 21 Nov. 1883 "with much enjoyment."

42. Spencer, *Data of Ethics,* 94.

43. Spencer, *Data of Ethics,* 84.

44. Untitled poem, in entry labeled "Sept. 22, '82, C[harlotte] A[nna] P[erkins]," loose scrap in front of CPG journal, 1882, vol. 18.

45. Mary J. Studley, *What Our Girls Ought to Know* (New York: M. L. Holbrook, 1878) used as a frontispiece this stanza from William Wordsworth:

A perfect woman, nobly planned,
To warn, to comfort, and command;
And yet a spirit still, and bright
With something of an angel light.

46. Untitled poem, in entry labeled "1882, Friday, Sept. 8," loose scrap in front of CPG journal, 1882, vol. 18.
47. Charlotte Perkins Stetson, "The Love Story," *Pacific Monthly* 2 (Sept. 1890): 176–77; quotation from 177.
48. CPG journal, 14, 16, 17, 18, 19 July 1882, vol. 18; George Eliot, *Adam Bede* (Edinburgh: Blackwood, 1859).
49. CPG to MLL, 16 Aug. 1881, CPG Letters, MSS 437, box 1, Rhode Island Historical Society, Providence, RI.
50. CWS diary, 2 Aug. 1882, in CWS, *Endure,* 80.
51. CWS diary, 10 Aug. 1882, in CWS, *Endure,* 82.
52. CPG journal, 16, 17 Oct. 1882, vol. 18.
53. CWS diary, 18 Oct. 1882, in CWS, *Endure,* 110–13.

Chapter 3

1. CPG journal, 30 Nov., 3 Dec. 1882, vol. 18, CPG Papers (177, Mf-1), Schlesinger Library, Radcliffe Institute, Harvard University, Cambridge, Mass. Walter had gone with her to the Hales but returned to Providence a day earlier.
2. CWS diary, 4 Dec. 1882, in CWS, *Endure: The Diaries of Charles Walter Stetson,* ed. Mary Armfield Hill (Philadelphia: Temple University Press, 1985), 119.
3. CPG to CWS, copied 6 Dec. 1882, in CWS, *Endure,* 121.
4. CWS diary, 4, 6 Dec. 1882, in CWS, *Endure,* 118, 120.
5. CWS diary, 12 Dec. 1882, in CWS, *Endure,* 122–23.
6. CWS diary, 21 Dec. 1882, in CWS, *Endure,* 124.
7. CPG journal, 31 Dec. 1882, vol. 18.
8. CWS diary, 30 Jan. 1883, in CWS, *Endure,* 133.
9. CWS diary, 19 Jan. 1883, in CWS, *Endure,* 129.
10. CPG journal, 11 Feb. 1883, vol. 18.
11. CWS diary, 12 Feb. 1883, in CWS, *Endure,* 135.
12. CWS diary, 12 Mar. 1883, in CWS, *Endure,* 139.
13. CPG journal, 4 Mar. 1883, vol. 18.
14. CPG journal, 28 Mar. 1883, vol. 18.
15. A. Fanny Alden to CPG, 10 Mar. 1883, CPG Papers, folder 160.
16. CPG journal, 18 Mar. 1883, vol. 18.
17. CWS diary, 19 Mar. 1883, in CWS, *Endure,* 143.
18. CWS diary, 22 Mar. 1883, in CWS, *Endure,* 144–45.
19. CWS transcribed the letter, interposing his own comments, in his diary, 31 Mar. and 2 Apr. 1883, in CWS, *Endure,* 148–54.
20. At this point in his diary, Walter wrote in parentheses: "that's very true."

21. CWS diary, 31 Mar. 1883, in CWS, *Endure*, 149.
22. CWS diary, 31 Mar. 1883, in CWS, *Endure*, 150.
23. CWS diary, 4 Apr. 1883, in CWS, *Endure*, 158.
24. CPG journal, 31 Mar. 1883, 1 Apr. 1883, vol. 18.
25. CWS diary, 4 Apr. 1883, 2 vols., 1:385, box 1, CWS Papers (93-M76), Schlesinger Library; the quotation not obscured by whorls can also be found in CWS, *Endure*, 158.
26. CWS diary, 9 Apr. 1883, 1:395, 394 (crossed-out passage), 395, CWS Papers; for the quotations not obscured by whorls, see also CWS, *Endure*, 161, 162.
27. CPG journal, 8 Apr. 1883, vol. 18. Perhaps it is significant that before telling of this, Charlotte first listed the chores of the day.
28. CPG journal, 10 Apr. 1883, vol. 18.
29. Helen Lefkowitz Horowitz, *Rereading Sex: Battles over Sexual Knowledge and Suppression in Nineteenth-century America* (New York: Knopf, 2002), 263–67.
30. Ann Braude, *Radical Spirits: Spiritualism and Women's Rights in Nineteenth-century America* (Boston: Beacon Press, 1989); John C. Spurlock, *Free Love: Marriage and Middle-class Radicalism in America, 1825–1860* (New York: New York University Press, 1988), 91–98, 143–45.
31. Mary Armfield Hill, *Charlotte Perkins Gilman: The Making of a Radical Feminist, 1860–1896* (Philadelphia: Temple University Press, 1980), 17. The relationship was such that in May 1879, Isabella, then under straitened circumstances, asked that Mary and Charlotte Perkins take over the Hooker's Hartford house, board them for rent, and take in other boarders to support the household. CPG, *The Diaries of Charlotte Perkins Gilman*, ed. Denise D. Knight, 2 vols. (Charlottesville: University of Virginia Press, 1994), 12.
32. Horowitz, *Rereading Sex*, chap. 15; Helen Lefkowitz Horowitz, "Victoria Woodhull and Free Love in the Feminine, First Person Singular," in *Forgotten Heroes*, ed. Susan Ware, for the Society of American Historians (New York: Free Press, 1998), 110–19.
33. Victoria Woodhull, "A Speech on the Principles of Social Freedom, Delivered in Steinway Hall, Monday, November 20, 1871," reprinted in *The Victoria Woodhull Reader*, ed. Madeleine B. Stern (Weston, Mass.: M & S Press, 1974), 13, 15, 16, 35.
34. CWS diary, 9 Apr. 1883, in CWS, *Endure*, 162.
35. CWS diary, 9 Apr. 1883, 1:399–400, CWS Papers; this passage is not found in CWS, *Endure*.
36. Horowitz, *Rereading Sex*, chap. 14.
37. CWS diary, 9 Apr. 1883, in CWS, *Endure*, 161–62.

38. CWS diary, 24 Mar. 1883, in CWS, *Endure,* 146.
39. CWS diary, 28 Mar. 1883, in CWS, *Endure,* 148.
40. In January 1882, for example, still suffering the loss of Martha Luther, she wrote in her journal: "am rather blue & lonely"; CPG journal, 20 Jan. 1882, vol. 18.
41. CPG to CWS, 26 Apr. 1883, in CWS, *Endure,* 178.
42. CPG to CWS, 26 Apr. 1883, in CWS, *Endure,* 178.

Chapter 4

1. CPG journal, 19 May 1883, vol. 18, CPG Papers (177, Mf-1), Schlesinger Library, Radcliffe Institute, Harvard University, Cambridge, Mass.
2. CPG journal, 15 Apr., 14, 20 May 1883, vol. 18.
3. CWS diary, 15 May 1883, in CWS, *Endure: The Diaries of Charles Walter Stetson,* ed. Mary Armfield Hill (Philadelphia: Temple University Press, 1985), 184.
4. CWS diary, 19 May 1883, in CWS, *Endure,* 187; 22 May 1883, 189–90, quotation from 190.
5. Henry James, *The Bostonians,* serialized, XLI, in *Century* 31 (Feb. 1886): 591–600; quotation from 600.
6. Charlotte A. Perkins, "In Duty Bound," *Woman's Journal,* Jan. 12, 1884, 14.
7. CPG journal, 23, 31 Oct., 16 Nov., 14 Dec. 1883, vol. 18. It was the first of her poems to be published.
8. Charlotte reported that Walter "wishes me to be gentler," CPG journal, 4 Nov. 1883, vol. 18. She discussed her picture in CPG journal, 9 Nov. 1883. Walter's description and comment: CWS diary, 12 Nov. 1883, in CWS, *Endure,* 244. See Denise D. Knight, " 'I Could Paint Still Life as Well as Any One on Earth': Charlotte Perkins Gilman and the World of Art," *Women's Studies* 35 (2006): 475–92, esp. 484–85.
9. CPG journal, 25 Nov. 1883, vol. 18.
10. CPG journal, 16 Dec. 1883, vol. 18.
11. CPG journal, 31 Dec. 1883, vol. 18.
12. CPG journal, 1 Jan. 1884, vol. 19; CPG to CWS, 1 Jan. 1884, in *The Selected Letters of Charlotte Perkins Gilman,* ed. Denise D. Knight and Jennifer S. Tuttle (Tuscaloosa: University of Alabama Press, 2009), 36–37.
13. CPG journal, 3 Dec. 1883, vol. 18.
14. CPG to GEC, 28 Feb. 1884, CPG Papers (Mf-6).
15. CPG journal, 2 May 1884, vol. 19.

16. Walter's diary records only his thoughts on this subject, not his actions, and does not allow knowledge of whether or not he sought other sexual outlets.

17. CWS diary, 24 Mar. 1883, in CWS, *Endure,* 146.

18. CWS diary, 23 June 1883, in CWS, *Endure,* 202.

19. CPG journal, 5 Apr. 1883, vol. 18.

20. CWS diary, 23 June 1883, in CWS, *Endure,* 201. Walter wrote of his disgust with "Whitman's tales of harlots and dithyrambic explanations of generation," his books "filled with gangrene and the odor of semen," 201–2.

21. Chiton: Greek for tunic, worn by men and women in ancient Greece and Rome. Walter had posed in one for a sketch class on 30 Jan. 1883, to what he thought was great effect (CWS diary, in CWS, *Endure,* 133). It seems from this telling that the legal ceremony did not involve Walter giving Charlotte a wedding ring.

22. CWS diary, 18 Aug. 1884, in CWS, *Endure,* 259–60.

23. CPG journal, 3 Aug. 1882, 2 Feb., 4 June 1883, vol. 18.

24. These practices included the controversial practice of laparotomy, the removal of both ovaries, in an attempt to cure insanity. Keller reported on one such case during the transcribed discussion following a paper by Anna M. Fullerton, "Report of the Work from the Woman's Hospital of Philadelphia," *Transactions of the Alumnae Association of the Woman's Medical College of Pennsylvania* 15 (1890): 83–84.

25. See the website of the Jamaica Plain Historical Society on the Bowditch School, www.jphs.org/victorian/bowditch-school.html (2 Mar. 2009); for information and a photograph of an attractive Dr. Keller see http://rememberjamaicaplain.blogspot.com/2008/02/dr-elizabeth-c-keller.html (2 Mar. 2009).

26. CPG journal, 4, 6 June 1883, vol. 18.

27. CPG journal, 28 May 1883, vol. 18.

28. CPG journal, 12 June 1883, vol. 18.

29. David J. Pivar, *Purity Crusade: Sexual Morality and Social Control, 1868–1900* (Westport, Conn.: Greenwood Press, 1973), 60–72. Regulation involved the medical inspection of prostitutes and thus the tacit legalization of prostitution; the Moral Education Society sought its absolute prohibition.

30. Anon., untitled, *Alpha* 8 (July 1883): 10–11.

31. A reference to the Beecher-Tilton scandal. Rev. Henry Ward Beecher, accused of an adulterous affair with a congregant Elizabeth Tilton, had characterized their intimacy as "nest-hiding."

32. Anon., "Alpha Teachings," *Alpha* 10 (Oct. 1884): 6–7.
33. And Dr. Winslow occasionally reprinted his ripostes. See "Dr. Foote's Reply to the Alphites," *Alpha* 6 (Oct. 1881): 8–10.
34. C.B.W., "Compromise," *Alpha* 9 (May 1884): 9–10.
35. Helen Lefkowitz Horowitz, *Rereading Sex: Battles over Sexual Knowledge and Suppression in Nineteenth-century America* (New York: Knopf, 2002), chap. 18.
36. Rebecca M. Ryan, "The Sex Right: A Legal History of the Marital Rape Exemption," *Law and Social Inquiry* 20 (1995): 941–1001, esp. 945–46.
37. Françoise Basch, "Women's Rights and the Wrongs of Marriage in Mid-nineteenth-century America," *History Workshop Journal* 22 (fall 1986): 18–40; on Stanton, 21; on Stone, 25.
38. CPG journal, 24 Nov. 1883, vol. 18; 5 Jan. 1884, vol. 19.
39. CPG, "One Girl of Many," *Alpha*, 9 (Feb. 1884): 14.
40. C.B.W., "Black Sheep," *Alpha* 8 (July 1883): 2–4; quotation from 4.

Chapter 5

1. CPG journal, 3 May 1884, vol. 19, CPG Papers (177, Mf-1), Schlesinger Library, Radcliffe Institute, Harvard University, Cambridge, Mass.
2. CPG journal, 9 May 1884, vol. 19.
3. CPG journal, 24 May 1884, vol. 19.
4. CPG journal, 15 May 1884, vol. 19.
5. CPG journal, 12, 13 June 1884, vol. 19.
6. She also reported that she removed herself from Walter: "Sleep about three hours on mattress in garret" (CPG journal, 15 June 1884, vol. 19).
7. CPG journal, 20 June, 31 July 1884, vol. 19.
8. George H. Napheys, *The Physical Life of Woman: Advice to Maiden, Wife, and Mother,* 6th ed. (Philadelphia: Maclean, 1872). Recommenders included the Hartford minister Horace Bushnell and the Providence physician Edwin M. Snow.
9. CWS diary, 21 Aug. 1884, in CWS, *Endure: The Diaries of Charles Walter Stetson,* ed. Mary Armfield Hill (Philadelphia: Temple University Press, 1985), 262.
10. CWS diary, 3 Sept. 1884, in CWS, *Endure,* 264.
11. Napheys, *Physical Life of Woman,* 104.
12. CWS diary, 17 Nov.1884, in CWS, *Endure,* 269.
13. Napheys, *Physical Life of Woman,* 151–53.

14. CPG journal, 4 Sept. 1884, vol. 19.
15. Napheys, *Physical Life of Woman,* 145.
16. CWS diary, 15 Sept. 1884, in CWS, *Endure,* 264.
17. CPG journal, 1 Jan. 1885, vol. 19.
18. CWS diary, 31 Oct. 1884, in CWS, *Endure,* 268–69.
19. CPG journal, 1 Jan. 1885, vol. 19.
20. CPG journal, 29 Jan., 1 Feb. 1885, vol. 19.
21. CPG journal, 2, 4, 17, 19, Feb. 1885, vol. 19.
22. CPG journal, 2 May 1885, vol. 19.
23. CPG journal, 5 Aug. 1885, vol. 19.
24. CPG journal, 28 Aug. 1885, vol. 19.
25. CWS diary, 24 Aug. 1885, in CWS, *Endure,* 279.
26. CWS diary, 24 Aug. 1885, in CWS, *Endure,* 279.
27. CWS diary, 24 Aug. 1885, in CWS, *Endure,* 279.
28. CWS diary, 24 Aug. 1885, in CWS, *Endure,* 280.
29. CWS diary, 24, 26 Aug. 1885, in CWS, *Endure,* 280. For context, see Carroll Smith-Rosenberg and Charles Rosenberg, "The Female Animal: Medical and Biological Views of Woman and Her Role in Nineteenth-century America," in *Women and Health in America: Historical Readings,* ed. Judith Walzer Leavitt (Madison: University of Wisconsin Press, 1984), 12–27.
30. CPG journal, 30 Aug. 1885, vol. 19.
31. Charlotte Perkins Stetson, "Advertising for Marriage," *Alpha* 11 (Sept. 1885): 7.
32. CPG journal, 4 Sept. 1885, vol. 19.
33. Henry James, *The Bostonians,* XXV, serialized in the *Century* 30 (Sept. 1885): 692–709; quotation from 693.
34. James, *Bostonians,* 705.
35. CWS diary, 12 Sept. 1885, in CWS, *Endure,* 290.
36. CWS diary, 12 Sept. 1885, 2 vols., 1:706, box 1, CWS Papers (93-M76), Schlesinger Library; quotation not in CWS, *Endure.*
37. CPG journal, 12, 22, 24 Sept. 1885, vol. 19.
38. Napheys, *Physical Life of Woman,* 272.
39. Napheys, *Physical Life of Woman,* 272–77.
40. CWS journal, 28 Sept. 1885, 1:715, CWS Papers; not in CWS, *Endure.*
41. CPG journal, 28 Sept. 1885, vol. 19.
42. Napheys, *Physical Life of Woman,* 283.
43. CPG journal, 8 Oct. 1885, vol. 19.
44. William F. Channing to S. Weir Mitchell, 16 June 1887, quoted in Jennifer S. Tuttle, "Rewriting the West Cure: Charlotte Perkins

Gilman, Owen Wister, and the Sexual Politics of Neurasthenia," in *The Mixed Legacy of Charlotte Perkins Gilman,* ed. Catherine J. Golden and Joanna Schneider Zangrando (Newark: University of Delaware Press, 2000), 111.

45. CPG to MLL, 13 Mar. 1886, CPG Letters, MSS 437, box 1, Rhode Island Historical Society, Providence, RI.
46. Playbill, "Changing Hands," box 13, folder 446, Grace Ellery Channing Papers (83-M201), Schlesinger Library.
47. CPG, "A Valentine," 14 Feb. 1886, CPG Papers (177, Mf-1), folder 205.
48. CPG to MLL, 13 Mar. 1886.
49. CPG journal, 3 Apr. 1886, vol. 19.
50. CWS diary, 2 June 1886, in CWS, *Endure,* 308.
51. CWS diary, 17 Aug. 1886, in CWS, *Endure,* 310.
52. CWS diary, 17 Aug. 1886, in CWS, *Endure,* 311.
53. CWS diary, 27 Aug. 1886, 1:756, CWS Papers; not in CWS, *Endure.*
54. CWS diary, 16 Sept. 1886, 1:759, CWS Papers; only partially quoted in *Endure,* without mention of the morphine compound.
55. CWS diary, 17 Aug. 1886, in CWS, *Endure,* 311–12.
56. CPG journal, 12, 19 Sept. 1886, vol. 19.
57. CPG, untitled manuscript, Aug. or Sept. 1886, CPG Papers (177, Mf-1), folder 222.
58. She sent her poem "Nevada" to the *Atlantic Monthly.* It was rejected, but the editor sent his praise.
59. Charlotte Perkins Stetson, "The Answer," *Woman's Journal,* Oct. 2, 1886, 313.
60. CPG journal, 2, 12 Oct. 1886, vol. 19. The *Providence Journal* sent her $3 in September for "On the Pawtucket," her first royalty for a manuscript. She wrote, "May it not be the last!" CPG journal, 4 Sept. 1886, vol. 19.
61. CPG journal, 27 Oct. 1886, vol. 19.
62. CPG journal, 27, 29 Oct. 1886, vol. 19.
63. CWS diary, 24 Nov. 1886, in CWS, *Endure,* 322.
64. CPG journal, 13 Dec. 1886, vol. 19.
65. CPG journal, 31 Dec. 1886, vol. 19.
66. This is also the way it has played out in the feminist literature that has emerged in the last thirty-five years.
67. CPG journal, 6 October 1886, vol. 19.
68. CPG journal, 1, 5, 23 Jan. 1887, 5 Feb. 1887, vol. 20.
69. Mary Armfield Hill, *Charlotte Perkins Gilman: The Making of a Radical Feminist,* 1860–1896 (Philadelphia: Temple University Press, 1980), 141–42.

70. CPG journal, 21 Feb. 1887, vol. 20.

71. CPG journal, 26 Feb. 1887, vol. 20.

72. CPG journal, 15 Feb. 1887, vol. 20.

73. CPG journal 20 Feb. 1887, vol. 20.

74. CPG journal, 21, 22 Mar. 1887, vol. 20.

75. CWS diary, 9 Feb. 1887, in CWS, *Endure,* 331.

76. CPG journal, 19 Mar. 1887, vol. 20; Judith A. Allen emphasizes the importance to Gilman of her suffrage work during this period in *The Feminism of Charlotte Perkins Gilman: Sexualities, Histories, Progressivism* (Chicago: University of Chicago Press, 2009), 37–39.

77. CPG journal, 9, 10, 20 Mar. 1887, vol. 20.

78. CPG journal, 5, 7, 8, 9 Apr. 1887, vol. 20.

79. CWS diary, 28 Apr. 1887, in CWS, *Endure,* 334. Interestingly enough, right before this description he wrote in his journal about his success with a portrait commission.

80. CPG journal, 11, 12 Apr. 1887, vol. 20. It is very possible that Caroline Hazard was the actual provider of the $100, either as a specific act or through the royalties for her biography of J. Lewis Diman that she assigned to his widow.

81. His entry is filled with moans for his own sorry state. "It is a terrible trial to the bodily 'virtue' of one of my temperament to be so bereft of wife and close love, and amid warm living beings who could love me I think.... It is not good for me. My mind is feverish and my body without peace. But who cares!" CWS diary, 28 Apr. 1887, in CWS, *Endure,* 335.

82. Biographical information on Mitchell draws from Ernest Earnest, *S. Weir Mitchell: Novelist and Physician* (Philadelphia: University of Pennsylvania Press, 1950); Richard D. Walter, *S. Weir Mitchell, M.D., Neurologist: A Medical Biography* (Springfield, Ill.: Thomas, 1970); S. Weir Mitchell, unpublished autobiography, S. Weir Mitchell Papers, 2/0241–93, box 16, Historical Library, College of Physicians, Philadelphia, Penn.

83. CPG journal, 13, 19 Apr. 1887, vol. 20.

84. CPG to S. Weir Mitchell, copy, 19 Apr. 1887, Zona Gale Papers, Wisconsin Historical Society Archives, Madison, copy in CPG Papers (A/G487c), Schlesinger Library. In discussing this letter, I am grateful to Denise D. Knight, " 'All the Facts of the Case': Gilman's Lost Letter to Dr. S. Weir Mitchell," *American Literary Realism* 37 (spring 2005): 259–70.

85. I am grateful to Knight, " 'All the Facts of the Case,' " for pointing out the way Charlotte demonizes her mother in the letter.

86. CPG journal, n.d. [between 16 and 20 Apr. 1887], vol. 20,
   pp. 38–39.

Chapter 6

1. CPG journal, n.d. [between 16 and 20 Apr. 1887], vol. 20,
   pp. 38–39, CPG Papers (177, Mf-1), Schlesinger Library, Radcliffe
   Institute, Harvard University, Cambridge, Mass.
2. George M. Beard, *American Nervousness: Its Causes and
   Consequences* (New York: Putnam,' 1881), 7–8. See Charles E.
   Rosenberg, "The Place of George M. Beard in Nineteenth-century
   Psychiatry," *Bulletin of the History of Medicine* 36 (1962): 245–59.
3. Dr. Bucknill, "Dean Swift's Disease," *Popular Science Monthly* 20
   (Apr. 1882): 806–17; quotation from 816. In today's language, Swift
   suffered a stroke.
4. When Conway Brown committed suicide, any evidence that he
   was insane and therefore had an incurable disease that made him
   not responsible for his act of self-destruction was a comfort to his
   parents (CPG journal, 3 Jan. 1884, vol. 19).
5. In Harriet Strong's case, Mitchell wrote to her husband,
   "Mrs. Strong has arrived here safely. I have made a careful
   Examination and, am glad to say, have been unable to find any
   organic lesion. I therefore hope that I can help her." He promised
   to let Mr. Strong know if at any time he found any "unfavorable
   ulcers," but from her present condition he did not "anticipate any
   serious trouble." S. Weir Mitchell to Charles Lyman Strong, 10
   Nov. 1882, HS 234, Huntington Library, San Marino, California.
6. Charlotte left her journal at home. Perhaps she knew that under
   Mitchell's care she would not be allowed to write. Walter reported
   her case from the remove of Providence.
7. Information from the 30 Apr. 1887 letter Walter received from
   Charlotte is in CWS diary, 30 Apr. 1887, in CWS, *Endure:
   The Diaries of Charles Walter Stetson,* ed. Mary Armfield Hill
   (Philadelphia: Temple University Press, 1985), 337.
8. CWS diary, 7 May 1887, in CWS, *Endure,* 337.
9. CWS diary, 7 May 1887, in CWS, *Endure,* 337.
10. CWS diary, 11 May 1887, in CWS, *Endure,* 339.
11. The manuscript diary reads "written by her own dear hand." CWS
    diary, 16 May 1887, 2 vols., 2:183, box 2, CWS Papers (93-M76),
    Schlesinger Library. This is in contrast to "neither by her own dear
    hand," in CWS, *Endure,* 340.

12. CWS diary, 16 May 1887, in CWS, *Endure,* 340.
13. S. Weir Mitchell, "Wear and Tear," *Lippincott's Magazine of Literature, Science and Education* 4 (Nov. 1869): 495.
14. Mitchell, "Wear and Tear," 496.
15. Mitchell, "Wear and Tear," 498.
16. S. Weir Mitchell, *Rest in Nervous Disease: Its Use and Abuse* (New York: Putnam, 1875), 20.
17. S. Weir Mitchell, "Rest in Nervous Disease: Its Use and Abuse" (Apr. 1875), no. 4 in *A Series of American Clinical Lectures,* ed. E. C. Sequin, 3 vols. (New York: Putnam, 1876–), 1:83–75; quotations from 94–95.
18. Mitchell used electricity to contract unused muscles. It was also, however, considered a "tonic" for sufferers from neurasthenia.
19. Mitchell, "Rest in Nervous Disease," 96.
20. S. Weir Mitchell, "The Evolution of the Rest Treatment," *Journal of Nervous and Mental Disease* 31 (1904): 368–73; quotations from 371, 372. In his successive retelling of the treatment, the initialed name changed, but Mitchell was likely referring to the same case.
21. The water cure (or hydropathy) was a popular form of alternative medicine in the early nineteenth century. Believing that disease was an aberration of the naturally healthy condition of the body, the cure's practitioners sought to dispel illness through internal and external applications of water. Sufferers able to afford it typically went to water-cure establishments. The movement was popularized by the *Water-cure Journal.*
22. Jennifer S. Tuttle, "Rewriting the West Cure: Charlotte Perkins Gilman, Owen Wister, and the Sexual Politics of Neurasthenia," in *The Mixed Legacy of Charlotte Perkins Gilman,* ed. Catherine J. Golden and Joanna Schneider Zangrando (Newark: University of Delaware Press, 2000), 103–21. Although the majority of his patients were women, Mitchell did prescribe the rest-cure to men, but typically did not require of them the same degree of isolation or rest.
23. S. Weir Mitchell, *Doctor and Patient* (1888; reprint, New York: Arno Press, 1972), 83–84; quotation from 83.
24. Emphasis added. Mitchell, *Doctor and Patient,* 13.
25. Anna Robeson Burr, *Weir Mitchell: His Life and Letters* (New York: Duffield, 1929), 373.
26. Mitchell, *Doctor and Patient,* 5.
27. S. Weir Mitchell, *Fat and Blood: And How to Make Them* (Philadelphia: Lippincott, 1882), 46, 45. This suggests that Mitchell did believe in listening to his patients, as had earlier physicians

without his somatic bias, but he did so not to enable them to express their distress and interpret it in a twentieth-century fashion but to redirect their will in a nineteenth-century way, to enable them to reassert self-control.

28. Mitchell, *Doctor and Patient,* 10.
29. Mitchell, *Doctor and Patient,* 11.
30. Mitchell, *Doctor and Patient,* 141.
31. Mitchell, *Doctor and Patient,* 85.
32. Mitchell, *Doctor and Patient,* 142, 143.
33. Mitchell, *Doctor and Patient,* 86.
34. Mitchell, "Rest in Nervous Disease," 12. Nosology is the systematic classification of diseases.
35. Ilza Veith, *Hysteria: The History of a Disease* (Chicago: University of Chicago Press, 1965); Sydenham quotation, 141; discussion of Charcot, 230–9. Today Charcot's hysterical convulsions appear as a testament to the power of suggestion.
36. Mitchell, *Doctor and Patient,* 119–20.
37. Mitchell, *Fat and Blood,* 30, 31.
38. Mitchell, *Fat and Blood,* 31–32. Alice James provides a clear example.
39. Mitchell, *Fat and Blood,* 30.
40. Mitchell, *Fat and Blood,* 42–43.
41. Mitchell, *Doctor and Patient,* 155.
42. Mitchell, *Doctor and Patient,* 155–57; quotations from 156, 157.
43. Mitchell, *Doctor and Patient,* 158–61; quotation from 161.
44. Mitchell, *Doctor and Patient,* 145.
45. Existing patient records of this institution cover this period, and she was not admitted. I have consulted the Record of patients treated in the Department for Nervous Diseases, ZDb/9, vols. 1–27, Department for Nervous Diseases, Philadelphia Orthopaedic Hospital and Infirmary for Nervous Diseases, MSS 6/0009–01, Historical Library, Philadelphia College of Physicians, Philadelphia, Penn.; and the Philadelphia Orthopaedic Hospital and Infirmary for Nervous Diseases, Casebook, 1885–1917, Trent Collection, History of Medicine Collections, Duke University Medical Center Library, Durham, North Carolina.
46. One forty-two-year-old woman admitted to the infirmary in May 1887, for example, had been suffering from malarial fever for three years, on top of which she had a recent attack of inflammatory rheumatism. What brought her to Mitchell was periodic loss of the use of her legs lasting several days. The specific example cited is in

Casebook, Neuralgia 4, Philadelphia Orthopaedic Hospital and
Infirmary for Nervous Diseases, 1885–1917, 25, Trent Collection.

47. For example, in September 1888 when a mother tried to get her
child admitted, Mitchell wrote to her that she should send a note
directly to the infirmary about her child, promising that her letter
would "receive prompt attention—If the case is a nervous one—or
mere [nerve?] deformity they will take it—on very moderate terms."
Nineteen months later, a letter from Dr. Zimmerman, the infirmary's
resident physician, informed the woman that a bed was available for
the child, who would be treated by one of Mitchell's associates
(Dr. W. W. Keen). S. Weir Mitchell to Mrs. Little, Sept. 1888,
item 260, shown in reproduction, and Dr. Zimmerman, Resident
Physician, to Mrs. Little, paraphrased, both in "Silas Weir Mitchell
(1829–1914), Physician, Author, Philadelphian, A Collection of His
Published Works, Correspondence, Family Photographs, Ephemera,
Etc." [sale catalogue], comp. Norman Kane, catalogued by David
J. Eilenberger (viewed Nov. 10, 2008, at the Library Company of
Philadelphia, Philadelphia, Penn.)

48. Pictures of the orthopedic hospital showing the nervous wards look
like pictures of any late-nineteenth-century hospital ward. Beds are
lined up against a wall perhaps eight feet apart, and nurses stand
at attention. Frederick P. Henry, ed., *Founders' Week Memorial
Volume* (Philadelphia: published by the city, 1909), plate opposite
796; the ward shown in this photograph may well have been in
a section of the hospital constructed after 1887, but the basic
arrangements would have been the same.

49. Harriet Williams (Russell) Strong to Charles Lyman Strong, 21 Dec.
1882, HS 844, Huntington Library.

50. William Dean Howells to William Cooper Howells, 25 Nov. 1888,
Howells Family Papers, bMS Am 1784.1 (78), by permission of the
Houghton Library, Harvard University, Cambridge, Mass.

51. And there she tragically died.

52. Helen Lefkowitz Horowitz, *Alma Mater: Design and Experience in
the Women's Colleges from Their Nineteenth-century Beginnings to
the 1930s* (New York: Knopf, 1984), 153–54.

53. The R. G. Dun Report has no entry for S. Weir Mitchell, for doctors
were professionals who were never regarded as being in business,
but in 1874 it listed his wife. A listing on 31 October stated that she
was married to "a first class Physician with a good practice, She is a
daughter of Genl. Thos Cadwallader who left a very valuable Estate,
& she is worth at least 100 m $ [$100,000], owns the residence &

other property." "Pennsylvania," listing for 31 Oct. 1874, 155:59, R. G. Dun & Co. Collection, Baker Library Historical Collections, Harvard Business School.

54. CWS diary, 26 May 1887, in CWS, *Endure*, 340.

55. The wording in Walter's diary is a bit confusing, for Charlotte certainly had no money to start a gymnasium. Mitchell may not have understood Charlotte's poverty, as she had been delivered to his establishment by the wealthy Mrs. George Vaux Cresson.

56. Mitchell, "Wear and Tear," 498; S. Weir Mitchell, *Wear and Tear, or Hints for the Overworked* (Philadelphia: Lippincott, 1887), 57.

Chapter 7

1. As discussed in Chapter 3, during the conflict in the spring of 1883, Walter had used these words to quote or paraphrase Charlotte's own, CWS diary, 22 March 1883, CWS, *Endure: The Diaries of Charles Walter Stetson, ed. Mary Armfield* Hill (Philadelphia : Temple University Press, 1985), 144–45; CWS diary, 21 June 1887, in CWS, *Endure*, 341.

2. The other versions vary slightly. CPG, "Why I Wrote the Yellow Wallpaper," *Forerunner* 4 (October 1913): 271; CPG to William Dean Howells, Oct. 17, 1919, Howells Family Papers, bMS Am 1784 (178), Houghton Library, Harvard University; CPG, *The Living of Charlotte Perkins Gilman: An Autobiography* (New York: Appleton-Century, 1935), 95–96, 121. The words quoted here are written at the bottom of the copy of the letter to Mitchell, p. 16. The handwriting bears a good resemblance to Gilman's right before her death. CPG to S. Weir Mitchell, copy, 19 Apr. 1887, Zona Gale Papers, Wisconsin Historical Society Archives, Madison, copy in CPG Papers (A/G487c), Schlesinger Library, Radcliffe Institute, Harvard University, Cambridge, Mass.

3. I am aware of the typewritten note entitled "TYW: Its History and Reception," with the handwritten "Note left by C.P.G." with Katharine's initials, folder 221, CPG Papers (177, Mf-1). It, too, was written quite late in Gilman's life, for it includes the statement that in some cases "it is used in college in rhetoric courses."

4. David Schuster, "Personalizing Illness and Modernity: S. Weir Mitchell, Literary Women, and Neurasthenia, 1870–1914," *Bulletin of the History of Medicine* 79 (2005): 695–722.

5. CWS diary, 23 June 1887, 2 vols., 2:193, 195, box 2, CWS Papers (93-M76), Schlesinger Library; not in CWS, *Endure*.

6. CWS diary, 10 Sept. 1887, in CWS, *Endure,* 351.
7. CWS diary, 30 June 1887, in CWS, *Endure,* 342.
8. CWS diary, 18, 19 July 1887, in CWS, *Endure,* 343.
9. CWS diary, 6 (?) Aug. 1887, in CWS, *Endure,* 347. (The editor was unsure of the date.)
10. CPG to GEC, 21 Nov. 1887, CPG Papers (Mf-6). I have put Alpha in boldface for emphasis.
11. CWS diary, 25 Feb. 1888, in CWS, *Endure,* 359.
12. CWS diary, 19 June 1888, 2:399–403, CWS Papers; not in CWS, *Endure.*
13. CPG to GEC, 21 Nov. 1887.
14. CPG to GEC, 21 Nov. 1887.
15. Denise D. Knight has written three articles about this book, in 1994, 2001, and most definitively in 2006: Denise D. Knight, "'I Could Paint Still Life as Well as Any One on Earth': Charlotte Perkins Gilman and the World of Art," *Women's Studies* 35 (2006): 475–92. The book was reissued by Reid and Reid in 1890 with a slight change of title: Mrs. Charles Walter Stetson, *Art Gems for the Home and Fireside* (Providence: J. A. & R. A. Reid, 1890). On the basis of my examination of the firm's 1881 book on President Garfield, of the same size, length, and basic type, I believe that the publishers assembled existing elements to create a book they hoped would have popular appeal and sell.
16. Stetson, *Art Gems,* 30.
17. Stetson, *Art Gems,* 18.
18. CWS diary, 2 Nov. 1888, 2:476, CWS Papers; not in CWS, *Endure.*
19. CWS diary, 30 Jan. 1888, in CWS, *Endure,* 355.
20. GEC to Mary Jane Tarr Channing, 6 June 1888, folder 61, GEC Papers (83-M201), Schlesinger Library.
21. Quoted in CWS diary, 15 June 1888, in CWS, *Endure,* 363–34.
22. GEC to Mary Jane Tarr Channing, 18 June 1888, folder 61.
23. GEC to Mary Jane Tarr Channing, 12 or 13 June 1888, folder 61. Exact dating is uncertain, as some letters are jumbled in the folder.
24. Grace Ellery Channing and Charlotte Perkins Stetson, "Noblesse Oblige," GEC Papers. In the longer version in the collection, written in Walter's fine hand, dated 1889, red ink for action alternates with black ink for dialogue; it seems clearly intended as a final draft.
25. When later revised, the play added a second serious element. Tied by engagement to an artist she no longer loves, Kate expresses her resigned willingness to keep her promise of marriage; she wishes, however, to be free to continue her medical education and to "live."

26. GEC to Mary Jane Tarr Channing, 13 July 1888, folder 62, GEC Papers.

27. Grace's full letter to her mother narrates the event, GEC to Mary Jane Tarr Channing, 26 Aug. 1888, folder 63, GEC Papers.

28. Deed and receipt, 14 Sept. 1888, for property in Hartford, Conn., Hazard Family Papers, Subgroup 6 (papers of Rowland G. Hazard II, 1829–98), Rhode Island Historical Society, Providence, RI.

29. Grace wrote home, in an apologetic letter to her mother, asking for Charlotte to be able to stay in the Channing household for a day or two: "I find her to my no little horror absolutely embarked without resources. It took her little all to pay her debts, and meet her expenses—and she literally has nothing to start with." GEC to Mary Jane Tarr Channing, 9 Oct. 1888, folder 64, GEC Papers, a letter written "On the Cars,"

30. CPG to GEC, 22 Sept. 1888, CPG Papers (Mf-6).

Chapter 8

1. GEC to Mary Jane Tarr Channing, 6 Oct. 1888, GEC Papers (83-M201), Schlesinger Library, Radcliffe Institute, Harvard University, Cambridge, Mass.

2. CPG to Rebecca Steere Stetson, 24 or 25 Apr. 1889, CWS Letters (BANC MSS 72/218c), Bancroft Library, University of California, Berkeley.

3. CPG to RSS, 30 Oct. 1888, CWS Letters.

4. Charles C. Eldredge, *Charles Walter Stetson: Color and Fantasy* (Lawrence, Kans.: Spencer Museum of Art, 1982), 49, discusses Walter's exhibit of 101 works on 3 Dec. 1888, at which enough works were sold to allow him to go to California.

5. CWS to RSS, 8 Jan. 1889, CWS Letters.

6. Grace chronicled these important connections at the time of the death of Jane Augusta Senter in "Tribute Paid by Friend," *Pasadena Star-News*, 25 Nov. 1935.

7. CWS to RSS, 9–10 Aug. 1889, CWS Letters.

8. CWS to RSS, 25 Aug. 1889, CWS Letters.

9. CWS to RSS, 4 Nov. 1889, CWS Letters.

10. CWS to RSS, 1 Mar. 1889, CWS Letters.

11. CWS to RSS, 4 Dec. 1889, CWS Letters.

12. Eldredge, *Stetson*, 59.

13. CWS to RSS, 30 Oct. 1889, CWS Letters.

14. CWS to RSS, 23 July 1889, CWS Letters.

15. Five months later, she wrote to Martha Lane that she had contacted the theater impresario Daniel Frohman about her plays, bragging that he liked her work. CPG to MLL, 10 Jan. 1890, CPG Letters, MSS 437, box 1, Rhode Island Historical Society, Providence, RI. In her diary entry of 17 Mar. 1890, Charlotte wrote, "Letter to Frohman." CPG diary, vol. 29, CPG Papers (177, Mf-1), Schlesinger Library.
16. CPG to MLL, 15 Aug. 1889, CPG Letters.
17. CPG to MLL, 15 Aug. 1889.
18. CPG to MLL, 20 Jan. 1890, CPG Letters. Perhaps to impress Martha, the letter was written on "The Californian" stationery.
19. Robley Dunglison, *A Dictionary of Medical Science* (Philadelphia: Henry C. Lea, 1874), a revision of a standard first published in 1833, made no distinction between melancholy and melancholia, in contrast to E. C. Seguin, "Treatment of Mild Cases of Melancholia at Home," in *A Series of American Clinical Lectures,* ed. Seguin (New York: Putnam, 1876), 2:40–65. Seguin presented two cases of women suffering from the disease of melancholia whose experience paralleled Charlotte's. One, with both "hysterical elements" and "strong morbid impulses," was brought back to normal functioning after she was relieved of child care and cohabitation with her husband and given rest, increased nutrition, drugs (including cannabis and opium), and moral treatment (46–48). Dr. Channing likely had knowledge of both works.
20. CPG to Marian Parker Whitney, 30 May 1890, in *The Selected Letters of Charlotte Perkins Gilman,* ed. Denise D. Knight and Jennifer S. Tuttle (Tuscaloosa: University of Alabama Press, 2009), 58–60, quotation from 59. The letter chirps about Grace, without suggesting their imminent separation, discusses Walter and his painting without a hint of the breakup of the marriage, and says that after he goes to Europe, she and Kate will follow.
21. CPG, "On Human Nature," 6–7, folder 172, CPG Papers. The many extracts from the lecture in "The Chief Events," *Los Angeles Times,* 8 July 1890, do not include this passage.
22. Gary Scharnhorst, "Making Her Fame: Charlotte Perkins Gilman in California," *California History* 64 (summer 1985): 192–201, 142–43.
23. "Wedded Bliss," *Kate Field's Washington,* 30 July 1890, 69.
24. "Reassurance," *Woman's Journal,* 5 July 1890, 214. This poem uncharacteristically ended on a conciliatory note. The "Coming Woman" rising would break the mold, return to original equality, and then forgive and be "better woman, wife and mother."

25. When published in *Kate Field's Washington,* 9 Apr. 1890, it was retitled "A Dramatic View" and issued as part 2 of "The Ceaseless Struggle of Sex."

26. "Grace over early. Start Colonial play." CPG diary, 26 Feb. 1890, vol. 29.

27. CPG to MLL, 15 Mar. 1890, CPG Letters.

28. Denise D. Knight, "New Evidence about the Origins of Gilman's 'The Giant Wistaria,'" *American Literary Realism* 40 (winter 2008): 173–79.

29. CPG to MLL, 15 Mar. 1890.

30. Fred Lewis Pattee, *The Development of the American Short Story: An Historical Survey* (New York: Harper, 1923), 292–93; Frederick B. Perkins, *Devil-puzzlers and Other Studies* (New York: Putnam, 1877), xvi, xviii–xix.

31. In a later letter, she declared Mar. 1, 1890, as the day she began writing professionally. CPG to Marian Parker Whitney, 28 Sept. 1890, in CPG, *Selected Letters,* 63.

32. "Record of Manuscripts," vol. 23, CPG Papers (177, Mf-1).

33. "Record of Manuscripts." In 1889, Hale and Edward D. Mead revived the magazine, and in 1890 Hale left active engagement, and Mead became its editor until 1901; Robert I. Rotberg, *Leadership for Peace: How Edwin Ginn Tried to Change the World* (Stanford: Stanford University Press, 2007), 44.

34. William Dean Howells to CPG, quoted in CPG to MLL, 17 June 1890, CPG Letters; CPG to William Dean Howells, 16 June 1890, Howells Family Papers, bMS Am 1784 (178), by permission of the Houghton Library, Harvard University. This comparison was very flattering. In 1848, at the beginning of his career, the revered poet James Russell Lowell opposed the Mexican War in *The Bigelow Papers.*

35. CPG diary, 24, 28 Aug. 1890, vol. 29.

36. CPG to MLL, 27 July 1890, CPG Letters.

37. "Attempted Outrage upon a Fifteen-year-old Girl on Villa Street," *Los Angeles Times,* 19 June 1890; "Notes and Comments," *Los Angeles Times,* 25 June 1890: "Personals: The Mass Meeting," *Los Angeles Times,* 26 June 1890.

38. CPG, "Causes and Cures," 3–4, folder 172, CPG Papers (177, Mf-1).

39. CPG, "Causes and Cures," 13–15.

40. CPG to MLL, 27 July 1890.

41. CPG journal, 8 Mar. 1879, vol. 15; Oct. 11, 1879, vol. 16.

42. Dated by Dock after she searched newspapers to find the two extraordinarily hot days in southern California; Julie Bates Dock, *Charlotte Perkins Gilman, "The Yellow Wall-paper" and*

the *History of Its Publication and Reception* (University Park: Pennsylvania State University Press, 1998), 4.

43. Denise D. Knight, "'Only a Husband's Opinion': Walter Stetson's View of Gilman's 'The Yellow Wall-Paper'—An Inscription," *American Literary Realism* 36 (fall 2003): 86–87.

44. "Record of Manuscripts."

Chapter 9

1. There is a rich, multilayered literary scholarship on this celebrated work in the years since 1973. I note only pieces of this vast corpus here and do so because I have been directly influenced by the cited writing (if only on occasion to counter it). Much of what has been written about Gilman's story is highly theoretical (feminist, Freudian, Lacanian, linguistic, queer), with little attention to historical chronology or context, and, as fascinating as some of it is, has little to do with my own effort to situate "The Yellow Wall-Paper" in Gilman's consciousness at the time and place of its writing. Most helpful to me for my purposes are the carefully grounded works of Denise D. Knight and Gary Scharnhorst, for which I am most grateful. I am also indebted to careful scholars, such as Catherine J. Golden, who have alerted me to many interesting elements of the story.

Though introduced to the story as a graduate student in the late 1960s (in a widely circulated photocopy of it), I began teaching it when I first constructed my women's history courses in the early 1970s, at the time the 1973 Feminist Press volume was published. Thus my reading of the story is likely to be shaped in part by the feminist interpretations that began in this formative period in my own work. In 1992, Elaine R. Hedges, who wrote the initial afterword to the Feminist Press edition of the story, offered a magnificent summary and analysis of the generations of scholarship on the work in relation to the political and cultural climate of shifting times in words that still hold today; "'Out at Last?' 'The Yellow Wallpaper' after Two Decades of Feminist Criticism," in *The Captive Imagination: A Casebook on The Yellow Wallpaper,* ed. Catherine Golden (New York: Feminist Press, 1992), 319–33. Golden's collection offers the best compendium of criticism before the early 1990s. Judith A. Allen has counted "nearly eight hundred publications and scholarly projects" on Gilman since 1975, a phenomenon she has labeled "Gilmania"; *The Feminism of Charlotte Perkins Gilman: Sexualities, Histories, Progressivism* (Chicago: University of Chicago Press, 2009), 327.

2. CPG to S. Weir Mitchell, copy, 19 Apr. 1887, Zona Gale Papers, Wisconsin Historical Society Archives, Madison, copy in CPG Papers (A/G487c), Schlesinger Library, Radcliffe Institute, Harvard University, Cambridge, Mass.

3. Because I am focusing on the creation, not the publication, of the story I use the manuscript version here rather than the first printed version, which appeared in *New England Magazine* in 1892. By contrast, Julie Bates Dock, *Charlotte Perkins Gilman, "The Yellow Wallpaper" and the History of Its Publication and Reception* (University Park: Pennsylvania State University Press, 1998), while providing an excellent study of the story, reproduces this first printed version. In choosing to use the manuscript, I agree with the judgment of Shawn St. Jean that "when the textual intentions of an author are what is most desired, one cannot go far wrong with an authorial manuscript." St. Jean argues that although in many cases the final version in print involves a true negotiation between writer and publisher to produce a text, in the case of "The Yellow Wall-Paper," Gilman had had no control over the editorial changes made by the publisher. There are more than four hundred documented changes between these two versions. See Shawn St. Jean, "Hanging 'The Yellow Wall-Paper': Feminism and Textual Studies," *Feminist Studies* 28 (summer 2002): 397–415 (quotation from 411); Shawn St. Jean, "Gilman's Manuscript of 'The Yellow Wall-Paper': Toward a Critical Edition," *Studies in Bibliography* 51 (1998): 260–73. I am grateful to be able to rely on the published version of the manuscript in *"The Yellow Wall-Paper" and Selected Stories of Charlotte Perkins Gilman,* edited with an introduction by Denise D. Knight (Newark: University of Delaware Press, 1994), 39–53.

4. CPG, "The Yellow Wall-Paper," in *"The Yellow Wall-Paper" and Selected Stories,* 39–53, quotation from 39 (cited hereafter with page numbers in parentheses in the text).

5. Charlotte read *Jane Eyre* in 1877, CPG journal, 19, 20 July 1877, vol. 27, CPG Papers (177, Mf-1).

6. Although much has been made of the possibility that the meaning of "the rings and things in the walls" meant that the room once held an insane person, given Gilman's knowledge of gymnasiums of her time, the better explanation is that of the Sargent gymnasium equipment. Two works carefully consider the horror/ghost genre and the way it structures the story: E. Suzanne Owens, "The Ghostly Double behind the Wallpaper in Charlotte Perkins Gilman's 'The Yellow Wallpaper,' " in *Haunting the House of Fiction,* ed. Lynette

Carpenter (Knoxville: University of Tennessee Press, 1991), 64–79; George Monteiro, "Context, Intention, and Purpose in 'The Yellow Wall-Paper,' A Tale in the Poe and Romantic Tradition," *Revisita Fragmentos* 17 (1999): 41–54.

7. She may have been aware of not only Poe's story "The Black Cat" but also European examples in which a narrator descends into madness, such as "The Sandman," by E. T. A. Hoffmann, and "The Horla, Or Modern Ghosts," by Guy de Maupassant.

8. CPG journal, 31 Dec. 1886, vol. 19, CPG Papers (177, Mf-1).

9. I have gained insight in my consideration of the unstable voice of the narrator from the perceptive piece by Annie G. Rogers, "In the 'I' of Madness: Shifting Subjectivities in Girls' and Women's Psychological Development in 'The Yellow Wallpaper,' " in *Analyzing the Different Voice: Feminist Psychological Theory and Literary Texts* (Lanham, Md.: Rowman and Littlefield, 1998), 45–65.

10. Many have written about the way Gilman controlled the language of the narrative to emphasize the initial strength of the husband's voice, but none with more perception than Catherine Golden, "The Writing of 'The Yellow Wallpaper': A Double Palimpsest," *Studies in American Fiction* 17 (autumn 1989): 193–201. Although subsequent scholarship has shown that some of the elements Golden relied on were not in Gilman's own version of the text, Golden's central perceptions hold.

11. Here I depart from the interpretation that Gilman imagined the narrator was insane at the outset of the story. The sense that the narrator descends into madness is strengthened by the use of the manuscript rather than the first published version of the text. The manuscript version has many fewer paragraph breaks, allowing the narrator to be coherent at the outset, providing initially "a well-paragraphed narrative." For this and other insights, I am grateful to St. Jean, "Hanging 'The Yellow Wall-Paper,' " quotation from 402.

12. Here and elsewhere I draw on the insight of Beverly A. Hume, "Managing Madness in Gilman's 'The Yellow Wall-Paper,' " *Studies in American Fiction* 30 (2002): 3–20, specifically here, 4–5. I do not, however, accept the piece's primary argument that Gilman sabotaged her feminist agenda in the "Yellow Wall-Paper," for I see her writing this deeply felt story for its own sake and for potential money, and then glossing it with a reformist overlay long after the fact. (The story certainly stands on its own as a profoundly feminist document against male hegemony in marriage and medicine.) I have also benefited from the linguistic reading of the story by Paula A.

Treichler, "Escaping the Sentence: Diagnosis and Discourse in "The Yellow Wallpaper," *Tulsa Studies in Women's Literature* 3 (spring–fall 1984): 61–77.

13. It has been with great pleasure that, after formulating my argument, I have found an author whose approach and judgments accord in some measure with my own: Michael Blackie, "Reading the Rest Cure," *Arizona Quarterly* 60 (summer 2004): 57–86.

14. Greg Johnson, "Gilman's Gothic Allegory: Rage and Redemption in 'The Yellow Wallpaper,' " *Studies in Short Fiction* 26 (fall 1989): 521–30, esp. 528–29, led me to see these asides.

15. Marty Roth goes so far as to link the arabesque pattern, favored by many designers, including William Morris, to Gilman's imperialistic vision: "Gilman's Arabesque Wallpaper," *Mosaic* 34 (2001): 145–62. Mary Jacobus considers yellow the "color of sickness...decay," for which there is some evidence, and for female sexuality, of which there is only inference. See Jacobus, "An Unnecessary Maze of Sign-Reading," in Golden, *Captive Imagination,* 277–95, esp. 282.

16. Hume, "Managing Madness," 7–8.

17. The contrast between daylight rationality and the gothic unconscious of the night is made by Johnson, "Gilman's Gothic Allegory."

18. Roth discusses synaesthesia and drug use in "Gilman's Arabesque Wallpaper," 151, 153–54. I have considered the interpretation that the "yellow" of the wallpaper represents the southern and eastern European immigrants and Asians; Susan S. Lanser, "Feminist Criticism, 'The Yellow Wallpaper,' and the Politics of Color in America," *Feminist Studies* 15 (fall 1989): 415–41. As a mature reformer, Gilman became a strong advocate for eugenics and supported some level of immigration restriction, but one should not read backward into this 1890s text positions she advocated beginning in 1900.

19. Catherine J. Golden, "Marking Her Territory: Feline Behavior in 'The Yellow Wall-Paper,' " *American Literary Realism* 40 (2007): 16–31. Dickens provided a precedent here in the character of Phil Squod in *Bleak House;* Michael Klotz, "Two Dickens Rooms in 'The Yellow Wall-Paper,' " *Notes and Queries* 52. 4 (December 2005), 490–91.

20. Hume rightly suggests that Gilman's own sense of the health-giving qualities of the outdoors is in contrast to the narrator's determination to remain indoors, choosing "yellow" over "green" (Hume, "Managing Madness," 15–16). Jacobus has emphasized

the importance in the story of "creeping" as it moves to the more figurative "creepy," or horror-inducing (Jacobus, "Unnecessary Maze," 282, 285–88).

21. Golden, "Writing of 'The Yellow Wallpaper,'" 198–99.

22. Hume, "Managing Madness," 8–9.

23. Much has been made of the invocation of "Jane," a name used only at the very end of the story, and some authors state that the narrator is Jane. It is possible, however, that Jane is the given name of the sister-in-law nicknamed Jennie, as suggested by Golden, "The Writing of 'The Yellow Wallpaper,'" 201 n. 9.

Chapter 10

1. Here, in considering her professional life, it seems the appropriate point to shift to "Gilman."

2. "Record of Manuscripts," vol. 23, CPG Papers (177, Mf-1), Schlesinger Library, Radcliffe Institute, Harvard University, Cambridge, Mass.; Howells's efforts to publish "The Yellow Wall-Paper" in the *Atlantic Monthly* and its actual publication in *New England Magazine* in 1892 are an interesting story, best told in Shawn St. Jean, "Hanging 'The Yellow Wall-Paper': Feminism and Textual Studies," *Feminist Studies* 28 (summer 2002): 397–415; See also St. Jean, "Gilman's Manuscript of 'The Yellow Wall-Paper': Toward a Critical Edition," *Studies in Bibliography* 51 (1998): 260–73. Mead was the younger cousin of Howells's wife.

3. The early reception is best summarized in Julie Bates Dock, " 'But One Expects That': Charlotte Perkins Gilman's 'The Yellow Wallpaper' and the Shifting Light of Scholarship," *PMLA* 111 (Jan. 1996): 52–65. I am grateful for Julie Bates Dock, *Charlotte Perkins Gilman's "The Yellow Wall-Paper" and the History of Its Publication and Reception: A Critical Edition and Documentary Casebook* (University Park: Pennsylvania State University Press, 1998); specific reference here, 103. Dock has argued that the space between M. and D. "signals that they are initials of a proper name that could as easily have been Margaret Dumont as Michael Douglas" (21). Gary Scharnhorst has challenged this, but his "M. D." and the "M. D." of this letter may not be the same person. See Scharnhorst, "A Note on Gilman's 'M. D.,'" *Charlotte Perkins Gilman Newsletter* 14 (2004): 5.

4. "Introduction: Why Do (These) Texts Matter," CPG, *"The Yellow Wall-Paper," by Charlotte Perkins Gilman: A Dual Text Critical*

Edition, ed. Shawn St. Jean (Athens: Ohio University Press, 2006), xv–xvii.

5. CPG to GEC, 3 Dec. 1890, CPG Papers (Mf-6).

6. CPG to George Houghton Gilman, 6 Mar. 1899, in *A Journey from Within: The Love Letters of Charlotte Perkins Gilman,* ed. Mary A. Hill (Lewisburg, Penn.: Bucknell University Press, 1995), 246; for a discussion of passion among women, see Helen Lefkowitz Horowitz, "Nous Autres: Reading, Passion, and the Creation of M. Carey Thomas," *Journal of American History* 79 (June 1992): 68–95.

7. This phase of Gilman's career is the principal subject of Judith A. Allen, *The Feminism of Charlotte Perkins Gilman: Sexualities, Histories, Progressivism* (Chicago: University of Chicago Press, 2009).

8. Dock, *Gilman's "The Yellow Wall-Paper,"* 19, 104–11; William Dean Howells, ed., *The Great Modern American Stories: An Anthology* (New York: Boni and Liveright, 1920), vii.

9. CPG to GHG, 16 June 1897, in CPG, *Journey,* 67. In using this source for GPG's letters to GHG, I have shifted the words by CPG printed in italics to underlinings.

10. CPG to GHG, 4 June 1897, in CPG, *Journey,* 63; 7 June 1897, in CPG, *Journey,* 65.

11. CPG to GHG, [26 June 1897], in CPG, *Journey,* 67–68; 11 July 1897, in CPG, *Journey,* 71.

12. CPG to GHG, 27 July 1897, in CPG, *Journey,* 74.

13. CPG to GHG, 23 Aug. 1897, in CPG, *Journey,* 80.

14. CPG to GHG, 2 Sept. 1897, in CPG, *Journey,* 93; 8 Sept. 1897, in CPG, *Journey,* 96; 11 Sept. 1897, in CPG, *Journey,* 99.

15. CPG to GHG, 21 Sept. 1897, in CPG, *Journey,* 102.

16. CPG to GHG, 12 Oct. 1897, in CPG, *Journey,* 106.

17. CPG to GHG, 3 Nov. 1897, in CPG, *Journey,* 114.

18. CPG to GHG, 8 Nov. 1897, in CPG, *Journey,* 117.

19. CPG to GHG, 14 Sept. 1898, in CPG, *Journey,* 173; 22 Sept. 1898, in CPG, *Journey,* 179.

20. CPG to GHG, 11 May 1898, in CPG, *Journey,* 135.

21. CPG to GHG, [16 Sept. 1898], in CPG, *Journey,* 175.

22. CPG to GHG, 18 Dec. 1898, in CPG, *Journey,* 217–18, quotation from 218.

23. CPG to GHG, 12, 15 Mar. 1899, in CPG, *Journey,* 248, 254.

24. CPG to GHG, 12–15 Mar. 1899, in CPG, *Journey,* 248–54; 2 Apr. 1899, in CPG, *Journey,* 266.

25. CPG to GHG, 20 Jan. 1900, in CPG, *Journey,* 341.

26. CPG to GHG, 21 Jan. 1900, in CPG, *Journey,* 342.

27. CPG to GHG, 27 Feb. 1900, in CPG, *Journey,* 350.

28. CPG to GHG, 16 May 1900, in CPG, *Journey,* 373.
29. CPG, *The Living of Charlotte Perkins Gilman: An Autobiography* (New York: Appleton-Century, 1935), 294. A particularly bright spot came in 1901, when Dr. Mary Putnam Jacobi's treatment gave her temporary relief.
30. For the most challenging consideration of these questions, see Ian Hacking, *Mad Travelers: Reflections on the Reality of Transient Mental Illnesses* (Charlottesville: University of Virginia Press, 1998).
31. Nancy C. Andreasen, *The Broken Brain: The Biological Revolution in Psychiatry* (New York: Harper and Row, 1984), and *Brave New Brain* (New York: Oxford, 2001).
32. Peter D. Kramer, *Listening to Prozac* (New York: Viking, 1993), 47–66, discusses this understanding, without necessarily agreeing with it.
33. *Diagnostic and Statistical Manual of Mental Disorder,* rev. 3rd ed. (Washington, D.C.: American Psychiatric Association, 1987), 232.
34. Jonathan Sadowsky, *Imperial Bedlam: Institutions of Madness in Colonial Southwest Nigeria* (Berkeley: University of California Press, 1999), offers a sustained consideration of these issues.
35. Laura D. Hirshbein, *American Melancholy: Constructions of Depression in the Twentieth Century* (New Brunswick: Rutgers University Press, 2009).
36. This was suggested to me by my Smith colleague Richard Millington, with whom I cotaught "The Yellow Wall-Paper" for many years. As he put it when I told him her story recently, it was perhaps Charlotte's very illness that offered her the necessary perspective to break through her era's fundamental belief system regarding gender. He reminded me of the great power of ideology over both institutions and individual psyches.
37. I am not the first to question the explanation by Gilman that turned the story to a reformist end. Greg Johnson, "Gilman's Gothic Allegory: Rage and Redemption in 'The Yellow Wallpaper,'" *Studies in Short Fiction* 26 (fall 1989): 530, sees her explanation after the fact as her denial of the power of imaginative creation in her determination to be good.
38. When she first wrote down this statement to Howells, she put Mitchell's words in the first person—"have my child with me all the time"—but then she corrected it on the page to the second person to make it conversational, as if it were a direct quotation. CPG to William Dean Howells, 17 Oct. 1919, Howells Family Papers, bMS Am 1784 (178), by permission of the Houghton Library, Harvard University.

39. At the bottom of the handwritten letter to Mitchell, CPG to S. Weir Mitchell, copy, 19 Apr. 1887, Zona Gale Papers, Wisconsin Historical Society Archives, Madison, copy in CPG Papers (A/G487c).

40. I am not the first author to challenge Gilman's telling of her own story in the *Forerunner* and her autobiography. Dock summarizes these in Dock et al., " 'But One Expects That,' " 52–65, esp. 58. Dock also penetrates the overlay of criticism beginning in the 1970s that has complicated the readings of the story. Denise D. Knight, Gilman's most careful scholar, in writing about Gilman's failure to ever acknowledge her first book, has written of the liberties Gilman took with her autobiography; Knight, " 'I Could Paint Still Life as Well as Any One on Earth': Charlotte Perkins Gilman and the World of Art," *Women's Studies* 35 (2006): 489.

41. Gilman's utopian novel *Herland* is a testament to that commitment.

42. Denise D. Knight supports the contention that Walter was the prototype for John in " 'Only a Husband's Opinion': Walter Stetson's View of Gilman's 'The Yellow Wall-Paper'—An Inscription," *American Literary Realism* 36 (2003): 86–87; and " 'I Am Getting Angry Enough to Do Something Desperate': The Question of Female 'Madness,' " in CPG, *"The Yellow Wall-Paper" by Charlotte Perkins Gilman: A Dual Text Critical Edition*, ed. Shawn St. Jean (Athens: Ohio University Press, 2006), 75–87, see esp. 83; Judith A. Allen concurs, *The Feminism of Charlotte Perkins Gilman: Sexualities, Histories, Progressivism* (Chicago: University of Chicago Press, 2009), 27.

INDEX ·····························